Understanding Minority Ethnic Achievement

The authors of this book take a refreshing approach to the issue of minority ethnic achievement as they examine the views, identities and educational experiences of those pupils who are undoubtedly 'achieving', but who tend to remain ignored and overlooked within popular concerns about under-achievement. By investigating the factors underpinning 'success', this ground-breaking book shows how a better understanding of high achievement can also inform our knowledge of under-achievement.

Understanding Minority Ethnic Achievement combines a broad analysis of minority ethnic pupils' achievement together with a novel, detailed case study of an educationally 'successful' group, the British-Chinese. Despite their apparent high achievement and social mobility, relatively little academic or policy attention has been given to the British-Chinese, who are popularly referred to as the 'invisible ethnic minority'. Yet their apparent success offers a fascinating angle to debates on the reproduction of social inequalities.

In this thought-provoking and highly accessible book, the authors:

*   Review the theoretical and policy context to issues of 'race', gender, social class and achievement
*   Discuss the role of teachers and schools
*   Explore Chinese parents' views of their children's education and explain how these families 'produce' and support achievement
*   Investigate British-Chinese pupils' views on their approaches to learning and their educational identities
*   Examine the relationship between aspirations and educational achievement
*   Consider the complexity and subtlety of racism experienced by 'successful' minority ethnic pupils.

Understanding Minority Ethnic Ach  students, education professionals and policy m tandings about educationally 'successful' minor

Louise Archer is at King's College London, UK.
Becky Francis is at Roehampton University, UK.

Understanding Minority Ethnic Achievement

Race, gender, class and 'success'

Louise Archer and Becky Francis

 Routledge
Taylor & Francis Group

LONDON AND NEW YORK

First published 2007
by Routledge
2 Park Square, Milton Park, Abingdon, Oxon OX14 4RN

Simultaneously published in the USA and Canada
by Routledge
270 Madison Ave, New York, NY 10016

Routledge is an imprint of the Taylor & Francis Group, an informa business

© 2007 Louise Archer and Becky Francis

Typeset in Garamond by
HWA Text and Data Management, Tunbridge Wells
Printed and bound in Great Britain by
TJ International, Padstow, Cornwall

British Library Cataloguing in Publication Data
A catalogue record for this book is available from the British Library

Library of Congress Cataloging-in-Publication Data
Archer, Louise, 1973–
   Understanding minority ethnic achievement : race, gender, class and
'success' / Louise Archer and Becky Francis.
      p. cm.
   Includes bibliographical references.
   1. Chinese students – Education – Great Britain – Case studies.
2. Chinese – Great Britain – Social conditions – Case studies. 3. Academic
achievement – Great Britain– Case studies. I. Francis, Becky. II. Title
LC3085.G7A73 2007
371.829'951041–dc22   2006011793

ISBN10: 0–415–37281–X (hbk)
ISBN10: 0–415–37282–8 (pbk)
ISBN10: 0–203–96839–5 (ebk)

ISBN13: 978–0–415–37281–7 (hbk)
ISBN13: 978-0–415–37282–4 (pbk)
ISBN13: 978–0–203–96839–0 (ebk)

for Matt, Danny, Ben and Louis, with love

Contents

Illustrations

Acknowledgements

We would like to thank everyone who has helped us in the production of this book.

The empirical data that we draw on were collected as part of a study funded by the Economic and Social Research Council (award no. R000239585), exploring constructions of gender, education and post-16 aspirations among British-Chinese pupils. We would like to extend our warmest thanks to all the British-Chinese young people, parents and teachers who generously gave their time and shared their views and experiences with us in this research – and we hope that we do them justice.

We would also like to thank Sau-Wah Lam for her excellent fieldwork in conducting (and translating) the interviews with Chinese parents – and for her comments and feedback on our analyses. We are also very grateful to the other British-Chinese advisers to the project, Yen-Wah Lam, Danny Hew and Sui-Mee Chan, for their advice across the project – from design and recruitment through to analyses. Thanks, in particular, are due to Sui-Mee for reading and commenting on draft work produced from the project.

We conducted the research study and began the initial writing of this book while we were both based at London Metropolitan University, in the Institute for Policy Studies in Education. We would like to thank all our former IPSE friends and colleagues for the various support they provided to us – especially Lindsay Melling for her organisation and coding of some of the data. We also thank our current colleagues at King's College London and Roehampton for providing us with the space and encouragement to complete the book.

Some of the data and discussion in the book are drawn from articles published in *British Journal of Sociology of Education*, *British Educational Research Journal*, *Sociological Review*, *Oxford Review of Education*, *Sociology* and *Race, Ethnicity and Education*. We thank the publishers (Sage, Blackwell and Taylor & Francis) for giving us their permission to reproduce material. We are also grateful to the DfES for allowing us to reproduce their tables on ethnicity and achievement in Chapter Two. We should like to extend thanks to colleagues at Routledge for commissioning the book and supporting its production.

Finally, thanks to our families and friends for their patience and support during the writing of this book.

Louise Archer and Becky Francis

Preface

It is evident that contemporary UK education policy is characterised by an 'obsession with academic achievement' (Mahony, 1998:39). This is amply illustrated by the proliferation of testing regimes, academic league tables and the regular, high profile publication of achievement statistics from children's earliest years through to GCSEs and into post-compulsory education. Indeed, we would assert that achievement is not just an educational issue – for the current government, it is *the* educational issue. As noted by Francis and Skelton (2005), however, the current policy concern with 'achievement' tends to be 'extraordinarily narrowly conceived', being treated 'as exclusively reflected by credentials from performance in examinations' (p. 2). As various critics have argued at length, the measurement and classification of achievement/ under-achievement within and between different groups of pupils remains a far more complex and contentious issue than education policy acknowledges (e.g. Epstein *et al.*, 1998; Francis and Skelton, 2005; Gillborn and Gipps, 1996; Gillborn and Mirza, 1992, 2000; Mirza 1992).

Beneath this umbrella concern with 'achievement', national moral panics have flourished regarding the apparent 'under-achievement' of particular groups of pupils – notably boys, working-class pupils and (some groups of) Black and minority ethnic (BME) young people. Within the broader concern with boys' achievement, the spotlight has been placed on the under-achievement of Black Caribbean boys (e.g. see Sewell, 1997, 1998; Phillips, 2005) – and to a lesser extent Asian Muslim pupils (e.g. see Archer, 2003). Inequalities in the educational experiences and outcomes of minority ethnic children have been documented and discussed throughout the twentieth century and into the twenty-first – although a range of radically different approaches and interpretations have been proffered. For instance, positivistic psychologists in the USA and Europe have attempted to explain differentiated achievement as the result of biological factors, reflecting inherent differences in intelligence, ability, or resulting from biologically different family structures and cultural psychologies. Whilst this work is mostly outdated and discredited (e.g. Eysenk, 1971; Jensen, 1973), it continues to re-emerge periodically (e.g. espousing innate racial differences in intelligence), attracting sensationalised media attention (e.g. Hernstein and Murray, 1994). Such approaches have for some considerable time been denounced as reflecting racist, homogenised and untenable assumptions about minority ethnic peoples (e.g. Mama, 1995; Omi and Winant, 1986). Indeed, as Rose

(2001) points out, ever since the end of the Second World War and the creation of the Geneva Conventions, there has been a growing popular concern to discredit and denounce essentialising approaches to understanding human behaviour, in acknowledgement of the horrific results of Fascist eugenicist ideology regarding racial hierarchies. However, as we discuss in this book, the potency of 'commonsense' racist discourses (Billig *et al.*, 1988) around minority ethnic pupils remains a pertinent concern, and continues to permeate education policy (Gillborn, 2005) and the everyday views of teachers, pupils and parents.

In this book we argue that policy approaches to 'under-achievement' tend to adopt a narrow, individualised approach to understanding the factors underlying and driving 'success' and 'under-achievement'. Thus the 'causes' of under-achievement among, for instance, Black Caribbean pupils and Muslim pupils, are often popularly assumed to be a product of personal attitudes, beliefs and cultural/family practices and values. Indeed, whilst conducting research and writing in this area, we have frequently been approached by journalists, policy makers and practitioners wanting to know the 'secret' of British-Chinese pupils' educational success and, more to the point, what messages and 'top tips' we can provide for application to 'other' groups. The popular assumption seems to be that there must be something that British-Chinese individuals and families are doing 'right' and that other groups are doing 'wrong'.

Our intention in writing this book is to bring a more complex understanding to the issue of minority ethnic educational 'success'. In particular, we try to place notions of 'culture' and individual agency within an appreciation of intermeshed structural identities and inequalities of 'race'/ethnicity, gender, sexuality, social class and age. We hope that the text provides a critical contrast to current dominant 'colour blind' approaches (which have entailed the erasure of 'race' from policy (Lewis, 2000)), whilst not falling into the trap of propagating essentialist and homogenised readings of racialised communities. Our intention is to help lever social justice concerns back into mainstream educational debates that have become dominated by the neo-liberal language of 'quality' – in which concerns with 'equality' have become evacuated and consigned to the margins.

The book also aims to provide researchers, policy makers and practitioners with insights and understandings about educationally 'successful' minority ethnic pupils – who are often ignored and overlooked within the prevalent concerns with 'under-achievement'. We also believe that understanding achievement is not only important in its own right, but can tell us more about under-achievement. As Gibson (1988) writes from the US context: 'many of these theories have originated in an effort to explain minority failure and have been generated without sufficient attention to cases of minority success' (Gibson, 1988, p. 168).

We would further argue that this focus on BME 'success'/achievement is politically, socially and academically important. For instance, the recognition and 'celebration'[1] of BME success provides an important challenge to the constant tirade of negative images and associations of BME young people as 'problems' and 'failing' pupils. It also provides a vital tool for highlighting some of the previously hidden and ignored injustices experienced by 'achieving' BME pupils – as we discuss at length within the book. Furthermore, the potential practical applications of this endeavour are underscored by the results of recent surveys of newly qualified teachers (NQTs) which are conducted each year in the UK by the Teacher Training Agency. These surveys continue to reveal that the majority of new teachers report feeling ill-prepared and ill-equipped to engage with multicultural classrooms and pupils from diverse backgrounds. This situation is perhaps understandable given the marginalisation and reduction of equality issues within initial teacher education courses (often as little as one session within an entire course) – a situation that is certainly not defensible in our opinion. This is not attempting to be a 'how-to' book, but we would hope that readers who are (student) teachers and professionals might be inspired to develop new knowledge and ways of 'thinking otherwise' (Renold, 2005) about minority ethnic pupils and parents and issues of achievement.

Whilst engaging with a broader literature pertaining to education and 'race'/ethnicity, gender and social class, we focus particularly on the case of the UK's highest educationally achieving 'ethnic group', the British-Chinese. As we note further in Chapter 2, British-Chinese identities remain under-theorised within the sociology of education and yet they offer a potentially interesting angle to debates around the (re)production of privileges/inequalities – especially given their apparent success in transcending barriers of racism and social class and achieving social mobility. Relatively little academic work has focused on the British-Chinese diaspora, although there is a growing critique that counters popular narrow, stereotypical representations of British-Chinese families and their 'success' (e.g. Archer and Francis, 2005a, 2005b, 2006; Chau and Yu, 2001; Cheng, 1996; Parker, 2000; Song, 1999; Wong, 1994).

The predominant academic silence around the British-Chinese is also matched by a wider silence within popular life. Despite a few tragic stories in the UK press over the last few years (e.g. the deaths of migrant Chinese workers and attempted 'illegal immigrants'[2]), the British-Chinese community attracts relatively little popular attention. This has led to their identification as 'the invisible ethnic minority'[3] – despite their notable academic and economic 'success'. Indeed, as the British-Chinese actor David Yip has complained, there are relatively few British-Chinese people represented to any meaningful degree within mainstream British cultural and popular life.

Structure of the book

We wrote this book with a potentially broad readership in mind. We hope that the ideas and understandings proposed within it will be relevant for a range of researchers/academics, students, practitioners, education professionals and policy makers. In practice, we recognise that this remains essentially an 'academic' text, discussing (and proposing) theoretical concepts and ways of reading, understanding and representing 'achieving' minority pupils. However, this academic text espouses a political and applied aim of contributing to, and helping to further develop, socially just practices with education. The following outline of the book's structure is intended to help readers to navigate their way through the text.

Chapter 1 effectively sets the scene for the book and discusses the policy context in relation to issues of 'race' and achievement. It explores current patterns of educational attainment by ethnicity and gender (including relevant statistical tables) and discusses this achievement in relation to 'social class'. These figures are critically discussed, with attention drawn to their contradictory use and interpretation within education policy. The chapter maps out key debates within the field, including the impact of the 'boys debate', the standards movement and educational credentialism – highlighting the pernicious effects of these discourses on BME pupils and discussions around ethnicity and achievement.

Chapter 2 provides the theoretical context to the book. It details the theoretical perspective that is brought to bear on our data and analyses and argues for the utility and importance of adopting an integrated approach which can simultaneously account for social axes of 'race'/ethnicity, gender, sexuality and social class. Key work is reviewed in relation to the theoretical approach adopted, notably on 'feminist poststructuralism', discourse analysis and, in relation to the conceptualisation of 'race'/ethnicity, gender, sexualities and social class. The chapter concludes with a discussion of the British-Chinese research context and provides an introduction and overview of the empirical study to be drawn on in the remainder of the book.

In Chapter 3 we explore teachers' views of BME pupil identities and achievement. The chapter reviews existing literature pertaining to teachers' roles and the impact on/ interaction of these with BME pupils. Teachers' attributions of BME success to the 'home'/ home culture are critically examined. Attention is also given to teachers' constructions of home–school relations. It is argued that despite praising British-Chinese pupils' educational success, teachers also unwittingly positioned it as problematic. Particular consideration is given to teachers' constructions of British-Chinese pupils and the ways in which these constructions are distinctly gendered. The chapter concludes by proposing a new conceptual model as a framework for understanding how dominant educational discourses of the ideal pupil positions both high *and* low achieving BME pupils as 'other'.

In Chapter 4 we examine BME parents' views of the British education system. The chapter reviews the education policy context with regard to parental involvement in schooling and reviews research conducted with both white and BME parents. Chinese parents' constructions of the value of education (and their transmission of this valuing to their children) and their mobilisation of economic capital to help support their children's achievement, are all explored. Attention is drawn to how Chinese parents mobilise this valuing of education within their constructions of racialised identities and ethnic boundaries. It is suggested that, despite not challenging schools overtly, many Chinese parents appear critical of the British education system (comparing it with Hong Kong/China) and express dissatisfaction with their children's schooling. In line with Ran (2001), it is suggested that irrespective of their children's high achievement, Chinese parents and schools appear to be travelling on 'parallel tracks', rather than engaging in equitable and reciprocal partnerships.

Chapter 5 focuses on BME young people's educational identities. Following an overview of relevant literature, the chapter examines British-Chinese pupils' learning preferences and learner identities. Their subject preferences, constructions of themselves as pupils and their stated approaches to learning are discussed and contextualised *vis-à-vis* research conducted with ethnically diverse pupil cohorts. The chapter also discusses in-depth pupils' views on the laddism debate and specifically whether, or not, laddishness applies to British-Chinese boys. Consideration is given to boys' and girls' constructions of British-Chinese masculinity and their explanations (and boys' performances of) British-Chinese laddishness. These questions are considered in terms of interweavings of 'race', class, gender and space within the construction of minority ethnic masculinities. The chapter explores these issues with the aid of a proposed conceptual dichotomy, discussing how British-Chinese approaches to learning and, in particular, British-Chinese boys' gender positions are othered/Orientalised.

Chapter 6 engages in linking identities, aspirations and achievement. In this chapter we bring together data from teachers, pupils and parents to explore the relationship between aspirations and achievement. The chapter introduces education policy in relation to aspirations – with particular reference to BME pupils and parents. The views of teachers, parents and pupils on the relationship between aspirations and British-Chinese approaches to learning and 'success', are then discussed in turn. These accounts reveal that whilst all parties agreed that British-Chinese pupils generally tend to hold 'high' aspirations (to go to university and achieve professional careers), parents and teachers tended to perceive pupils as holding a narrower range of occupational aspirations than pupils themselves. Differences were also evident in terms of how parents, teachers and pupils perceived and explained points of agreement (or disagreement) between British-Chinese pupils and their families regarding their future aspirations. The chapter discusses how a desire for familial social mobility (fostered by the diasporic cultural habitus) is a key driver of 'high aspirations' and attention is given to the role of social class and gender within British-Chinese boys' and girls' constructions of their aspirations. Discussion focuses on British-Chinese families' use of social capital and of 'known'/'safe' routes – proposing that these reveal agentic responses within a constraining context of structural inequalities.

Chapter 7 explores how we might understand and address educational inequalities of racism, sexism and classism. It notes that there is a relative silence within policy texts on issues of racism – which stands in stark contrast to research studies documenting BME pupils' experiences of racism in their schools and classrooms. As many teachers assumed, British-Chinese pupils are not often considered to experience racism – presumably on account of their high levels of achievement. However, as this chapter demonstrates, for many pupil respondents racism was an everyday issue. These experiences of racism took many forms – both subtle and overt. In particular, we suggest that their experiences can be understood as revealing a specific local (or micro) form of Orientalism (Said 1978) and we attempt to unpick the key features of these local manifestations of Orientalist discourses within the lives of contemporary British-Chinese pupils. Attention is drawn to 'negative-positives' in relation to the stereotypes applied to the British-Chinese, and to the gendered cultural exoticisation of British-Chinese performances of masculinity and femininity. The chapter also discusses pupils' resistances and responses to these racisms and concludes by reflecting on challenges for schools.

Finally, the key contributions of our findings are drawn together in Chapter 8. The implications of our analysis are teased out in relation to researchers, policy makers and practitioners and the argument is made that a more institutionally critical and reflexive approach might usefully be brought to bear on the complex and multifaceted issues of 'race', racisms, and achievement in education.

1 'Race' and achievement

The policy context

'Race', ethnicity and achievement in policy discourse

The presence of minority ethnic pupils in Western schools has long been characterised in negative racist terms, with concerns being expressed about their problematic behaviours and achievement and their potential negative impact on schools and other (i.e. White) pupils as a result of their 'alien' demands and identities. As highlighted by high profile cases such as *Brown v. Board of Education*, the USA historically adopted a policy of formally segregating minority ethnic and White pupils – a policy which was successfully challenged as Black families mounted a series of legal cases to demand equality of opportunity for their children (see e.g. Chapman, 2005 for review and discussion).[1] In Britain, the schooling of minority ethnic and White pupils was not formally segregated to the same extent; however, research and testimonies have documented how discrimination against minority ethnic groups was systematised within mainstream British education for decades (e.g. Swan Report, 1985; Mullard, 1985; Troyna and Hatcher, 1992). Mullard (1985), for instance, discusses how Black children were assumed to be detrimental to, and a burden on, White schools, so were 'bussed' to different areas in order to spread and minimise the impact across schools. White authorities also hoped that such dispersal would encourage (or force) the children concerned to 'assimilate', and adopt the dominant White culture (Mullard, 1985; see also Rattansi, 1992 for a discussion of the history of multicultural education policy in Britain).

As we shall argue, whilst policy approaches to 'race' have changed over the years, the pathologisation of minority ethnic pupils within education policy remains an issue today – although debates have taken on a more subtle and complex form. For instance, it is notable that issues of race/ethnicity are only really acknowledged or addressed by education policy within the context of 'under-achievement'. In this chapter we examine the ways in which issues of ethnicity and achievement are framed and understood within contemporary education policy discourse. Reviewing statistical evidence and recent policy initiatives, we argue that issues of 'race'/ethnicity have been subject to a pernicious turn in policy discourse which removes the means for engaging with inequalities, naturalises differences in achievement between ethnic groups and places the responsibility or blame for achievement differentials with minority ethnic individuals. This discourse effectively denies racism as a potential cause of differences in achievement and hides inequalities within congratulatory public statements. We also trace how issues of 'race'/ethnicity, social class and achievement (and achievement issues pertaining to girls) have been eclipsed by the 'boys' under-achievement' debate – although, as we discuss, this debate is profoundly racialised and classed.

Current patterns of educational attainment according to ethnicity

The following tables are drawn from the Department for Education and Skills (DfES) website, and depict pupils' achievement at Key Stages 1–4, according to ethnicity and gender. They provide a vivid illustration of current attainment patterns, and our commentary attempts to draw out some of the complexities that the figures reflect, as well as key points of note. What needs to be kept in mind when looking at the percentage figures is that some groups are far bigger than others (e.g. 473,665 'White' pupils eligible at Key Stage 1, compared to 42,044 'Asian', and 1,819 Chinese). We can also see in each case how the 'Total' (bold) figure is relatively useless (or misleading), given that the group categories are so broad as to include groups with vastly differing performance levels (e.g. White British and Gypsy/Roma under the title 'White'; or Indian and Bangladeshi pupils under the title 'Asian').

The first set of tables depict pupils' achievements at Key Stage 1 (level 2 and above). We can see from these figures that in all ethnic groups girls outscore boys at reading, though for some groups this gender difference is marginal (e.g. Chinese), where in others it is profound (e.g. Gypsy/Roma). This is also the case for writing at Key Stage 1, where the gender gap is even more pronounced. In maths, too, a higher percentage of girls achieve level 2 and above across most ethnic groups (the exception being Travellers of Irish Heritage); although here the gaps are far smaller, and in some cases insignificant. In terms of ethnicity, a pattern emerges across Key Stage 1 – Chinese pupils perform best as a group; followed by Indian pupils; followed by White British and dual heritage pupils. Next comes a cluster falling below the average for percentage achieving level 2, including Black Caribbean pupils, Black African pupils, Pakistani pupils and Bangladeshi pupils (mainly, but not exclusively in that order); and finally following a substantial attainment gap, Traveller of Irish Heritage and Gypsy/Roma pupils.

These patterns are largely replicated at Key Stage 2, with the same patterns emerging for comparative attainment among the various ethnic groups at Maths, English and Science. There are a few exceptions, for example Indian pupils achieve the highest proportion of level 4s and above for English at Key Stage 2.

The gender gap at Key Stage 2 English is even more evident than in writing at Key Stage 1, and girls' superior attainment is particularly dramatic in certain ethnic groups. For example, 79 per cent Black Caribbean girls achieve level 4 and above compared to only 58 per cent of Black Caribbean boys (fewer Black girls attain this level in comparison with groups such as White British, dual heritage, Indian and Chinese girls, but they out-perform White British boys as a group – of whom only 73 per cent achieve level 4 and above – and even Chinese boys, who are the highest achieving male group for English). Performance at Key Stage 2 Science is very similar

Table 1.1   Achievements at Key Stage 1 Level 2 and above in 2004, by ethnicity and gender

| | Reading | | | | | |
| | Eligible pupils | | | % Achieving | | |
Key Stage 1	Boys	Girls	Total	Boys	Girls	Total
White	**242,693**	**230,972**	**473,665**	**81**	**90**	**85**
White British	234,307	223,179	457,486	82	90	86
Irish	1,112	1,015	2,127	82	90	85
Traveller of Irish Heritage	190	178	368	25	38	31
Gypsy/Roma	351	354	705	36	53	45
Any other White background	6,733	6,246	12,979	77	84	80
Mixed	**9,977**	**9,760**	**19,737**	**81**	**89**	**85**
White and Black Caribbean	3,408	3,413	6,821	77	89	83
White and Black African	1,019	1,001	2,020	81	88	84
White and Asian	2,045	1,955	4,000	85	93	89
Any other mixed background	3,505	3,391	6,896	82	89	86
Asian	**21,468**	**20,576**	**42,044**	**78**	**85**	**81**
Indian	6,490	6,151	12,641	86	92	89
Pakistani	8,953	8,586	17,539	73	81	77
Bangladeshi	3,845	3,800	7,645	72	81	76
Any other Asian background	2,180	2,039	4,219	80	86	83
Black	**11,836**	**11,416**	**23,252**	**75**	**84**	**79**
Black Caribbean	4,328	4,156	8,484	76	86	81
Black African	6,203	6,009	12,212	74	82	78
Any other Black background	1,305	1,251	2,556	76	86	81
Chinese	**903**	**916**	**1,819**	**87**	**92**	**90**
Any other ethnic group	**2,683**	**2,581**	**5,264**	**72**	**78**	**75**
Unclassified[1]	**7,971**	**7,392**	**15,363**	**72**	**82**	**77**
All pupils	**297,531**	**283,613**	**581,144**	**81**	**89**	**85**

1 Includes information refused or not obtained.

Table 1.1 continued

| Key Stage 1 | Writing | | | | | |
| | Eligible pupils | | | % Achieving | | |
	Boys	Girls	Total	Boys	Girls	Total
White	**242,694**	**230,972**	**473,666**	**77**	**88**	**83**
White British	234,307	223,179	457,486	77	88	83
Irish	1,112	1,015	2,127	78	88	83
Traveller of Irish Heritage	190	178	368	22	38	29
Gypsy/Roma	352	354	706	32	54	43
Any other White background	6,733	6,246	12,979	72	83	78
Mixed	**9,977**	**9,760**	**19,737**	**76**	**88**	**82**
White and Black Caribbean	3,408	3,413	6,821	71	86	79
White and Black African	1,019	1,001	2,020	75	86	81
White and Asian	2,045	1,955	4,000	80	91	85
Any other mixed background	3,505	3,391	6,896	78	88	82
Asian	**21,469**	**20,576**	**42,045**	**73**	**83**	**78**
Indian	6,490	6,151	12,641	81	91	86
Pakistani	8,954	8,586	17,540	68	79	73
Bangladeshi	3,845	3,800	7,645	68	80	74
Any other Asian background	2,180	2,039	4,219	76	85	80
Black	**11,836**	**11,417**	**23,253**	**68**	**81**	**74**
Black Caribbean	4,328	4,156	8,484	69	82	75
Black African	6,203	6,009	12,212	68	79	74
Any other Black background	1,305	1,252	2,557	69	83	76
Chinese	**903**	**916**	**1,819**	**85**	**92**	**88**
Any other ethnic group	**2,683**	**2,581**	**5,264**	**66**	**77**	**71**
Unclassified[1]	**7,971**	**7,392**	**15,363**	**67**	**80**	**73**
All pupils	**297,533**	**283,614**	**581,147**	**76**	**87**	**82**

1 Includes information refused or not obtained.

| Key Stage 1 | Mathematics | | | | | |
| | Eligible pupils | | | % Achieving | | |
	Boys	Girls	Total	Boys	Girls	Total
White	**242,694**	**230,972**	**473,666**	**90**	**92**	**91**
White British	234,307	223,179	457,486	90	92	91
Irish	1,112	1,015	2,127	90	93	91
Traveller of Irish Heritage	190	178	368	51	49	50
Gypsy/Roma	352	354	706	60	67	64
Any other White background	6,733	6,246	12,979	88	90	89
Mixed	**9,977**	**9,760**	**19,737**	**89**	**92**	**90**
White and Black Caribbean	3,408	3,413	6,821	87	90	88
White and Black African	1,019	1,001	2,020	87	91	89
White and Asian	2,045	1,955	4,000	90	94	92
Any other mixed background	3,505	3,391	6,896	90	92	91
Asian	**21,469**	**20,576**	**42,045**	**85**	**88**	**86**
Indian	6,490	6,151	12,641	91	93	92
Pakistani	8,954	8,586	17,540	82	84	83
Bangladeshi	3,845	3,800	7,645	82	85	83
Any other Asian background	2,180	2,039	4,219	89	90	90
Black	**11,836**	**11,417**	**23,253**	**82**	**86**	**84**
Black Caribbean	4,328	4,156	8,484	83	88	85
Black African	6,203	6,009	12,212	81	86	83
Any other Black background	1,305	1,252	2,557	84	87	85
Chinese	**903**	**916**	**1,819**	**95**	**96**	**95**
Any other ethnic group	**2,683**	**2,581**	**5,264**	**85**	**85**	**85**
Unclassified[1]	**7,971**	**7,392**	**15,363**	**83**	**85**	**84**
All pupils	**297,533**	**283,614**	**581,147**	**89**	**91**	**90**

1 Includes information refused or not obtained.

between girls and boys, although where there are differences the marginal gap favours girls. Again, Black Caribbean pupils provide an example here with 6 per cent more girls than boys achieving level 4 and above for Science. Maths performance is likewise very similar according to gender, although in this case where there are differences these tend to favour boys. It is noticeable that Black Caribbean and African pupils buck this trend, however, with Black girls out-performing their male counterparts in maths as well as other subjects.

What is also striking is that the achievement across *all* ethnic groups is reduced if we compare the percentages achieving level 4 and above at Key Stage 2 with those achieving level 2 and above at Key Stage 1 (Francis and Skelton, 2005). Scores at writing and reading were higher in Key Stage 1 than at English at Key Stage 2, and the slippage in achievement for maths is even more pronounced. This reduced achievement does not affect all groups in the same way. For example, if we look at maths (where comparison is most straightforward), 18 per cent less White British girls, and 15 per cent less White British boys, achieve level 4 Maths at Key Stage 2 than those achieving level 2 at Key Stage 1 – a dramatic difference, especially for girls. But for Black Caribbean pupils the slippage is even greater, with 25 per cent fewer boys, and 24 per cent fewer girls, achieving the desired result than at Key Stage 1. And for Gypsy/Roma children, the difference is 36 per cent for boys, and 40 per cent for girls. These results are gravely worrying, suggesting as they do that for some groups progress through Key Stage 2 exacerbates, rather than reduces, inequality.

Turning now to Key Stage 4 GCSE grades, higher proportions of girls than boys achieve 5 or more A*–C GCSEs in all ethnic groups except Gypsy/Roma children. For a detailed discussion of issues concerning the 'gender gap' at GCSE, see Francis and Skelton (2005). For our purposes it may suffice to note that Table 1.3, focusing on the number and level of GCSE A*–C grades, does not illustrate the gendered complexities concerning achievement at particular subjects, and indeed the numbers of pupils entered in these various (gendered) subject areas. The same is, of course, true of ethnicity. Various researchers have demonstrated that pupils from particular minority ethnic groups may tend to prefer and do well at – or dislike/perform badly at – contrasting curriculum subjects to the majority White pupil population (Mirza, 1992; Lightbody and Durndell, 1996; Francis and Archer, 2005a).

Table 1.3 illustrates how the patterns of comparative achievement of various ethnic groups identified at Key Stage 1, largely replicated at Key Stage 2, and noted previously by researchers such as Gillborn and Gipps (1996); Gillborn and Mirza (2000); and Bhattacharyya *et al.* (2003), remain fairly steady at GCSE level. Chinese and Indian pupils do best (74 per cent of Chinese pupils and 67 per cent Indian pupils gain 5 or more GCSE A*–C grades; and 98 per cent Indian pupils and 96 per cent Chinese pupils gain passes at GCSE). Bangladeshi and Pakistani pupils, Black pupils, and especially Traveller and Gypsy/Roma children under-perform in comparison with the average. (It is important to note that there is far less diversity between groups achieving 'any passes', than between those achieving the desired 5 A*–C grades. The vast majority of pupils in all groups achieve at least one pass, so the differentiated patterns lie in the quantity and quality of passes.) However, where in earlier stages of schooling Black children (especially Black Caribbean children) tended to marginally

Table 1.2   Achievements at Key Stage 2 Level 4 and above in 2004, by ethnicity and gender

| | English | | | | | |
| | Eligible pupils | | | % Achieving | | |
Key Stage 2	Boys	Girls	Total	Boys	Girls	Total
White	**250,394**	**239,493**	**489,887**	**72**	**84**	**78**
White British	242,944	232,398	475,342	73	84	78
Irish	1,139	1,032	2,171	77	87	82
Traveller of Irish Heritage	191	183	374	17	30	23
Gypsy/Roma	349	323	672	22	38	30
Any other White background	5,771	5,557	11,328	70	80	75
Mixed	**8,424**	**8,284**	**16,708**	**74**	**85**	**79**
White and Black Caribbean	3,029	3,097	6,126	68	82	76
White and Black African	715	790	1,505	70	85	78
White and Asian	1,668	1,569	3,237	81	88	84
Any other mixed background	3,012	2,828	5,840	76	85	80
Asian	**19,673**	**19,048**	**38,721**	**68**	**79**	**74**
Indian	6,454	6,271	12,725	79	87	83
Pakistani	8,340	7,967	16,307	61	74	68
Bangladeshi	2,980	2,999	5,979	66	77	71
Any other Asian background	1,899	1,811	3,710	70	81	75
Black	**10,851**	**10,724**	**21,575**	**62**	**77**	**70**
Black Caribbean	4,404	4,335	8,739	61	79	70
Black African	5,348	5,269	10,617	63	76	69
Any other Black background	1,099	1,120	2,219	64	78	71
Chinese	**966**	**972**	**1,938**	**76**	**87**	**81**
Any other ethnic group	**2,467**	**2,337**	**4,804**	**61**	**71**	**66**
Unclassified[1]	**9,907**	**8,623**	**18,530**	**65**	**78**	**71**
All pupils	**302,682**	**289,481**	**592,163**	**72**	**83**	**77**

1 Includes information refused or not obtained.

Table 1.2 continued

| Key Stage 2 | Mathematics | | | | | |
| | Eligible pupils | | | % Achieving | | |
	Boys	Girls	Total	Boys	Girls	Total
White	**250,547**	**239,611**	**490,158**	**75**	**74**	**74**
White British	243,075	232,485	475,560	75	74	75
Irish	1,140	1,032	2,172	79	78	78
Traveller of Irish Heritage	191	187	378	23	23	23
Gypsy/Roma	350	321	671	24	27	25
Any other White background	5,791	5,586	11,377	74	72	73
Mixed	**8,428**	**8,286**	**16,714**	**73**	**74**	**74**
White and Black Caribbean	3,034	3,098	6,132	68	69	69
White and Black African	715	791	1,506	71	74	72
White and Asian	1,667	1,569	3,236	80	80	80
Any other mixed background	3,012	2,828	5,840	75	75	75
Asian	**19,681**	**19,054**	**38,735**	**70**	**69**	**69**
Indian	6,454	6,271	12,725	80	79	80
Pakistani	8,344	7,967	16,311	62	60	61
Bangladeshi	2,985	3,002	5,987	68	65	66
Any other Asian background	1,898	1,814	3,712	77	77	77
Black	**10,858**	**10,745**	**21,603**	**61**	**65**	**63**
Black Caribbean	4,407	4,342	8,749	58	64	61
Black African	5,355	5,282	10,637	62	65	64
Any other Black background	1,096	1,121	2,217	63	65	64
Chinese	**968**	**972**	**1,940**	**89**	**90**	**89**
Any other ethnic group	**2,476**	**2,344**	**4,820**	**70**	**69**	**70**
Unclassified[1]	**9,913**	**8,640**	**18,553**	**68**	**67**	**68**
All pupils	**302,871**	**289,652**	**592,523**	**74**	**73**	**73**

1 Includes information refused or not obtained.

| Key Stage 2 | Science | | | | | |
| | Eligible pupils | | | % Achieving | | |
	Boys	Girls	Total	Boys	Girls	Total
White	250,612	239,658	490,270	87	87	87
White British	243,141	232,532	475,673	87	87	87
Irish	1,140	1,033	2,173	88	88	88
Traveller of Irish Heritage	191	186	377	36	40	38
Gypsy/Roma	350	323	673	42	48	45
Any other White background	5,790	5,584	11,374	83	83	83
Mixed	8,428	8,285	16,713	86	87	86
White and Black Caribbean	3,033	3,097	6,130	83	85	84
White and Black African	715	791	1,506	83	86	85
White and Asian	1,668	1,569	3,237	89	89	89
Any other mixed background	3,012	2,828	5,840	87	88	87
Asian	19,677	19,051	38,728	79	79	79
Indian	6,456	6,269	12,725	87	87	87
Pakistani	8,337	7,967	16,304	72	73	72
Bangladeshi	2,984	3,001	5,985	77	77	77
Any other Asian background	1,900	1,814	3,714	82	82	82
Black	10,865	10,746	21,611	75	79	77
Black Caribbean	4,408	4,343	8,751	75	81	78
Black African	5,358	5,282	10,640	74	76	75
Any other Black background	1,099	1,121	2,220	77	82	80
Chinese	966	972	1,938	88	90	89
Any other ethnic group	2,474	2,343	4,817	75	76	76
Unclassified[1]	9,921	8,638	18,559	81	82	81
All pupils	302,943	289,693	592,636	85	86	86

1 Includes information refused or not obtained.

out-perform Bangladeshi and Pakistani children, by GCSE this situation is reversed. It is to be noted that 48 per cent of Bangladeshi pupils, and 45 per cent of Pakistani pupils achieve 5 A*–C GCSEs, compared to 36 per cent Black Caribbean and 43 per cent Black African pupils. Hence the attainment of Black pupils can be seen to comparatively reduce further and further throughout compulsory schooling. As Table 1.3 shows, the gender gap among Black Caribbean pupils is particularly substantial, with only 27 per cent of Black Caribbean boys gaining 5 A*–C grades, compared with 44 per cent of Black Caribbean girls. However, it is important to note that in contrast to Mirza's (1992) findings a decade ago that Black girls do as well as their White counterparts, this is certainly not the case today. White British boys, objects of such heightened concern over their apparent 'under-achievement', do better than Black Caribbean girls at GCSE level, and White British girls as a group substantially out-perform them. It is interesting to observe that the proportion of Travellers of Irish Heritage gaining 5 A*–C grades is not far from matching the results of African Caribbean pupils, in comparison with a far more substantial achievement gap at Key Stages 1 and 2, illustrating the way in which Black Caribbean achievement slips disproportionately over the years of formal schooling. Finally, Gypsy/Roma children under-perform dramatically – Gypsy/Roma girls achieve the lowest credentials with only 13 per cent achieving 5+ A*–C grades, compared to White British girls at 57 per cent, and the highest achieving group Chinese girls at 79 per cent.

Although social class continues to have a profound effect on school achievement, in our contemporary society it is increasingly difficult to define and categorise (see Chapter 2). This is especially the case for minority ethnic groups, whose trajectories and experiences often defy traditional British categories of social class as delineated by the Registrar General Scale (Archer and Francis, 2006). Categorisation of 'poverty' by the uptake of free school meals (FSM), as utilised by the DfES, may be particularly problematic for any analysis of ethnicity issues, as some groups may be more likely than others to draw on state services such as free school meals. For example, a propensity has been noted by some commentators that some Chinese families may try to avoid reliance on the state, and indeed lack awareness of what benefits may be on offer (Chau and Yu, 2001). Such examples may, of course, apply equally to other minority ethnic groups. However, for the purposes of providing a rough indicator of relative poverty, the delineator of FSM serves a basic function. Indeed, Table 1.4 vividly illustrates how social class/socio-economic status is for the majority of British children the clearest indicator of educational achievement (Gillborn and Gipps, 1996; Gillborn and Mirza, 2000). The figures depicted in Table 1.4 concerning the largest (White British) group of pupils should provoke national shame. Whereas over half of White British pupils not taking free school meals achieve 5+ A*–C grades at GCSE, only just over one-fifth of those taking free school meals achieve these results. These figures also reveal clearly how in this case gender is a relatively minor issue in comparison to social class/socio-economic status. Although, whether taking free school meals or not, girls in virtually all ethnic groups outperform their male counterparts, non-FSM boys usually out-perform FSM girls from the same ethnic group, often very substantially. For example, 51 per cent of non-FSM White British boys achieve 5+ A*–C grades, compared to only 25 per cent FSM White British girls.

Table 1.3   Achievements at GCSE and equivalent in 2004, by ethnicity and gender

| GCSE and equivalent | Level 2: 5 or more grades A*–C at GCSE and equivalent | | | | | |
| | Number of 15 year olds | | | % achieving | | |
	Boys	Girls	Total	Boys	Girls	Total
White	249,797	243,672	493,469	47.4	57.4	**52.3**
White British	242,622	236,915	479,537	47.3	57.3	52.3
Irish	1,146	1,163	2,309	54.0	62.5	58.3
Traveller of Irish Heritage	86	63	149	23.3	39.7	30.2
Gypsy/Roma	100	166	266	15.0	12.7	13.5
Any other White background	5,843	5,365	11,208	49.3	61.3	55.0
Mixed	5,566	5,862	11,428	44.8	54.4	**49.7**
White and Black Caribbean	2,026	2,169	4,195	34.1	44.9	39.7
White and Black African	492	471	963	43.5	51.0	47.1
White and Asian	1,065	1,071	2,136	61.4	69.9	65.7
Any other mixed background	1,983	2,151	4,134	47.1	57.1	52.3
Asian	18,568	17,770	36,338	49.4	61.4	**55.3**
Indian	7,147	6,871	14,018	61.6	71.9	66.6
Pakistani	7,084	6,556	13,640	38.8	52.1	45.2
Bangladeshi	2,536	2,754	5,290	41.0	55.2	48.4
Any other Asian background	1,801	1,589	3,390	54.8	65.9	60.0
Black	9,712	10,039	19,751	31.9	45.9	**39.0**
Black Caribbean	4,317	4,459	8,776	27.3	43.8	35.7
Black African	4,104	4,382	8,486	37.3	48.9	43.3
Any other Black background	1,291	1,198	2,489	29.8	43.0	36.2
Chinese	1,095	1,029	2,124	69.5	79.1	**74.2**
Any other ethnic group	2,358	2,118	4,476	43.0	54.4	**48.4**
Unclassified[1]	12,665	11,523	24,188	42.7	52.0	47.1
All pupils	299,761	292,013	591,774	46.8	57.0	51.9

1 Includes information refused or not obtained.

Table 1 .3 continued

| GCSE and equivalent | Any passes | | | | | |
| | Number of 15 year olds | | | % achieving | | |
	Boys	Girls	Total	Boys	Girls	Total
White	249,797	243,672	493,469	95.5	96.9	96.2
White British	242,622	236,915	479,537	95.6	96.9	96.2
Irish	1,146	1,163	2,309	95.6	96.8	96.2
Traveller of Irish Heritage	86	63	149	76.7	82.5	79.2
Gypsy/Roma	100	166	266	74.0	81.3	78.6
Any other White background	5,843	5,365	11,208	93.5	95.9	94.6
Mixed	5,566	5,862	11,428	94.1	95.9	95.0
White and Black Caribbean	2,026	2,169	4,195	92.9	95.3	94.2
White and Black African	492	471	963	93.1	93.8	93.5
White and Asian	1,065	1,071	2,136	96.2	97.2	96.7
Any other mixed background	1,983	2,151	4,134	94.4	96.2	95.3
Asian	18,568	17,770	36,338	96.8	98.0	97.4
Indian	7,147	6,871	14,018	98.0	98.8	98.4
Pakistani	7,084	6,556	13,640	96.4	97.7	97.0
Bangladeshi	2,536	2,754	5,290	96.5	97.8	97.2
Any other Asian background	1,801	1,589	3,390	94.6	96.1	95.3
Black	9,712	10,039	19,751	94.1	96.0	95.1
Black Caribbean	4,317	4,459	8,776	94.2	96.9	95.6
Black African	4,104	4,382	8,486	94.3	95.2	94.8
Any other Black background	1,291	1,198	2,489	93.1	95.5	94.3
Chinese	1,095	1,029	2,124	95.4	96.9	96.1
Any other ethnic group	2,358	2,118	4,476	91.5	93.9	92.6
Unclassified[1]	12,665	11,523	24,188	93.9	95.4	94.6
All pupils	299,761	292,013	591,774	95.4	96.8	96.1

1 Includes information refused or not obtained.

Interestingly though, the figures suggest that social class/economic status is a more salient predictor of achievement for the majority White British population than is the case for minority ethnic groups. Although FSM pupils in these groups consistently perform less well generally than their non-FSM counterparts, the gaps tend to be far smaller (e.g. only 5 per cent more Bangladeshi non-FSM pupils achieve 5+ A*–C GCSEs than do Bangladeshis taking free school meals, and for Pakistani pupils the gap is a more representative difference of 14 percentage points). Moreover, although many researchers concerned with social justice have made the point which we reiterate above – that social class has the most significant outcome and a far greater bearing than does gender on the educational achievement of the majority of children in Britain – this is not necessarily the case for minority ethnic groups (see also Bhattacharyya *et al.*, 2003). For as well as the FSM/non-FSM gaps often being far smaller among these groups, in some cases (e.g. Bangladeshi, Black Caribbean, other Black background and Chinese) girls taking free school meals do as well as, or exceed the attainment of, boys in the same groups who are not taking free school meals. Hence, when considering achievement in relation to social identity factors, it is imperative to keep in mind two key points. First, as many researchers have previously noted, social class, gender and ethnicity inflect together to impact on the achievement of different pupils. Second, as more recent qualitative work is highlighting, ethnicity impacts on constructions and performances of gender and social class, in some cases making the latter variables less salient predictors of educational achievement.

Hence the emergent pattern in the comparative achievement across various ethnic groups through English schooling is a strong and persistent one, with Chinese and Indian pupils tending to significantly outperform the White British majority, and Black pupils, Bangladeshi, Pakistani and Traveller and Gypsy children tending to underperform. As we have seen, these patterns are highly gendered and classed, but nevertheless are clearly delineated on ethnic lines. Moreover, worryingly, for some groups (notably Black Caribbean children) the achievement gap actually broadens, rather than narrows, as children progress through compulsory education.[2] Of course, it is of concern that for *all* pupils the proportion achieving the desired results reduces, rather than increases, at each assessed stage of compulsory schooling. However, that the 'ethnicity gap' expands rather than narrows for some groups during schooling is a particular indictment of a failure of the British education system to address these pupils' needs and ensure fairness for all.

A radically different interpretation of these figures is expressed on the 'Ethnic Minority Achievement' section of the DfES 'Standards Site' (2005), where under the self-congratulatory title 'Minority Ethnic Pupils Make Further Progress at GCSE', the commentary trumpets how minority ethnic groups are making 'great progress' and 'closing' achievement gaps. This was due to quoted figures such as the 2.8 per cent increase in Black Caribbean children gaining 5+ A*–C grades at GCSE (to 36 per cent), and 2.6 per cent increase among Black African pupils (to 43 per cent). Yet, as the figures depicted actually showed, there had been a 1 per cent increase among the 'White' group (to 52 per cent), exacerbating the marginality of the apparent 'narrowing' of ethnicity gaps, and – in spite of the lack of acknowledgement of the stark picture in the DfES commentary – vividly depicting the persistent enormity

Table 1.4 Achievements at GCSE and equivalent in 2004, by ethnicity, Free School Meal provision and gender

| GCSE and equivalent | Non FSM | | | | | | FSM | | | | | |
| | 15 year olds | | | % achieving | | | 15 year olds | | | % achieving | | |
Level 2: 5 or more grades A*–C	Boys	Girls	Total	Boys	Girls	Total	Boys	Girls	Total	Boys	Girls	Total
White	220,755	215,129	435,884	51.2	61.6	56.3	29,042	28,541	57,583	18.7	25.7	22.2
White British	215,036	209,621	424,657	51.1	61.5	56.2	27,586	27,292	54,878	18.3	25.3	21.8
Irish	936	966	1,902	60.7	69.0	64.9	210	197	407	24.3	30.5	27.3
Traveller of Irish Heritage	54	43	97	37.0	55.8	45.4	32	20	52	0.0	5.0	1.9
Gypsy/Roma	53	92	145	24.5	19.6	21.4	47	74	121	4.3	4.1	4.1
Any other White background	4,676	4,407	9,083	54.4	66.1	60.1	1,167	958	2,125	29.1	38.9	33.6
Mixed	4,249	4,484	8,733	51.2	61.2	56.3	1,317	1,378	2,695	24.2	32.4	28.4
White and Black Caribbean	1,434	1,583	3,017	39.9	50.7	45.6	592	586	1,178	20.1	29.0	24.5
White and Black African	357	336	693	49.9	57.4	53.5	135	135	270	26.7	34.8	30.7
White and Asian	884	887	1,771	67.4	76.0	71.7	181	184	365	32.0	40.8	36.4
Any other mixed background	1,574	1,678	3,252	52.6	64.0	58.5	409	473	882	25.9	32.8	29.6
Asian	12,838	12,187	25,025	55.7	67.3	61.3	5,730	5,583	11,313	35.4	48.6	41.9
Indian	6,240	5,984	12,224	64.3	74.2	69.2	907	887	1,794	42.3	56.3	49.2
Pakistani	4,252	3,931	8,183	43.6	58.6	50.8	2,832	2,625	5,457	31.7	42.3	36.8
Bangladeshi	970	1,050	2,020	45.6	57.2	51.6	1,566	1,704	3,270	38.1	53.9	46.3
Any other Asian background	1,376	1,222	2,598	60.7	70.3	65.2	425	367	792	35.8	51.2	42.9
Black	6,491	6,801	13,292	35.6	51.3	43.6	3,220	3,238	6,458	24.4	34.7	29.6
Black Caribbean	3,164	3,304	6,468	30.2	47.7	39.1	1,153	1,155	2,308	19.3	32.7	26.0

Black African	2,423	2,675	5,098	43.5	56.9	50.5	1,680	1,707	3,387	28.4	36.3	32.4
Any other Black background	904	822	1,726	33.2	47.3	39.9	387	376	763	22.0	33.5	27.7
Chinese	950	906	1,856	69.9	80.4	75.0	145	123	268	66.9	69.9	68.3
Any other ethnic group	1,460	1,381	2,841	51.0	60.2	55.5	898	737	1,635	30.1	43.4	36.1
Unclassified[1]	10,709	9,720	20,429	46.0	55.8	50.7	1,404	1,382	2,786	20.0	26.3	23.1
All pupils	257,452	250,608	508,060	50.8	61.4	56.1	41,756	40,982	82,738	22.1	30.2	26.1

Notes
1 Includes information refused or not obtained and pupils categorised using the old ethnic group classifications.

of the ethnicity gap between some groups (e.g. 16 per cent more of 'White' pupils gaining 5+ A*–C grades than Black Caribbean pupils). That the DfES can present this picture as a positive one illustrating 'great progress' is shocking, and lends support to Gillborn's (2005) accusation of 'tacit intentionality'. In other words, reading the figures in this perverse way does indeed suggest intentional distortion, as well as indicating a tolerance of these clear inequities.

Indeed, in spite of these differentiated patterns in school achievement there has recently been a tendency for inequalities according to 'race' to be played down within British education research and policy. As Majors (2001) and Gillborn (2001) complain, the New Labour administration has tended to maintain the 'colour-blind' stance adopted by the previous Conservative Governments. Gillborn (2005) goes further, maintaining that the apparent acceptance of race inequity within British education policy reflects 'tacit intentionality' on the part of the Government – intentionality to maintain power structures that privilege Whites. Hence while acknowledging issues such as the disproportionate exclusion of Black boys (DfES, 2003), or the findings of the Macpherson Report (1999), the Government has been unwilling to set targets for improvement in relation to any of the statistics outlined. Instead, the response has been that a focus on improving standards, facilitated by programmes such as 'Excellence in Cities' and 'Aim Higher', will aid the achievement of *all* pupils including Black students (Gillborn, 2001).[3] Targeted initiatives, such as 'Aiming High' (see Chapter 6) and small discrete pots of funding, such as the Black Pupils' Achievement Programme and the Ethnic Minority Achievement Grant Funding (EMAG), are available in recognition of the issue, to provide targeted support, but these are small-scale and localised. Indeed, work by Tikley *et al.* (2005) shows that the EMAG funds have made little impact in closing ethnic achievement gaps, and indeed that the achievement of some groups, 'notably Black Caribbean pupils, has not improved at all since the introduction of the grant'. This 'tokenism' and refusal to regard race equity in achievement as a valid issue demanding attention and significant resources in its own right is a contrasting picture to that in the USA, where differentiated patterns of educational achievement according to 'race' dominate concerns about social identity and achievement. Indeed, until recently, concerns about 'race' and achievement outstripped those of gender (i.e. boys' achievement) which (as we shall see) have had such a profound impact in Britain and elsewhere.[4]

There has been a great deal of analysis of the development of educational policy in relation to 'race' issues – although the contested nature of debates remains a common theme over the years. In 1979, the UK Department of Education and Science set up the Rampton inquiry to investigate the causes of minority ethnic (but particularly 'West Indian') under-achievement. The inquiry underwent a series of changes over the years (including replacing the chair, Anthony Rampton with Lord Swann), resulting in the publication of the Swann Report (DES 1985) – a report which had broadened its remit to an investigation of multi-cultural education more generally. Despite attracting considerable (and justifiable) criticism for its tendency to represent ethnic groups in essentialist terms (and its inability to engage with achievement differentials within 'Asian' groups), the Swann Report did at least bring issues of 'race' and racism into the mainstream education policy arena, emphasising how multi-ethnic education is an issue 'for all', not just for minority ethnic pupils. Alongside these developments, high profile reports such as the MacDonald Report (1989) (set up in response to the murder of Ahmed Iqbal Ullah by a White school peer in the playground of his school) delivered condemning analyses of the ineffectiveness of the current anti-racist policies of that time. More recently the murder of Black British teenager Stephen Lawrence, and the subsequent release of the Macpherson Report (1999) has also underlined the failures within public institutions to adequately tackle racism and promote good race relations. As Gillborn (2001) discusses, most commentators organise their account of UK education policy concerning ethnicity into different key phases, but Gillborn is right to warn that such straightforward categorisation and the linear development which it invokes does not necessarily represent an accurate picture. For influential and thorough accounts of such policy developments see Tomlinson (1977), Mullard (1985), Rattansi (1992) or, more recently, Gillborn (2001). Rather than rehearsing these details here, we wish to focus on current education policy, both as it directly relates to 'race' and in terms of some of the policy discourses impacting on such relations. As we have seen, the stance of the present government has been to play down race inequities in achievement, in spite of their clear and easily illustratable persistence. In the ensuing sections we shall turn to broader policy movements which may shed light on this approach.

The impact of 'the boys debate'

The debate (some would say 'moral panic') around 'boys' under-achievement' is well established in the UK and in Australia, and is rapidly developing elsewhere, including in the USA (Hayes and Lingard, 2003; Francis and Skelton, 2005). In Britain the concern at boys' apparent under-performance in mainstream education in comparison with girls was precipitated by the introduction of the mandatory publication of school 'league tables' in 1992. These documented pupil performance at GCSE exams (the exams which mark the end of compulsory schooling at 16 in the UK) for each school, and included a breakdown of results according to gender. These statistics suggested that, overall, girls were catching up with boys at maths and science (and by the mid-1990s they had caught up), and were out-performing boys dramatically in some other subjects areas. These findings caused a furore in the national media, with journalists speculating wildly about the supposed size and potential consequences of the 'gender gap' and about the various explanations for this apparently sudden turn of events (Epstein et al., 1998).[5]

The size of any 'gender gap' has been debated, and has been argued to be inflated by the reporting and sometimes misinterpretation of statistics (Gorard et al., 1999; Arnot et al., 1999; Connolly, 2004). Attention has been drawn to the way in which a profound gender gap at language and literacy subjects (favouring girls) – which the OECD PISA report demonstrates is largely consistent across OECD nations – skews the results of boys overall (Francis and Skelton, 2005), leading many commentators to assume that they are under-performing across the curriculum. But controversies about the 'gender gap' aside, it is interesting to consider what is included in league table data and what is not. League tables include a breakdown according to gender, but not according to 'race', gender and social class. This focus has meant that gender has dominated debate on achievement whereas other aspects of social identity have been marginalised from it. As we have seen, for the majority of pupils in Britain ethnicity and social class continue to be stronger predictors of educational achievement than gender (Griffin, 1998; Epstein *et al.*, 1998; Lucey, 2001; Francis and Skelton, 2005). This attention to nuance and the interweaving of social identity variables in achievement patterns has led many feminist and pro-feminist researchers to call for nuanced attention to 'which girls?' and 'which boys?' under-achieve (Collins *et al.*, 2000; Lingard *et al.*, 2002). So what has led to this policy focus on gender and achievement?

The impact of the 'standards' movement and educational credentialism

Of course, in analysing this question (and issues around 'race' and schooling more generally) we also need to consider the socio-economic context and the prevalent policy discourses – for the decision to publish school league tables did not occur randomly.

Since the early 1980s, Britain has been subject to policy drives and discourses emerging from the movement which we now call neo-liberalism. The rise of neo-liberalism and its infusion in educational policy in the West has been well documented (e.g. Weiler, 1993; Fraser, 1994; Ball *et al.*, 2000; Mahony, 1998; Mahony and Hextall, 2000; Giroux, 2002; Hayes and Lingard, 2003).

As researchers such as Ball (1999), Ainley (1998) and Mahony (1998) discuss, a foundational aspect of neo-liberalism is a confidence in the logic of human capital theory. From this perspective global economic competition demands the development and maintenance of a highly qualified, flexible workforce in order to ensure Western nations' position at the forefront of this competitive global marketplace. This belief in human capital theory (as Brine (2005) observes, now the staple position of the EU), and the consequent requirement for a highly qualified workforce, has resulted in a policy obsession with educational achievement (Mahony and Hextall, 2000; Francis, 2006).

Within this movement 'achievement' is extraordinarily narrowly conceived – almost exclusively in terms of academic attainment measured by exam credentials. In order to facilitate such achievement among their pupils, educational institutions must be focused on this over-riding credentialist principle and on successfully driving children towards academic attainment. There is little room here for broader views of education as facilitating citizenship, general knowledge, social skills, or any other of the raft of potential functions (Francis and Skelton, 2005). Instead, tropes of *excellence* and *high standards* pepper policy documents and the speeches of education ministers. Weiler (1993) documented the rise of concerns with educational 'standards' and testing in the USA in line with neo-liberal social policy and the marketisation of education (see Giroux, 2002). These trends have spread internationally with neo-liberalism, and have had a profound impact in Britain (Ball *et al.*, 2000; Mahony and Hextall, 2000).

As these authors note, the preoccupation with standards and accountability has gone hand-in-hand with that other new-managerialist practice, the audit culture. Within education a culture of 'rigorous' surveillance and testing has been developed, ostensibly to ensure that appropriate standards are developed and upheld. The publication of league tables cataloguing the attainment of pupils at difference schools was just one of a range of measures incepted due to the 'standards' agenda. The practice is based on a number of inter-connected premises: first that in having to advertise their results in this way schools with poor results would be 'named and shamed', hence presumably schools would be motivated to raise or maintain standards in order to avoid embarrassment. Second, reflecting policy makers' enthusiasm for the development of an educational 'market', parents ('customers') would be able to use league table results to inform their choices over which school to send their children to. Third, and relatedly, schools in a competitive market need to ensure that their exam results are good in order to attract prospective students ('customers').

These neo-liberal policy drives and the discourses on which they are premised have also had an important impact in the area of conceptions of social identities (including 'race') and citizenship. It has often been observed that workers in post-industrial societies can no longer expect 'a job for life', but must rather expect to 'upskill' and remake themselves for a succession of jobs in an insecure marketplace (Beck, 1992). These socio-economic practices become fundamental in the social construction of 'appropriate personhood', and internalised by individuals. This internalisation of responsibility for survival and success is a product of neo-liberalism's location of responsibility in the individual (Rose, 1999; Walkerdine, 2003). Neo-liberal discourse positions insecurity and instability as inevitable within a competitive global economy. It is the duty of the individual to be sufficiently flexible to maximise the opportunities available to her or him – any failure resides in the individual rather than in the socio-economic structures such as those which privilege/discriminate on the basis of 'race', gender, sexuality, social class and so on (see e.g. Rose, 1999; Bauman, 2001, 2005; Giroux, 2002 for critiques of this position). Within this neo-liberal 'individualised' model the self is not fixed, but is rather a work in progress, constantly being made and remade (Beck, 1992). As DuGay (1996) has summarised, this view positions individuals as the 'entrepreneurs of the self'. In this reading, there are no foundational aspects of selfhood such as 'race' or gender that preclude an individual from taking up the opportunities available to them – failure to do so simply reflects an individual lack of enterprise. Work by Dewan (2005) has shown how minority ethnic women[6] internalise these discourses of individualism and meritocracy, subscribing to the meritocratic view in spite of their experiences of racism, and hence attributing any lack of progress on their parts as a reflection of their own individual limitations, rather than institutional racism or discrimination.

As Bauman (2005) has argued, the neo-liberal state benefits in the transference of responsibility for 'failure' from the state to individuals because these discursive practices justify what he calls a 'washing clean of hands' in relation to those not thriving in this socio-economic environment. Indeed a discourse of meritocracy enables society to blame the disadvantaged for their social position. As the disadvantaged are thus positioned as irresponsible rather than unfortunate, so there has been a corresponding shift in policy thinking about how to deal with them (Bauman, 2005). Again, the shift from a notion of 'entitlement' to that of 'obligation' was initiated in the USA (Fraser, 1993, 1994), but has been enthusiastically adopted by neo-liberal governments elsewhere. The New Labour administration in the UK has been preoccupied with 'Something for Something' welfare policies (evoking a supposedly prior 'something for nothing' approach). This theme is mirrored in Australia in the shape of the 'Mutual Obligations' movement (with the ensuing catch-phrase 'no rights without responsibilities'). Hence a new approach to welfare has developed, involving drives to delineate the 'deserving' and 'undeserving' poor (Mendes, 2003). As Bauman (2005) describes, these policy practices have involved the creation of a raft of punitive policies that involve the surveillance, regulation, circumscription and punishment of those deemed 'undeserving'.[7]

Within this policy climate, then, it appears no surprise that improving the educational achievement of particular minority ethnic or social class groups has fallen off the agenda (Dewan, 2005) or been subsumed within a generic concern with 'social exclusion' (Lewis, 2000). Under-achievement can be positioned as the failure of individuals (or even particular communities) to take responsibility for their own achievement, and/or as a demonstration of inadequacy within a meritocratic model. To be fair, there are of course concerned and dedicated individuals working at the DfES and at other organisations aiming to impact on policy (such as the Commission for Racial Equality) to improve the achievement of particular minority ethnic groups. The late 1990s saw the publication of a host of important reports relating to minority ethnic engagement and achievement at school, often commissioned by government departments (e.g. Gillborn and Gipps, 1996; OFSTED, 1999; Blair and Bourne, 1998; Weeks and Wright, 1998; The Macpherson Report, 1999; Hamilton et al., 1999; Gillborn and Mirza, 2000; Bhattacharyya et al., 2003; Tikly et al., 2004). However, the neo-liberal, individualist tenor of current policy discourse means that it is little wonder that this work appears to be having little purchase in terms of either impacting on the hegemonic policy approach or in affecting achievement outcomes.

The hegemony of individualism in current educational policy has gradually erased specific allusion and concern with particular factors of social identity, including very notably the absence of 'race', from policy documents (Dewan, 2005; Lewis 2000). As Francis and Skelton (2005) report, in 2004 David Hopkins (then Head of the Standards and Effectiveness Unit at the DfES) openly articulated his distrust of analysis of achievement 'gaps' between different groups, and his preference for a position which sees all children as individuals coming from 'different starting points'. While this initially may sound like a sensitive and responsive view, we would argue that such an approach not only jettisons the conceptual tools to analyse inequality (the social structures of race, class, gender and so on), but also *naturalises* such inequality. Such a position discursively produces 'different [educational] starting points' for children as inevitable and natural, and from this flows a logic that the end results will 'naturally' be different too. Education policy and practice may develop and improve the achievements of each individual child, but this discourse consigns the vision of *equal* attainment to history along with associated unfashionable conceptions such as comprehensive education. These individualised discursive drives and their policy outcomes are interwoven. In a neo-liberal policy environment inequality is produced as inevitable, even as positive from a meritocratic perspective; and the persistent shadowy structural patterns that form behind these outcomes are obscured by the dazzle of equal opportunities rhetoric.

What might be asked though, and in conjunction with our previous question about the data included and excluded from league tables, is: *why is gender currently maintained and prioritised as an issue in policy around educational achievement, when other aspects of social identity are not?*

Why the focus on 'boys'?

It might be argued that gender has subsumed 'race' (and social class) as a point of government policy concern with achievement because it is a more nebulous and less directly political category. By the latter, we mean that gender permeates all social classes and ethnicities, so that it can be seen to affect all citizens. Whereas redistribution of resources to aid equity of achievement according to social class or ethnicity risks angering and alienating the most powerful groups in society, and those with the greatest political influence – White and middle-class people.

This skewing of concern to gender ('boys') away from other social identity variables in relation to achievement is clearly evidenced by the silencing of debate around the latter, in favour of continuing media and policy fanfare over gender and education attainment. While the continuing hegemony of the educational standards agenda means that the policy spotlight remains fixed on achievement, and rafts of resources and school-based materials are provided to facilitate the achievement of boys, there has been a dearth of mainstream discussion and materials focusing on achievement according to ethnicity (Gillborn, 2001, 2005). Indeed, when the head of the Commission for Racial Equality, Trevor Phillips, suggested the creation of Black schools to address needs of Black boys he was met with widespread media outrage and accused of supporting 'educational apartheid'. This is in spite of the fact that many of the newspapers concerned take an extremely positive approach to suggestions for increasing single-sex education and the inception of single-sex classes in co-educational schools, ostensibly to raise the achievement of boys.[8] This is not considered 'gender apartheid'. And while double standards appear to be applied in regard to the views of the press on segregated schooling, the language and morality of (race and gender) anti-discrimination is increasingly being drawn on by the media in application to their concerns about *boys*, to sustain what Epstein *et al.* (1998) branded the 'poor boys' discourse. A good example of this appropriation is provided by comment in the *Daily Mail*:

> Imagine that your child has a teacher who has a grudge against him. Now imagine this teacher deliberately sets him work only in his weak subjects, never capitalises on the things he is good at, makes him feel inadequate and, eventually, leads him to give up on his education altogether. You'd protest, wouldn't you … Now imagine if it isn't a teacher who has it in for your son, but the school system itself.

Where do you go now? The fact is that many parents and education experts alike now believe our school system is inherently prejudiced against boys .

(http://www.dailymail.co.uk/pages/standard/article.html)

At this point it seems important to reiterate that such presentations of *boys as a group* as under-achieving or as experiencing low self-esteem are not based on evidence. Indeed, national statistics continue to show groups of boys achieving high attainment (as we have seen, middle-class White boys dramatically out-perform working-class White girls, and certain minority ethnic groups of boys tend to out-perform White girls and boys as well as pupils from other minority ethnic groups). Further, studies continue to support Sadker and Sadker's (AAUW, 1992) findings that boys tend to hold higher self-esteem in relation to learning than do girls (e.g. Barber, 1994; Chaplin, 2000; Walkerdine *et al.*, 2001), and indeed that they tend to find schooling affirming to their (masculine) identities and feelings of self-worth (Davies and Saltmarsh, 2006). But educational policy makers and commentators persist in presenting boys generally as vulnerable and disaffected in spite of this counter-evidence.

However, increasingly developing alongside this dominant discourse of 'poor boys', are those which position *particular groups of boys* as problems and potentially to blame for their own under-achievement (Francis and Skelton, 2005; Francis, 2006). For example, where most of the policy and media commentary in this area is directed at criticising 'feminised' teaching practices and school environments for boys' comparative under-performance (criticisms which again have been shown by research to be deeply misplaced, see Francis and Skelton (2005) for discussion), a reproachful note aimed at certain boys is increasingly evident:

> Boys who are failing to reach their full potential often cause problems in the classroom through disruptive and anti-social behaviour … Every day people working in and with schools are spending valuable time and money picking up the pieces after routine acts of disruption and vandalism which are mostly carried out by boys.
>
> (Connolly,1995, p. 2)

> Secondary schools often contain groups of boys who create a culture that is anti-work, anti-establishment and disruptive to both boys' and girls' education – the antithesis of the positive achievement culture and ethos that a school is hoping to create.
>
> (DfES, 2003, p. 14)

As Francis (2006) observes, within these new discourses, 'problem boys' are positioned as not only irresponsibly impeding their own individual growth, but also those of their peers (and indeed, from a human capitalist perspective, of the nation!). In Britain these 'problem' boys are clearly classed and racialised, indicatively being working-class White, Black/dual-heritage and Muslim (especially Pakistani/ Bangladeshi) boys (these groups hold the largest proportions of low-achieving boys; see also Gillborn and Mirza, 2000). Particular concern has been expressed by researchers and policy makers at the extent to which Black boys are disproportionately over-represented in exclusions from school (Parsons *et al.*, 2003; DfES, 2005), fuelling stereotypes of Black boys as the archetypal 'problem pupil'. Indeed, studies have demonstrated how Black Caribbean boys are particularly likely to be stereotyped by teachers as 'problems' (e.g. Sewell, 1997) and classroom observational research has shown that teachers direct more discipline at Black boys than at other pupils, and that these pupils tend to be dealt with more punitively than other pupils for similar offences (Connolly, 1995; Blair, 2001a). Increasingly, in the current climate of Islamaphobia following the terror attacks of 11 September 2001 and the bombings in London of 7 July 2005, Muslim boys are also joining the ranks of demonised 'problem boys' (Archer, 2003).

Discourses at work in policy around 'ethnicity and achievement'

We saw above how anti-discriminatory discourse is being diverted from its original application to marginalised groups (in education minority ethnic pupils, all girls and sometimes working-class pupils) to boys.[9] What is important to note is the demise of this discourse in relation to ethnicity and achievement (Dewan, 2005). Equal opportunities discourse remains evident (although often interwoven with meritocracy narratives). However, as Davies (1989) and Francis (1998) have argued, equal opportunities discourses are limited in their effects due to their liberal assumption of facilitating change within existing systems, rather than questioning and challenging those systems and values which perpetuate inequalities. The case of the Ethnic Minority Achievement Grant provides an example here, as it 'builds on statutory responsibilities placed on LEAs and schools by the Race Relations (Amendment) Act 2000 to promote race equality' (DfES, 2005b). Explicitly observing that 'Raising the achievement of minority ethnic pupils has historically been viewed as a marginal issue' (p. 5), the EMAG is specifically intended to 'narrow achievement gaps'. On the other hand, as Tikly *et al.* (2005) have shown, the money available is limited, and has been frozen in recent years, raising questions about the government's commitment to it. Further, the grant bears all the limitations of equal opportunities approaches, as it simply resources extra help within the existing system (such as paying for dedicated EAL teachers, etc.), rather than being used to challenge systemised inequalities and institutional racism inherent within the education system. Consequently, its effects have been limited (Tikly *et al.*, 2005).

So what are the discourses often replacing those of anti-discrimination? If we return to the 'Ethnic Minority Achievement' page of the DfES 'Standards' Website that heralds 'Minority Ethnic Pupils Make Further Progress at GCSE', Foucauldian discourse analysis enables the illumination of various narratives underpinning the complacent commentary. For example, the quoting of a government education minister congratulating minority ethnic groups for 'making great progress' educationally reflects a narrative of meritocracy and work ethic, which positions minority ethnic groups as responsible for their own educational performance. The patronising tone lacks any acknowledgement of the particular challenges they may face in making progress. Furthermore, the positioning of responsibility for 'progress' within 'minority ethnic groups', rather than with teachers, schools, or education policy, locates the potential to 'progress' (and hence also any failure to progress) squarely with minority ethnic groups themselves. Hence while the overt message of the text is one of congratulation, the discursive 'unsaid' is that the continuing under-achievement of some minority ethnic groups reflects their own failure, rather than that of the education system.

Conclusion

In this chapter we have reviewed the statistical evidence and have discussed how issues of ethnicity and achievement are framed and understood within contemporary education policy discourse. We have argued that issues of 'race'/ethnicity have been subject to a pernicious turn in policy discourse – in which the terms have been largely erased (Lewis, 2000) and eclipsed by competing concerns (e.g. with boys' under-achievement), and the means for engaging with racism and related inequalities has been removed. In particular, we traced how such approaches seek to naturalise differences in achievement between ethnic groups and place the responsibility or blame for achievement differentials with minority ethnic pupils and their families. Indeed, we have argued that inequalities (and the role of potential structural factors in generating and sustaining unequal patterns of achievement) have been rendered invisible – being buried beneath congratulatory public statements.

2 Theoretical perspectives on race, gender, class and achievement

There are established interdisciplinary bodies of work on the theorisation of race/ethnicity, gender and social class. These mostly undertake a detailed focus on social divisions as separate entitites, i.e. focusing on either gender, or social class or race/ethnicity. Some writers actually argue against addressing all three aspects and suggest instead that either there is conflation between social categories, or that they fall into hierarchies of importance. For example, Lynch and O'Neill (1994) argue that social class is qualitatively different to other indices of social difference, particularly in relation to education, and should thus be addressed separately. However, in this chapter – and indeed in the book as a whole – we want to argue for the utility and importance of addressing race/ethnicity, gender and social class as integrally related issues that need to be collectively theorised if we are to understand pupils' identities and achievement in schools. We feel that this is important, not just at a theoretical or conceptual level, but also in social terms, as a prerequisite for social justice approaches to educational policy and practice.

This chapter begins by outlining the theoretical tools that we are bringing to bear upon our examination of minority ethnic pupils' achievement. We then devote specific attention to theorisations of race/ethnicity, gender/sexuality and social class, outlining the key thinking in each area that we shall be drawing on. Finally, we present our model for an integrated analysis and introduce the empirical study that we shall be drawing on in the remainder of the book.

'Feminist post-structuralism' and discursive analysis

Our conceptual starting point is that of social constructionism and post-structuralism. These bodies of thought have developed to challenge positivism and enlightenment approaches to understanding the social world. Positivistic and enlightenment approaches adopt a 'scientific' approach to understanding the social world and are organised around principles of rationality, objectivity and coherence. Post-structuralist and social constructionist approaches, in comparison, question the existence of a singular or unitary 'reality' and draw attention instead to multiple, competing and contradictory realities which, it is argued, are produced through discourse. Within this approach, social identities, divisions and inequalities (of race/ethnicity, social class, gender and sexuality) are understood as being brought into being through social life – through talk, actions, policies, practices, and so on. Social constructionist thinking proposes that social identities and inequalities are not fixed or based on biology (i.e. identities are not 'essentialised'), rather they are socially constructed and always 'in process'. Some social constructionist perspectives have drawn on a Foucauldian conception of power (Burr, 1995) to note how power is produced (and produces people) via discourses. Hence it is not simply held by one group or individual at the expense of another; rather it is complex, multi-faceted and shifting, and can be both constraining ('power over') and productive ('power to', e.g. generating resistance) (e.g. Foucault, 1980). Such an approach is particularly useful for understanding minority ethnic pupil achievement because it enables us to look at the complexities of power (its slipperiness and diffusion – its 'net like' organisation (Foucault, 1980)) and how pupils, teachers, schools and societies are located within complex matrices of power across various indices of difference.

As noted above, the social world is constituted through discourse. We conceptualise discourse as referring to socially organised patterns/frameworks of language, knowledge and meaning. Discourses constitute how particular ways of thinking about the world come to be taken for granted or seen as 'natural'. Discourses are not fixed or passive and they are not simply reproduced. Rather, they are 'active' in the sense that they perform actions, have consequences and are subject to change and interpretation (see Burman and Parker, 1993; Wetherell and Potter, 1992). Whilst there are many different sorts of discourse analysis (Burr, 1995), here we employ an analysis of discourse (e.g. Burman and Parker, 1993) that involves identifying and analysing discourses as practices that bear power. The goal of this form of analysis is to open up meanings and understandings as part of a critical project of 'deconstruction'. It is also worth explaining at this point that we are intepreting the notion of 'texts' in its broadest possible sense. Whilst in the vast majority of this book we discuss analyses of verbal texts (e.g. the written or spoken word, policies, interview transcripts, etc.), we would emphasise that texts can also be visual and non-verbal (e.g. pictures, photographs, video, paintings), all of which can be analysed discursively (see Barthes, 1981 and Gleeson *et al.*, 2005).

We feel that discourse analysis provides a useful means for looking at power and its role in creating and sustaining relationships of inequality and hence is highly appropriate for understanding pupil achievement. A post-structuralist approach to discourse analysis states that power is never absolute and draws attention to the intimate interlinking between power and resistance (Foucault, 1980). Post-structuralism thus allows us to engage with the complexity of people's social lives and the workings of social inequalities. It also facilitates an awareness of the ways in which people are multi-positioned – for example, how we are positioned within and by discourses, how we position ourselves and how we position others.

The version of post-structuralism that we use in our work is a specifically *feminist* post-structuralism – although this conjugation also constitutes a conceptual oxymoron. As we have argued elsewhere, 'pure' post-structuralism is conceptually incompatible with feminism because it can seek to deconstruct all claims to 'truth' – even supposedly emancipatory ones (see Francis, 1999 for discussion). Thus in order to engage with social justice concerns (e.g. racial discrimination, gender inequalities, and so on), like many other feminists, we advocate an approach that draws on aspects of post-structuralism (and deconstruction) and which acknowledges the permanent partiality and situatedness of all knowledge (Haraway, 1988, 1990; Harding, 1986) – whilst also retaining certain 'baseline realities' (e.g. Bordo, 1990; Fricker, 1994) or a form of 'strategic essentialism' (Spivak, 1993) that avoids sliding into endless reductionism (see also Archer, 2005; Burman, 1992; Gill, 1995; Francis, 2002). This allows us to recognise both how social identities and inequalities are socially constructed – and hence 'not real' – but also how these identities and inequalities can have very 'real' effects on people's lives and life chances. To borrow from Whitehead (1998), identities may be illusory but they can have a profound material actuality. Some of the implications of this theoretical position for actually conducting research in schools are developed towards the end of this chapter.

The theoretical approach we employ also maintains a dual concern with people as agentic beings (i.e. possessing agency, some element of free will and the capacity to undertake action) whilst recognising the location of individuals and groups within wider social structures of power and inequality that shape and constrain our thinking, sense of self and behaviours. We subscribe to a feminist educational research paradigm that understands pupils (children and young people) as active agents who are involved in the construction of their own sociality and experiences (e.g. Davies, 1989), whilst also being shaped by the discourses produced by and within their social contexts. This attention to context embraces social, temporal and geographical aspects – recognising how people are located within time, space and place. Furthermore, our understandings of pupils' identities and achievement bring together the social, cultural and embodied aspects of children and young people's experiences. In other words, we advocate approaching identities as located not only with individuals, but also within *structures, cultures* and *bodies*. Hence we do not treat identities as 'free-floating' or universally available, rather we understand them as produced within contexts, with the capacity for particular 'authentic' performances being shaped by embodied social and material relations.

Finally, we have found that psycho-social approaches within feminist educational research – as espoused in the work of Helen Lucey, Valerie Walkerdine and others – seem to offer a useful tool for bridging the gap between the conscious and rational aspects of identity and experience and the inner world of the unconscious, emotions and the psychic elements of people's lives. Thus we agree the need:

> [...] to get beyond conscious, rational explanations to a greater understanding of the influences and behaviours of ourselves, both the psychic and social processes of how they have come about.
>
> (Lucey *et al.*, 2003, p. 286)

Integral to this approach is a rejection of the Cartesian dualism that separates the body and mind, and a recognition that the psychic and the social are recursively linked:

[...] social and cultural analysis needs an understanding of emotional processes presented in a way which does not reduce the psychic to the social and vice versa, but recognises their interweavement.

(Lucey *et al.*, 2003, p. 286)

Thus psycho-social perspectives enable us to develop an understanding of the psychic and the social as multi-mediated by one another (Hollway and Jefferson, 2000).

Conceptualising 'race'/ethnicity

Our starting point for theorising race and ethnicity is the pivotal work of Stuart Hall (e.g. 1992, 1996) and the developments and extensions of his thinking by others within the fields of post-colonial theory, sociology and cultural studies. This body of work has made an important contribution by disrupting fixed notions of race, ethnicity, culture and racism. In particular, 'traditional' and 'commonsense' notions about race as a biological phenomenon have been challenged (Miles, 1989). Instead, it has been argued that race is an ideological, not a scientific, construct (denoted as 'race') and attention has been drawn to the ways in which 'race' is constituted, challenged and reformed through multiple discourses across time and space. 'Race' is thus unstable and 'constantly being transformed by political struggle' (Omi and Winant, 1986, p. 68). However, as Hall's work also reminds us, 'race' is a fiction that has very 'real' material and symbolic consequences (e.g. Hall, 1990, p. 226).

Hall's (1992) conceputalisation of 'new ethnicities' also provides a key theoretical orientation point – this non-essentialised approach to ethnicity allows us to understand ethnic identities as forever 'in process', constructed through the social, cultural and discursive, and integrally tied to the production of identity. Ethnic identities are thus never complete, they are 'always in process and always constituted within, not outside, representation' (Hall, 1990, p. 222). This perspective challenges popular views of ethnic groups as homogenous entitities, proposing instead that ethnic boundaries are contextual, contested and ever changing. Ethnic groups are re-framed as loose collectivities that are forever 'becoming'. These collectivities are often organised around some notion of common belonging or origin and are inflected by gender and social class (Anthias and Yuval-Davis, 1992). To use Anderson's terminology, racialised and ethnic groups are 'imagined communities':

> the members of even the smallest nation will never know most of their fellow-members, meet them, or even hear of them, yet in the minds of each lives the image of their communion.
>
> (Anderson, 1991, p. 6)

These developments in the theorisation of race/ethnicity have been accompanied by political and conceptual debates around the terminology and naming of ethnic identities. For instance, in the 1980s 'Black' identity became widely proposed as a political identity under which non-White groups could unite to challenge racism. However, its political potential was challenged by 'other' minority ethnic groups, like 'Asians', who argued that their interests are not fully represented or engaged with sufficiently under the banner of 'Black' (e.g. Modood, 1994). More recently, attention has been drawn to the challenge posed by contemporary identities that – whilst 'racialised' to some extent – also break away from, and disrupt, unitary notions of collectivity that are organised around colour-based, national or geographical origins and belongings. For instance, Muslim religious identities and 'new' migrants, such as refugees and asylum-seekers are all subject to exclusionary and racialised practices – but do not fit comfortably within previous, more static or binary notions of cultural and biological racism. Calls have also been made for further critical attention to be given to dominant ethnicities, such as whiteness, which tend to remain otherwise 'hidden' and unexamined within analyses of racialised identities and inequalities (Fine *et al.*, 1997; Anthias, 1992).

One response to the challenge of how to engage with the complexity of contemporary global 'intercultural' ethnicities and identities, and the settlement and growth of second and third generation communities, has been the concept of hybridity. As Hall (1990, p. 235) suggests, 'identity lives with and through, not despite, difference: by hybridity'. This notion of hybridity is expanded upon by Bhabha:

> the hybrid strategy or discourse opens up a space of negotiation where power is unequal but its articulation may be equivocal. Such negotiation is neither assimilation nor collaboration.
>
> (Bhabha, 1996, p. 58)

The syncretic nature of these identities is often conveyed as hyphenated identities (Modood, 1992), such as British-Asian, Black-British. Hybrid identities combine elements of other cultures in new, creative ways, to produce an identity that is more than just the sum of its (cultural) parts. Particular attention has been given to the creation of 'new' cultural forms that blend, synthesise and fuse together different cultural elements (e.g. music, dress, language, food, etc.). Proponents suggest that hybrid identities can be transgressive and/or liberatory because they challenge and transcend 'old' boundaries and ways of thinking about race/ethnicity and offer a 'third space' (Bhabha, 1990) from which to theorise identities. However, as we shall now discuss, the concept of hybridity has also attracted considerable criticism (e.g. Ahmed, 1999; Werbner and Modood, 1997; Anthias, 2001; Yuval-Davis, 1997).

One of the key criticisms levelled against the concept of hybridity is that it risks bringing in essentialism 'through the back door' (Yuval-Davis, 1997, p. 202) due to its invocation of a fusion, or grafting together, of two (or more) fixed and/or bounded 'cultures'. Furthermore, as Anthias (2001) argues, the focus on hybridised cultural styles and identities can unintentionally detract attention away from power inequalities and injustices. In particular, she draws attention to how different hybrid forms may be produced through asymmetrical social relations and she warns that not all new or hybrid cultural forms are necessarily progressive. Anthias calls for a wider recognition of how hybridity is rooted within, and produced through, 'cultural hierarchies and hegemonic practices' (p. 619). Finally, she critiques the emphasis that many proponents of hybridity place on 'culture' as the key mechanism through which hybrid identities are formed – arguing that political, social, economic and other aspects need also to be taken into account.

Instead, Anthias proposes the conceptual tool of 'translocational positionality' as a means for engaging with complex contemporary identities, paying attention to 'spatial and contextual dimensions, treating the issues involved in terms of processes rather than possessive properties of individuals' (2001, p. 633). The notion of translocational positionality holds within it notions of fluidity and process (the idea of subject positions, rather than essentialised, fixed identities) and recognises the importance of context and change. It points to movements and dialogues across time and space and addresses both the importance of social positions and processes of social positioning:

> [...] it acknowledges that identification is an enactment that does not entail fixity or permanence, as well as the role of the local and the contextual in the processes involved. Narratives of belonging (and its disclaimers) may then be seen as forms of social action, that is, as actively participating in the very construction of subject positionalities.
>
> (Anthais, 2001, p. 633)

In particular, as will be discussed further below, the particular strength of Anthias' contribution lies in the recognition of 'the interplay of a range of locations and dislocations in relation to gender, ethnicity, national belonging, class and racialization' (2001, p. 634). It is this approach that we suggest is particularly useful for any analysis and engagement with the identities and achievement of pupils in relation to ethnicity.

Alongside the issue of ethnic identities, it should also be noted that considerable debate has taken place with regard to how we might talk about (and engage with) inequalities of 'race'. In line with the re-theorisations of ethnicity, 'race' and identity discussed above, it has been argued that it is not possible to speak of any singular or coherent notion of 'racism' either. Rather, critical sociological and psychological thinking has moved towards an understanding of multiple racisms, which include subtle and complex articulations and formations that are not just attitudinal, interpersonal or behavioural, but can also be unwitting and structural – enacted via policies and institutions as well as by individuals or groups. As Said (1978) discussed in the classic text '*Orientalism*', racist discourses of the Other can be complex and apparently contradictory – for example, masquerading beneath a veneer of objectivity or positivity. In particular, Said drew attention to the ways in which the Oriental Other is repeatedly exoticised and pathologised within Western discourse – a point we shall return to in Chapter 7.

More recently, the Macpherson Report (1999), published in response to the murder of the young Black student Stephen Lawrence, brought the notion of institutional racism into the public consciousness, defining it as:

The collective failure of an organisation to provide an appropriate and professional service to people because of their colour, culture or ethnic origin. It can be seen or detected in processes, attitudes and behaviour, ignorance, thoughtlessness and racist stereotyping which disadvantage minority ethnic people.

(Macpherson, 1999, p. 28)

However, this has been refined further by academics such as Levitas (2005), who points to the importance of delineating between, and recognising, both *institutional* and *institutionalised* forms of racism – in order to engage with those forms of racism and patterns of inequality that are embedded and upheld within societies through the very way in which society and its structures are organised and normalised.

Conceptualising gender and sexualities

Mirroring the critiques of 'race' and ethnicity discussed above, critical theorists working within the fields of gender and sexuality have also engaged in disrupting the biological basis of 'sex' and gender and troubling the supposed dichotomy between sex (as biological) and gender (as social). It is not our intention here to rehearse a whole range of different theoretical and ideological approaches to sex/gender (see instead Francis and Skelton, 2005 for a broad-ranging review). Rather, we use this section to focus on the specific approaches that will be drawn upon within this book, and which we consider to be particularly useful to apply and integrate in to analyses of (minority ethnic) boys' and girls' identities and educational achievement.

In line with the discursive, social constructionist approach to 'race' and ethnicity outlined above, we also subscribe to a theorisation of sex, gender and sexuality as non-essential, fluid, contested, processual and produced through discourse. Challenging the notion that differences between men and women stem from 'nature', post-structuralist writers, such as Butler (1990, 1997) have argued that sex might be better understood as a product of gender, rather than the other way round. In other words, sex, gender and sexuality do not simply derive from genetic or biological differences – rather they are 'real fictions' that are produced and constructed through social life and relations of power (Foucault, 1978; Weeks, 1981, 1986).

Foucault posits that identities can be understood as the product of social relations of power, as a 'set of effects produced in bodies, behaviours and social relations' (Foucault, 1978, p. 127). He suggests that identities are learnt and taken up through the enactment of 'polymorphous techniques of power' (Foucault, 1978, p. 11), as the social relations and structures which act upon the self are internalised and performed through a self-regulation of thinking, behaviour and the body. These ideas have been applied and used to explain how children learn to police their gender identities within schools via regimes of self-surveillance (e.g. Davies, 1989; Martino and Palotta-Chiarolli, 2003).

The work of Judith Butler (1990, 1993) has been highly influential within the field of gender theory. Butler posits that gender can be understood as performative – as produced through acts and (bodily) performances of people as social actors. This production of gender through performance and action is encapsulated by the notion of 'doing boy' and 'doing girl'. Whilst we may feel and experience people's (and our own) performances of gender as conveying a sense of a 'real' or coherent gendered self, Butler explains that such readings are illusory. However, as she also points out, it is not that people are knowingly complicit in these performances – both actors and audience 'come to believe and perform in the mode of belief' (Butler, 1990, p. 141). For Butler, a key element within her theorisation concerns the transformative, subversive and liberatory potential of gender as performance. In particular, she argues that transgressions to dominant gender performances can be knowingly performed, which can destabilise the 'reality' of gender. Furthermore, because gender performances are rarely perfect or absolute, the gaps between these performances provide spaces within which to enact 'alternative' performances of gender.

Butler's work is undoubtedly useful and important, although it has attracted some criticism. In particular, she has been accused of over-emphasising 'performance' to the neglect of wider structures of social power and inequality that also shape the repertoire of gendered performances open to different social actors. The transgressive potential of gender performances has also been called into question. For example, Renold (2005, p. 5) highlights how primary school children in her study 'were more than ready to expose the gaps, and transgressions of other children who constantly struggled to pull off convincing gender performances'. However, as Renold argues, this often resulted in the reinforcement, rather than challenging, of gender norms.

The ways in which children 'do boy/masculinity' and 'do girl/femininity' within education and schools has received considerable feminist attention – not least in response to the policy debates and panics outlined in the preceding chapter. Feminist researchers have highlighted how gender identities and subject positions are constructed relationally to one another (e.g. Davies, 1989, 1993; Francis and Skelton, 2001; Walkerdine, 1990). That is, notions of 'maleness' and 'masculinity' can only be produced and understood in relation to notions of 'femaleness' and 'femininity' (and vice versa).

A key concern within these discussions of gender and schooling is that of power and hegemony. Feminists (like ourselves) are especially interested in how the performance of gender identities is inextricably bound up with the enactment of relations of power. Part of this endeavour requires an understanding of how gender identities are simultaneously 'in process' yet also entrenched – being continually produced and reproduced in ways that keep traditional gender and sexual inequalities in place (see Archer, 2005).

Attention has thus been drawn to the hierarchies and gradations that are produced within performances of gender. Not all performances of gender are equal: some carry more weight and power than others. Indeed, the very power of more dominant identities might be understood as based upon the subordination and/ or marginalisation of other subject positions. In this respect, a conceptualisation of hegemony (and hegemonic identities) is useful. Within the field of gender, the most common application of Gramsci's (1971) conceptualisation of hegemony has been within the context of hegemonic masculinities, following the pivotal work of Connell (1987, 1989, 1995; Carrigan *et al.*, 1985). Hegemonic masculinities are 'those dominant and dominating modes of masculinity which claim the highest status and exercise the greatest influence and authority' within particular contexts (Skelton, 2001, p. 50). Dominant forms of masculinity tend to be organised around the discursive subordination of Others, notably women and gay men (Connell, 1989; Edley and Wetherell, 1995; Paechter, 1998). They are also constituted via racialised hierarchies and relations (Cohen, 1988; Kimmel, 1994; Archer, 2003) – although not in any coherent or simplistic ways. Indeed, the dominance and power of 'hegemonic' identities is often highly localised, being produced in particular contexts of time, space and social relations (Archer, 2003).

As Gramsci notes, hegemony is never complete or absolute – it is always under threat and demands constant re-working and defence. Thus, dominant gender identities occupy a 'contested territory … an ideological battlefield' (Edley and Wetherell, 1995, p. 17) and are involved in constant struggles against competing alternative discourses. This multiplicity of gender identities (hegemonic or otherwise) can be denoted as 'masculinities' and 'femininities' – although the value of this pluralisation is contested (indeed, even between ourselves as authors, Becky uses the singular and Louise the plural). As Connell (2007) observes, his concept of different versions of masculinity work has been criticised due to its evocation of typologies; a point one of us has made in relation to much educational work influenced by his theories (Francis, 2000a). Certainly, the notion of different 'types' of masculinity is out of step with a view of identity as constantly shifting and produced (and reproduced) via discourse. For this reason we see plurality in the *performance* of gender, rather than these various performances being indicative of discrete types of masculinity or femininity (Francis, 2007).[1]

Issues of power, multiplicity and performance have also been explored in relation to the conceptualisation of sexuality. In particular, academics working within the field of queer theory have engaged in disrupting dominant notions of heterosexuality and developing ways of 'thinking Otherwise' about gender (see e.g. Halberstam, 2005). It has been argued that heterosexuality should be understood as a form of institution (Jackson and Scott, 2004) – a notion that is encapsulated within Adrienne Rich's classic notion of 'compulsory heterosexuality' (Rich, 1986). Compulsory heterosexuality refers to the ways in which heterosexuality is institutionalised within society, being 'imposed, managed, organised, propagandised and maintained by force' (Rich, 1986, p. 21). This notion is developed further by Butler (1990) in her conceptualisation of the 'heterosexual matrix', as the mechanism through which gender identites are naturalised:

> a hegemonic, discursive/epistemological model of gender intelligibility that assumes that for bodies to cohere and make sense there must be a stable sex expressed through a stable gender (masculine expresses male, feminine expresses female) that is oppositionally and hierarchically defined through the compulsory practice of heterosexuality.
>
> (1990, p. 151)

Attention has also been drawn to the intersection of 'race' and sexuality. For instance, Barrett (1998) examines the meanings of blackness across different historical times and spaces, and hooks (1992) discusses the ways in which representations of 'whiteness' and 'blackness' are bound up with sexuality (see also Mercer, 1988).

Issues of sexuality and identity have also been taken up and addressed in relation to schooling and education, with research demonstrating that sexuality is not merely an issue for older, secondary school age pupils, but is integral to gender relations and identities among primary aged and young children too. For example, research by Holland *et al.* (1998) and Epstein *et al.* (2003) demonstrates how heterosexuality is normalised within primary schools and highlights the ways in which children's sexual cultures are bound up with wider social and cultural relations and power structures. As Emma Renold's research also shows, dominant gender identities and relations are integrally interwoven with heterosexuality – hence the importance of analysing gender and sexuality as inter-related issues:

> [...] all gendered subject positions (e.g. 'tomboys', 'squares', or 'sissies') are to some extent subject to the heterosexual male gaze and all are produced within a heteronormative framework of 'compulsory heterosexuality'.
>
> (Renold, 2005, p. 35)

Conceptualising social class

Social class has long been a core concern within sociological thinking (Edgell, 1993), but more recent debates have questioned the conceptual relevance (or not) of social class in today's world. On the one hand, there are those who argue that social class is 'dead' and irrelevant to contemporary, highly individualised, modes of society (Pakulski and Waters, 1996). On the other hand, it might be argued that class has never really left the policy or research agenda. For instance, classificatory work has continued with regard to developing ever more precise measurements of social class that can be used in policy and research (e.g. Goldthorpe, 1996; NS-SEC, 2001). Furthermore, as we shall explain below, recent years have also witnessed a re-invigoration of social class theory through the emergence of a 'culturalist' form of class analysis (Devine and Savage, 2000; Savage, 2000; Skeggs, 1997, 2004). We would align ourselves with this latter, 'culturalist' approach (Archer *et al.*, forthcoming; Archer and Francis, 2006), and assert the importance and relevance of social class for the study of social identities and inequalities. However, as we shall argue in later chapters, we feel that theories of social class have been primarily formulated with reference to White communities, and hence care must be taken when extending these notions to minority ethnic communities.

The cultural school of class analysis addresses one of the contemporary paradoxes of social class, namely that:

> the structural importance of class to people's lives appears not to be recognised by people themselves. Culturally, class does not appear to be a self-conscious principle of social identity. Structurally, however, it appears to be highly pertinent.
>
> (Savage, 2000, p. xii)

Savage proposes that the reason for this apparent demise of class as an everyday language within people's lives is precisely due to class processes. Namely, he argues that middle-class modes of individualisation are increasingly normative 'ways of being' and that these shape the formation of privileged or excluded identities and render 'other', working-class identities unthinkable and unsayable.

Whilst traditionally class has been addressed in occupational terms, the new cultural analysis understands social class as produced through a combination of social, cultural and economic practices and relations of power. This cultural school of class analysis has been centrally informed by the work of Pierre Bourdieu (e.g. 1986, 1993). Bourdieu proposed a theoretical framework in which social and educational inequalities can be understood as contextually produced (within and across social fields) through interactions between the 'habitus' and forms of resource, or 'capital' (economic, social, cultural and symbolic).

Money and economic forms of capital are obviously important to the reproduction of educational inequalities as they can be used to purchase various forms of advantage and mobility (and conversely can be deployed to protect against risks, costs and fixity). Social capital (in Bourdieu's usage) refers to forms of social participation and connection, such as membership of networks, groups, communities, families and so on, which provides another important type of resource. Cultural capital is slightly more complex and can:

> exist in three forms: in an embodied state, i.e. in the form of long-lasting dispositions of the mind and the body; in an objectified state, in the form of cultural goods; and in the institutionalized state, resulting in such things as educational qualifications.
>
> (Skeggs, 2004, p. 16)

However, as Skeggs (2004) argues, the value afforded to different forms of capital is dependent upon context and is produced through relations of power. In other words, the value and weight of different forms of capital will depend upon the extent to which they are recognised as symbolically legitimate or dominant. Working-class forms of social or cultural capital, for instance, tend to only be valued, or generate status and benefits, at a 'local' level because they are not legitimated within dominant, middle-class relations of representation. As Skeggs explains, the processes through which capitals are afforded different forms of 'value' are central to understanding the production of social class. Hence the most powerful forms of capital are those in which intrinsic value can be converted, or generated, into a symbolic and recognised form (ie. having 'exchange-value'). In comparison, other forms of capital may only convey a 'use-value', wherein the value is only locally recognised (e.g. by those who possess it) and does not translate or gain recognition within dominant contexts and fields. Hence symbolic capital denotes 'the form the different types of capital take once they are perceived and recognized as legitimate' (Skeggs, 2004, p. 17). Thus the crucial point to note here is, Skeggs argues, the conversion process of legitimation, rather than the actual form or content of the capitals themselves. For Skeggs, social class is produced through processes of inscription, exchange, evaluation and perspective (see

2004 for full discussion) and – like gender and race/ethnicity – is in a continuous process of production, has fuzzy boundaries and is produced through struggle. It is thus through different relations of exchange (power) that particular types of subject are produced.

The application of Bourdieu's concepts of capital to education has highlighted how social class inequalities are produced within schooling and post-compulsory education. For example, attention has been brought to bear on how the middle classes generate and defend their privileged positions thanks to their possession and deployment of dominant (symbolically legitimated) forms of economic, cultural and social capital, which they use to successfully negotiate educational markets. As Stephen Ball suggests, the middle classes are 'adept at taking up and making the most of the opportunities of advantage that policies present to them' (Ball, 2003, p. 26). Middle-class families are able to make 'the best' educational choices and access the most elite educational spaces (e.g. 'elite' schools and universities) thanks to their differential possession of embodied forms of cultural capital. For example, studies reveal how middle-class families invest considerable time and resources in producing a child's cultural capital through 'enriched' CVs (Vincent and Ball, 2005) and how they are able to negotiate access to privileged educational spaces and secure advantages for their children at school thanks to being seen as the 'right sort of person' (Reay, 1997). In contrast, the working classes lack of (institutionally valued) forms of capital (or having the 'wrong sort' of capital) is implicated in the production of working-class disadvantage (Reay, 1997) and exclusion from the 'best' educational spaces (see Reay and Lucey, 2000, 2001).

In addition to the role of capitals, Bourdieu proposes that classed identities and inequalities are also produced through interplays between the 'habitus' and the social field. As discussed by Reay (2004), the habitus can be understood as an amalgamation of the past and present, which shapes future engagement with the social world and what is perceived to be normal, desirable and possible. It encompasses both the individual and the collective, as experiences, histories and ways of thinking combine to shape present and future perceptions and possibilities. Habitus plays an important role within the reproduction of social inequalities – for example the middle classes enjoy greater synergy between their own lifeworlds and those of dominant insitutions of society. Hence the middle-class habitus encounters less friction or disjuncture when it comes into contact with, for example, the educational field. In this way, the middle classes may experience education as 'natural' and can move within it 'like a fish in water' (Bourdieu and Wacquant, 1992, p. 127). In comparison, a working-class habitus may experience disjunctures and discomfort and may not enjoy the same 'feeling for', and expertise in, 'playing the game' as the middle-class subject.

Bourdieu's ideas are becoming increasingly popular and frequently found within sociology of education – indeed, as Valerie Hey has warned, Bourdieuian references can often be found indiscriminately peppered through academic articles, like 'academic hairspray' (Hey, 2002). However, as Bourdieu himself noted, his ideas are 'intended for exercise, or even better, for putting into practice' (Bourdieu, 1993, p. 271). An important body of theorising has been building up in terms of the extension of Bourdieuian thought to analyses of gender and class (e.g. Skeggs, 1997; Lawler, 1999; Reay, 1997, 2003). However, a task that we undertake in this book is to consider the utility of extending Bourdieu's concepts to an analysis of the achievement of minority ethnic boys and girls – which often appears to 'overcome' classed inequalities.

An integrated analytic approach

It should be clear, from the previous sections, that there are obviously a number of key commonalities between our conceptualisations of 'race'/ethnicity, gender, sexuality and social class. For instance, we are treating them all as fuzzy, 'in process' and contested identities and inequalities, as fictions with material consequences that are constantly remade and performed whilst also being embodied and temporally and spatially located within structures. However, the challenge remains as to how to employ a workable model that holds together these social divisions and allows us to attend to the points of overlap and interrelations between them. For example, it is commonly recognised that social divisions cannot be separated out and do not exist in isolation from one another (e.g. Hall writes that 'Dominant ethnicities are always underpinned by a particular sexual economy, a particular figured masculinity, a particular class identity' 1996, pp. 473–4) – but what form does this relationship take?

Various debates have arisen as to whether social identities and inequalities should be described as cross-cutting, intersecting or inter-relating. For example, Bradley (1996) suggests the notion of fracture and fragmentation and advocates a terminology of a 'both/and' approach. Cealey-Harrison and Hood-Williams (1998), however, argue that systematic analysis of intersecting, multiple social categories is, in practice, potentially unworkable as a large number of categories could be of equal importance. As we discuss elsewhere (Francis, 2001; Archer *et al.*, 2001), the notion of multiple, intersecting categories can also imply that the separate components are somehow fixed and unitary in themselves, such that these entities remain unchanged and can just 'slot' (or interlock) together, or be 'added on' to one another *ad infinitum*. This does not appear to begin to engage with the 'simultaneity of oppression and resistance' within social experience (Brewer, 1993, p. 28). And as Bordo (1990) argues, the notion that all categories can be equally attended to implies that an objective 'view from nowhere' is possible and achievable.

The challenge of finding a 'good-enough' language for this task is ongoing, but our purpose in highlighting it here is both to keep this particular theoretical project salient, and also to qualify and problematise our own terminology and usage of discursively produced, 'inter-relating' identities and inequalities (of social class, gender, sexuality and 'race'/ethnicity) within the book. In other words, we seek to convey that our conceptualisation of the relationship between social divisions is that they are inseparable to the extent that, for example, gender can be understood as inherently racialised, classed and formed through notions of sexuality, and so on. Thus, we wish to grapple with the ways in which gender, sexuality and social class are all central principles within the construction of ethnic boundaries, and how discourses of 'culture' and 'minority ethnic identity' cannot be understood as divorced from material and discursive practices around gender, sexuality and class.

Thus we might talk of 'classed, racialised masculinities' or 'gendered, classed ethnicities', or 'racialised, gendered class identities'. The utility of this is that if we want to talk about 'boys', it compels us to consider, 'which boys?' If talking about working-class rates of progression into HE, for instance, it prompts us to think about whether we are 'really' talking about White students or males. Who are we excluding and why/how? How, for example, would a working-class Chinese girl with high achievement fit into this account? It may help to draw our attention back to relations of power and what can so easily be excluded or unspoken within our imperfect everyday shorthands.

Engaging with race, class and gender in the educational field

In the following chapters of this book, we will be drawing upon our recent empirical study conducted with British-Chinese pupils, parents and teachers to illustrate our arguments around minority ethnic achievement. This section provides an introduction and background information to study.

As noted in Chapter 1, British-Chinese pupils currently record the highest levels of achievement within the compulsory schooling sector. Their performance appears to overcome some of the disadvantages associated with economic deprivation, as Chinese pupils on free school meals (FSM) out-perform their counterparts from other ethnic groups. This educational success extends beyond compulsory schooling, with over 90 per cent of British-Chinese students now continuing into full-time post-compulsory education (Owen, 1994). This is proportionally more than any other ethnic group in Britain (Gillborn and Gipps, 1996), but represents a rapid change since the 1980s, when HE participation was relatively rare amongst the UK Chinese community (Taylor, 1987). Indeed, British-Chinese students are the only ethnic group (majority and minority) to be proportionally more likely to attend pre-1992 universities (Connor et al., 2004).

The British-Chinese are popularly represented as an economic success story – a notion that has been fuelled by figures showing higher rates of economic activity (and greater representation among professional occupations) among Chinese men and women than among White men and women (Cheng, 1996). Such figures do, however, need to be treated with care – not least because, as Cheng (1996) points out, they mask important differences and inequalities. For example, whilst the Chinese appear to be successful in terms of gaining access to the professional class, they are more likely to be concentrated towards the lower end of the hierarchy in comparison to their White counterparts. Furthermore, high rates of economic activity amongst non-professional Chinese do not simply reflect the 'success' of the Chinese catering trade. This trade is itself the product of particular racialised and classed inequalities and histories, which have shaped 'a low-paid, racialized catering class' (Tam, 1998, p. 84) who experience lower levels of home ownership and increased difficulties in accessing public and social services (Cheng, 1996; Chau and Yu, 2001; Cheng and Heath, 1993). The term 'Chinese' also masks a great diversity between migrant groups (e.g. geographical, linguistic, national, social, regional) and often too little attention is given to the social and historical relations within which patterns of employment and migration are produced.

Despite the fact that they occupy a highly unique and interesting position in British society, the British-Chinese community receives relatively little popular attention. Indeed, they have been termed 'the invisible ethnic minority'[2] who enjoy both academic and economic 'success' but who remain marginalised within popular, media and policy spheres. In academic writing too, relatively little work has focused on the British-Chinese diaspora, although there is a growing critique that counters popular narrow, stereotypical representations of Chinese families and their 'success' (e.g. Archer and Francis, 2005a, 2005b; Chau and Yu, 2000; Francis and Archer, 2005a, 2005b; Parker, 2000; Song, 1999; Wong, 1994).

The study that we conducted was funded by the Economic and Social Research Council (ESRC, R000239585) and explored constructions of gender, education and post-16 aspirations among British-Chinese pupils. The study was conducted in London, where almost half the total Chinese population in Britain are concentrated (Chau and Yu, 2001). We conducted semi-structured individual interviews with 80 British-Chinese young people (48 girls, 32 boys) from Years 10 and 11 (14–16-year-olds) in 26 schools. The sample of schools included both mixed and single-sex schools and the majority were comprehensive state schools (two were selective independent schools). Most of the pupils were second-generation British-Chinese whose parents hailed from the New Territories of Hong Kong or Hong Kong Island. The sample also included some third-generation pupils (whose parents had been born or grown up in Britain), pupils from mainland China and a small number of pupils whose parents came from ethnic Chinese communities living in other countries (e.g. Malaysia). We asked the young people about their perceptions of gender issues, their educational preferences and experiences, their attitudes to learning, and their educational and occupational aspirations post-16.

As we discuss in more detail elsewhere (Archer and Francis, 2006), the young people came from a range of 'social class' backgrounds – although considerable care and caution needs to be applied when extending notions of social class across ethnic boundaries. Using a very loose and approximate notion of social class/socio-economic status (derived from parental occupations and information from schools and interviewees), the young people's family backgrounds could be roughly characterised as professional (around 20 per cent of the sample), 'working class' (e.g. manual, skilled and semi-skilled, around 27 per cent) and small business owners (around 31 per cent).[3] The point that we would like to emphasise, however, is that – in line with existing figures on achievement – British-Chinese young people in our sample were disproportionately represented in the higher achievement bands. Indeed, 60 per cent of the entire sample were in top and top/middle ability sets and only two young people out of the entire sample were in the lower ability bands at school.[4]

We conducted further semi-structured, individual interviews with 30 teachers (20 women, 10 men), drawn from 19 schools. In terms of ethnicity, the teachers described themselves as White British/English/UK (20), Irish (3), British-Chinese/Chinese-Taiwanese (3), British-Pakistani (1), Greek Cypriot (1), South American

(1) and White French (1). Most of the teachers taught Year 10 or 11, although a few had English as an Additional Language (EAL) responsibilities. Teachers were questioned on a range of issues and topics, including the achievement and aspirations of British-Chinese pupils, Chinese parents, racism and general perceptions on gender and learning (e.g. the notion of 'laddishness').

Interviews were also conducted with 30 Chinese parents/guardians (nine fathers, and 21 mothers, all from Hong Kong), who were asked about their views on education and their expectations for their children's educational achievement and future occupations. These parental interviews were conducted by a British-Chinese researcher (Sau-Wah Lam), who is fluent in Cantonese and Hakka as well as English, and to whom we are extremely grateful. All the interviews (with pupils, parents and teachers) were audio-recorded and fully transcribed, and processed via the NVivo package. Pseudonyms were assigned to all participants and to the schools who took part.

We are highly aware that interactions of 'race'/ethnicity, gender, age and social class between researchers and participants raise important issues around power and ethics that require sensitive and reflexive consideration (see Archer, 2002a, 2003; Phoenix, 1994; Reay, 1996). This project was no exception and as White, middle-class, female researchers we have attempted to employ reflexivity and sensitivity to these concerns throughout the design, conduct and analysis. Several British-Chinese consultants (both academic and 'lay') were employed throughout the project and their views and input were sought across all stages of the process.

As feminists we were concerned to build in reflexivity throughout the research process – but we also recognise the political problems that arise where White researchers undertake research with minority ethnic groups (Archer, 2002a, 2003), especially in relation to issues like racism (Essed, 1990). However, at a conceptual level, we suggest that 'matching' of researchers and participants is neither intrinsically possible nor desirable – not least because the researcher is always partial (Harding, 1991). Furthermore, power differentials will remain even between researchers and participants from similar backgrounds due to the very nature of the research process (Oliver, 1992; Yuval-Davis, 1994; Phoenix, 1994). Instead, we subscribe to Diane Reay's suggestion of employing reflexivity as a means for working towards 'uncovering/recognising the difference your differences make' (Reay, 1996, p. 443) and to Kum-Kum Bhavnani's argument with regard to using our different positionings to engage with social relations within the research process (Bhavnani, 1988). This entails interrogating how and why different types of knowledge are produced within the research process and considering what the effects and consequences of these knowledges might be (Maynard and Purvis, 1994).

3 Teachers' views on pupil identities and achievement

In this chapter we look at teachers' views of British-Chinese pupils and their families. First we consider how teachers unanimously attributed British-Chinese educational success to 'home' and 'culture'. We then discuss their constructions of home–school relations. In both of these sections we argue that, despite recognising British-Chinese success, teachers (albeit unwittingly) framed this success as problematic. We then look specifically at the ways in which teachers' constructions of British-Chinese pupils were distinctly gendered. Finally, we propose our conceptual model (a trichotomy) as a framework for understanding how dominant educational discourses of the 'ideal pupil' work to position both high and lower achieving minority ethnic pupils as 'other'.

Teachers and minority ethnic pupils

Research and literature concerning the role of teachers in relation to minority ethnic achievement has tended to focus on how teachers may be implicated within the production of *under*-achievement among minority ethnic pupils. For example, attention has been drawn to how teachers' (conscious or unconscious) stereotypes and assumptions about minority ethnic groups can impact negatively on pupils' achievement. American and UK literature has catalogued the systematic inequalities and degradations inflicted by education on Black children (e.g. Eggleston, *et al.*, 1986; Wright, 1987b) and the impact of teacher expectations on minority ethnic pupils' (lack of) success (e.g. Brittan, 1989; Ladson-Billings, 1994; Rosenthal and Jacobson, 1968; Wright, 1987a), with core themes being consolidated within more recent critical research and thinking (e.g. hooks, 1982; Ferguson, 2000; Luttrell, 2005).

In the UK, Bernard Coard's landmark publication *How the West Indian Child is made Educationally Sub-Normal in the British School System* (1971) publically recognised the systematic and institutionalised unequal treatment of Black pupils. Since then, studies of 'race' and education have catalogued the ways in which minority ethnic children experience racism from White teachers and pupils (e.g. Gillborn, 1990; Osler, 1989; Siraj-Blatchford, 1993; Wright, 1986; Youdell 2003). For instance, Wright (1986) documented teachers' complaints about the 'alien' ways, troublesome attitudes and academic inferiority of 'immigrant' pupils. Subsquent research also continues to develop and document how teachers' racial stereotyping of pupils can impact negatively on the educational achievement and experiences of minority ethnic children and young people (e.g. Archer, 2003; Blair and Bourne, 1998; Connolly, 1998; Majors, 2001; Osborne, 2001; Sewell, 1997). Indeed, it has been argued that minority ethnic pupils are often painfully aware of the stereotypes and particular expectations that some teachers hold about them (Archer and Francis, 2006; Wrench and Hassan, 1996), and these perceptions inevitably impact upon performance (Tikly *et al.*, 2004).

In particular, research has focused on how teachers may tend to both hold and convey lower expectations for Black (especially Black Caribbean) pupils, and how they may tend to read these pupils' behaviours and appearance in specific racist (and/or sexist) ways. For example, OFSTED (1999) documents how teachers' assessments of Black students' potential are consistently lower than their actual exam results. Furthermore, there is considerable evidence that teachers may be more likely to interpret the behaviours of Black boys (Mac an Ghaill, 1988; Sewell, 1997) and Black girls (Mirza, 1992) in negative ways, for example as aggressive and challenging. It has been argued that these findings reflect Western racist stereotypes of Black people, particularly Black men/boys, as aggressive and uncontrollable (Blair and Bourne, 1998; Majors, 2001; Osborne, 2001; Sewell, 1997) – a discourse which resonates back to historical racist constructions of Black people as 'bestial' and 'savage' (hooks, 1982). Feminist researchers have also drawn attention to how Black girls are often viewed negatively by teachers as being aggressive and over-assertive (Lees, 1992; Mirza, 1992; Wright, 1997). As Reay (2002) and Ali (2003) argue, this often arises where Black girls' behaviours are perceived as not conforming with idealised Western constructions of femininity (e.g. as passive and quiet).

As we discuss elsewhere (Archer, 2003), research indicates that teachers' perceptions of 'Asian' pupils have undergone some notable shifts over the past 15 years or so. Prior to the Salman Rushdie Affair[1] of 1989 (which marked a watershed in British race relations, Modood 1992), pupils from South Asian backgrounds (e.g. India, Bangladesh, Pakistan) had tended to be lumped together as 'Asians' and were generally perceived by teachers as being 'behavers and achievers' (e.g. Gillborn, 1990; Siraj-Blatchford, 1993). However, the Rushdie affair brought religious differences to the fore of public awareness, and contributed to a subsequent delineation in popular views between 'believers' (Muslim pupils, mostly from Pakistani and Bangladeshi backgrounds) and 'achievers' (Hindu and Sikh pupils, mostly from Indian backgrounds). The former (Muslim pupils) have been particularly demonised as 'problem pupils' due to their apparent lower achievement and lower rates of progression into post-16 education and on account of a rising public Islamphobic hysteria, exacerbated by the terrorist attacks of 9/11 and the July 2005 London bombings. Against this backdrop, research has drawn attention to the specifically gendered nature of teachers' racialised perceptions of both 'Asian' and Muslim pupils. For instance, Muslim boys are often associated with fears of fundamentalism and sexism (e.g. Archer, 2003) whereas 'Asian' and Muslim girls are assumed to be oppressed by their families and culture (e.g. Ahmad, 2001; Brah, 1994; Brah and Minhas, 1986; Basit, 1997a, 1997b; Dwyer, 1998; Haw, 1998; Shain, 2003). In contrast, Indian pupils have tended to remain positioned within the behavers and achievers discourse (Connolly, 1998; Siraj-Blatchford, 1993). However, it is notable that considerably little research has been conducted with 'successful' groups of minority ethnic pupils, like British-Chinese and Indian pupils (cf. Won Gibson's 1988 research with Punjabi Sikh pupils in America) and very few examined the factors promoting educational success among Black pupils forthcoming).

As we shall argue in this chapter, to understand interactions between teachers and higher achieving minority ethnic pupils, it is insufficient to simply 'draw across' from previous studies conducted with other groups of pupils. Furthermore, as our analyses of teacher interview transcripts indicate, there are various pertinent issues and problems that could usefully be addressed with regard to relations and interactions between teachers and higher achieving minority ethnic pupils and families.

Before we continue, however, we would like to sound a note of caution with regard to the data and interpretations discussed in this chapter. When we conducted the 30 teacher interviews, many of our teacher respondents expressed a genuine concern that their views might be read as stereotyping British-Chinese pupils. This, they worried, would be because they had experience of teaching only a very small number of British-Chinese pupils. We recognise the validity of this concern and suggest that the following analyses should be read within this context. However, we also found that teachers across the board, did tend to express quite stereotypical views about British-Chinese pupils and that these stereotypes held sway even in the face of teachers' conflicting experiences with British-Chinese pupils (e.g. one teacher, Mr Anderson, referred to a British-Chinese boy he had taught, but who did not conform to the stereotype, as an 'outlier'). Hence we feel it to be an important and valid exercise to delve deeper beneath these stereotypes. Our aim is thus to provide ways to better support teachers to understand how, and why, particular views are generated and how they may be detrimental to British-Chinese pupils. In other words, by analysing the (unconscious) biases within teachers' constructions of pupils, we hope to support teachers to develop ways of 'thinking otherwise' about minority ethnic pupils.

Teachers' views on 'race', ethnicity and achievement: 'it must come from the home'

All the teachers we interviewed suggested that British-Chinese pupils' high achievement can be attributed to 'the home'. Within this discourse, 'home' was signified by 'Chinese parents' and 'Chinese culture'. Indeed, the teachers' talk revealed a frequent collapsing together of Chinese 'culture', 'the home' and 'parents' – where each of these were used interchangeably, as synonymous with one another. This view echoes popular constructions of 'Asian' pupils, in which South Asians are characterised as 'culture-rich' communities (Benson, 1996).

There were three main elements within teachers' suggestions that British-Chinese success is produced by the home. First, a familial/parental or cultural *valuing of education* was felt to produce an ethos of respect for education and qualifications and a fostering of high expectations for children's achievement. Second, Chinese parents/culture were felt to subscribe to a particular *moral order*, which produces a respect for elders, a valuing and practising of discipline, stable family structures and a 'work ethic'. However, as will be discussed below, these values and practices were also seen as a source of problems (notably the danger of over-work/exhaustion and a lack of 'balance' in young people's lives). Third, the exertion of *parental will/'pushing'* was perceived as producing a strong encouragement for children and ensuring that families operate as a cohesive unit. This pushing was also, however, positioned as potentially negative – as aggressive, producing the 'wrong sort' of learning, being too 'enclosed' and denying children individuality. Each of the three elements will now be discussed in turn.

(i) Family, parental, cultural valuing of education and planning

Teachers widely agreed that Chinese parents strongly valued education and it was felt that this valuing of education produced an ethos of respect for education and qualifications within families.

> I think this thing that qualifications – they do respect people who have qualifications.   (Mrs Singleton)

> I do believe the whole background is more geared up about the importance of education and the aspirations and you know.   (Mr Anderson)

> … Education is valued much more highly by the parents, as a way forward.
>   (Ms Ellis)

> And there is, there is an inherent respect for educators you may not find in other cultures.   (Mr Cant)

Teachers often suggested that this strong valuing of education set Chinese families apart from other ethnic groups (e.g. 'I particularly work with Afro-Caribbean groups and I know there's huge problems within that, you know, culture there, to try and get the kids motivated, especially boys', Mr Noakes). This theme was also picked up on and reiterated by Chinese parents (Chapter 4) and pupils (Chapter 5), although it was notable that parents and pupils expressed this sentiment in slightly less essentialised terms than did teachers (Francis and Archer, 2005a).

Teachers felt that this valuing of education fostered high expectations for British-Chinese children's educational achievement – although (as we discuss shortly) concerns were expressed that this could tip over into an all-consuming obsession with 'success'. These high expectations and desire for success were, however, regarded as helping to motivate and drive pupils to behave and achieve well at school.

> The high expectations regarding academic success, [children] are expected to do well … whether it's to do with whether their sons behaving well, or trying hard, it's all to do with success.   (Mr Hunt)

Ms Perkins flagged up how these high expectations were linked to aspirations for social mobility, which set working-class Chinese families apart from other working-class ethnic groups by virtue of their 'middle-class' aspirations and imagined educational and occupational paths. Her perceptions of their aspirations evoke the 'unquestioned' middle-class educational habitus of Reay's (1998a) middle-class young

people who were 'always knowing' that they would follow the 'gold standard' route of
A levels to university to professional jobs.

> but I think the idea [is] that it comes from home. They are expected to achieve,
> they're not expected to sort of go into the cycle of maybe the lower-paid jobs,
> the more menial jobs. They're expected to push themselves, go on to sixth form,
> go on to A levels and beyond, and for them it's not questioned. It's part of what
> they grow up with rather than thinking oh maybe I won't go to college, maybe
> I won't go to college, well what are you going to do when you're 16. ... So, it's
> not so much 'will I go to college?' for the Chinese boys, it's more, 'where will I
> go?' They're thinking about where, which college, which courses are on offer and
> which college and they're thinking about it ... They think about it before other
> boys do. They get themselves sorted quicker than other boys.

Other teachers, like Ms Philbin, also referred to Chinese pupils and parents 'having
a goal, having a long-term goal'. This strategy and planning can play a role in the
production of social mobility and advantage by helping some pupils to 'get ahead' of
others. By virtue of being 'sorted quicker than other boys', they are able to maximise
their choices in the educational marketplace (see also Ball, 2003). As noted by Archer
et al. (2005), many working-class pupils occupy structurally riskier positions which
feed into the adoption of a 'wait and see' approach to educational choices and a
deferment of post-16 plans. To some extent, this 'wait and see' approach represents a
pragmatic strategy for the management of risk and disappointment (being designed
to keep as many options open as possible and not to hang all hopes on a particular
favoured option). However, it can also place pupils at a disadvantage within a system
that favours strategic planning and choice-making. As Ms Perkins notes, however, the
British-Chinese pupils she has met seem to be circumventing this issue and adopting
a middle-class mode of engagement with the education system, irrespective of their
own class positioning.

(ii) Moral order

A second element to this discourse was the notion that Chinese parents/culture were
felt to subscribe to a particular moral order. This moral code was seen as producing
'respect' (especially for elders), a valuing and practising of discipline, stable family
structures and a 'work ethic', all of which can foster success.

> [Parents] teaching them, you know, right and wrong ... You know, having very
> high moral standards.   (Ms Philbin, Chinese teacher)

> I think that's a cultural thing, that they're a very respectful sort of society.
>   (Mrs Singleton)

> The family's enclosed. I think they [pupils] would want to please their parents.
> There's still, there's a lot of respect for their parents and their parents' wishes.
>   (Ms Ellis)

> They are very well behaved and respectful towards adults.   (Ms Lynch)

Within this discourse of morality, several White teachers also made specific mention of Chinese families as being more cohesive and stable family units, as compared to families from other ethnic backgrounds. For instance, Ms Benjamin compared Chinese families to other ethnic groups with more 'polygamous' family structures.[2] 'Stable' family units were felt to benefit British-Chinese children as they would be less likely to have to suffer the trauma of households breaking apart:

> I think, I suspect that would be another difference, there probably is less family break up and dysfunction for Chinese families and ethnic groups … [but] again, that's just, you know, it may be that we're not made aware of it .   (Ms Ellis)

> It's a highly supportive family and they're usually very stable families, very supportive.   (Mr Hunt)

Notions of stability and morality are closely associated with (idealised) constructions of (White) middle-class identities, against which other (White and Black) working-class families are often pathologised as immoral, feckless and unstable (see Skeggs, 2004; Phoenix, 1987). In this way, these teachers might be read as explaining British-Chinese success as due to their perceived enactment or embodiment of idealised 'family values' as part of a 'culture rich' (Benson, 1996) construction of Chinese ethnicity. This is illustrated particularly within Ms Ellis' extract, below:

> I mean I do think it seems to come from this sort of tight family structure. Right from the beginning they sort of discipline – there's better health care, they're fed properly, they don't eat garbage – you notice that, they often bring in their own pack lunches.   (Ms Ellis)

Within this extract, Ms Ellis suggests that families' attention to their children's food (e.g. through the provision of packed lunches) can be read within a moral discourse, as indicative of 'care of children'. She identifies discipline, health and nutrition as key elements within the production of children's educational success – a point with which many people might agree. However, her constructions also contain an unsaid, implicit pathologisation of the families of those pupils who are not achieving (i.e. White and Black working-class pupils). The implication is that such pupils come from families that are looser in structure, lack discipline, eat 'garbage' and eat school dinners.[3] As such, her comments could be read as blaming poor families for making 'wrong' choices, e.g. with regard to food, discipline and health, rather than blaming the inadequacies of the system (e.g. the quality and/or cost of school dinners).[4] Thus this construction implies that those who cannot provide packed lunches (e.g. families entitled to free school meals) are in some way less 'caring'/careful and attentive to the needs, healthcare and nutrition of their children.

A construction of 'Chineseness' as integrally associated with notions of morality, discipline and respect was used to align British-Chinese identities with the qualities that are congruent with a 'good' and desirable learner/pupil. For instance, as will be discussed further below on the section on *Home-School relations*, teachers suggested that the perceived moral order of Chinese families 'fitted' well with the school ethos and this congruence could help minimise potential misunderstandings and smooth home-school interactions. The assumed focus on discipline and structure within Chinese families was also mentioned as helping British-Chinese pupils to fit effortlessly into the school discipline structure (as good, compliant pupils would not challenge authority):

> I presume that the Chinese children have quite maybe, they may have quite a structured life outside school and because their life is quite structured, they are able to be quite structured inside school ... What I find is that they're a lot more focused in class and they will follow instructions more accurately than the other children and I think they have, whether they believe it or not, you know they seem to have more respect for the teacher and I think they're more you know, they won't talk back or have any confrontation in any way at all and even if they do misbehave, if you tell them off you can tell that it affects them a lot more than maybe a child from a different culture.
>
> (Mr Anderson)

A key element within this assumed cultural practice of discipline and respect was the notion of a Chinese 'work ethic'[5] (e.g. 'I think that there is by and large, this very good work ethic and, you know, good determination to use the opportunities which they get'). This was commonly felt to promote pupils' willingness and readiness to work hard at school. In some cases, the notion of a Chinese work ethic was almost essentialised as a 'natural' aspect of Chineseness that was not present in other ethnic groups, or which could be 'diluted' within dual heritage families. For instance, Mr Groome identified one boy, Ben, as 'not quite as hard working' as other British-Chinese boys at school, which Mr Groome attributed to Ben's 'not totally Chinese' home (notably a reconstituted family structure and a White step-father):

> [Ben is] not quite as hard working as the others that I am thinking of. I think his – although academically he is perfectly competent – it always seems to me with the other Chinese boys in the past that this is a very definite work [ethic] here which is no doubt engendered by parents. Ben has got quite a good work ethic ... but there are occasions where he can be a little bit lazy, possibly connected with his own family background, which is not totally Chinese. His mother is Chinese but his [step]father is English.

Despite teachers' exhortations of discipline, morality and respect as factors that promoted achievement and enabled pupils to 'fit' with schools, these values and practices were conversely also seen as a source of potential problems from British-Chinese boys and girls. For instance, an over-emphasis on discipline (and children's conformity to this discipline) was positioned as being at odds with a child-centred 'learning through (assertive) questioning' pedagogical model. Furthermore, a number of teachers warned against the danger of over-work and exhaustion that might result from the Chinese 'work ethic' and several worried that there may be a lack of 'balance' in young people's lives. For instance, Mrs Brennan described the Chinese as 'selfless, as a race' and worried that a Chinese cultural ethos of respect and discipline to the collective could create too many competing demands in British-Chinese children. She cited the example of a British-Chinese girl at her school who, Mrs Brennan worried, was 'making herself ill' through her over-work and exertions as she tried to balance a dedication to schoolwork, helping out in her family's restaurant and 'working out' in the gym to 'stay slim'. (We shall return to this example again below, in our discussion of teachers' constructions of British-Chinese femininities.)

(iii) Parental 'pushing' and collectivism

It was commonly felt that Chinese parents' valuing of education was backed up with a distinct 'pushing' of children to produce success ('if their parents are quite controlling that most probably will have quite a major effect [...] they are very pushy, though', Mr Anderson). This pushing was felt to include the regulation of children's schoolwork, for example ensuring that all homework is completed ('I would think that they [children] are *made* to do homework', Mrs Singleton) and a general pushing of children to achieve their maximum potential. As Ms Perkins put it:

> the boys usually are quite successful in class, but I think parents, from what I've seen of parents' evening, they do want them to do better. They do want them to push themselves that bit more, even if they are coming out with predicted five A–Cs or whatever across the board, they're still saying make the C a B, make the B an A, y'know, and they're pushing them from that ... I think it's just the culture that they come from and the family background. As I said, parents will always look and see what could be done better rather than oh this is a good report, I mean yes this is a good report but you could push this now. You know you can move yourself on a grade. What does he need to do to do that? Are you listening? This sort of stuff, that tends to be the sort of support you get from the parents when they come in to parents' evenings and meetings and progress checks and stuff like that.

However, whilst 'parents who push their children' are applauded and welcomed within education policy discourse, as Miriam David notes, 'pushy parents' (particularly 'pushy mothers') may actually be demonised within schools and the media. We thus suggest that there seems to be a fine discursive line between constructions of beneficial/'good' pushing versus excessive/'bad' pushing – a tension that is reflected within some of the teachers' constructions of Chinese parents (e.g. Mr Anderson's reflection that 'they are pushy, though').

Various studies have highlighted how minority ethnic parents tend to hold higher expectations than schools for their children – whilst schools tend to hold lower expectations for pupils and position parents as 'overambitious' and wanting 'too much' (e.g. Mirza, 1992; Archer *et al.*, 2004). These lower expectations can negatively impact on minority ethnic pupils' progression within compulsory and post-compulsory education (see e.g. Archer, *et al.*, 2003). However, as Ms Perkins went on to explain, she had recently undertaken a closer analysis of the attainment data as part of her new role as EMA co-ordinator, and had actually found that some of the British-Chinese boys were indeed under-performing relative to their predicted ability levels:

> last year, when my job changed into ethnic minority [achievement] away from more the EAL, I did a lot of analysis work, and that was one thing that came out

when I analysed the results for 2002. We had two boys, two Chinese boys, which I know is a very small statistic, but they got their 100 per cent A–Cs. But when I looked at their CAT tests, their SATs predictions for GCSEs, they actually under-achieved by 50 per cent.

In this respect, we suggest that minority ethnic parents' 'pushing' and high expectations might provide useful points for teachers and schools to use to reflect on whether their own expectations for minority ethnic pupils could/should be raised.

Within the teachers' transcripts, this notion of 'pushing' parents was linked with the image of a 'tight' and 'cohesive' family unit that prioritises collectivism over individualism. In other words, Chinese families were felt to treat a child's educational success as something that is achieved for the good of the family (or to repay parental sacrifices), rather than for the individual (e.g. 'it's almost as if the boys are duty bound, because their parents are clearly making sacrifices to send them here, to ensure that they do the very best for themselves that they possibly can do', Mr Groome). A collectivist orientation towards 'home culture' was felt to provide the means through which both boys and girls can resist 'peer pressure':

> Because the family structure's so much closer. … they're prouder of their culture, their self-esteem is higher, and so I don't think they would suffer the need for, you know, for peer pressure to quite such an extent. (Ms Ellis)

On the one hand, teachers expressed admiration for Chinese families' cohesion and pushing of children to produce success, but on the other hand, these qualities were faintly disapproved of, as teachers implied that some form of inter-generational conflict is a more 'normal' model of family relations:

> What I've seen has been sort of interactions during let's say parents' evenings if it's like a parents' evening and the boys come along with the parents, but I haven't seen any sparks flying at all so – I don't know what goes on behind the scenes, but generally they tend to present a united front, you know? … All of them, mother, father, son, they're all asking the same questions about the future and they appear to want the same things. But as I say, I don't know really what goes on [Interviewer: Is that fairly typical of most of the boys here?] Not necessarily, I mean, sometimes the boys generally aren't afraid to disagree with the parents, teachers, virtually anybody they can find to disagree with! So it's not so much the norm as it once was. (Mr Baxter)

> [British-Chinese pupils are] following very much in parents' footsteps in that respect. Almost as if this had been indicated to them in advance [that] this is what you should do. (Mr Groome)

Mr Baxter's and Mr Groome's extracts seem to suggest that perhaps the 'united front' that teachers encounter during parents' evenings is not 'what goes on behind the scenes'. They both insinuate that perhaps some boys have been told what to say 'in advance' of these public encounters and might be 'afraid to disagree'. In this sense, British-Chinese pupils and their families become positioned as almost anachronistic, or archaic – representing 'old fashioned' relations of respect, compared with the norm of contemporary, challenging youth. Indeed, British-Chinese pupils who appear to agree with their parents' wishes are almost positioned as outside the boundaries of 'normal' youth identity – which in itself reveals how dominant conceptualisations of youth are often based on Eurocentric assumptions that privilege notions of individuality and rebellion as 'normal'.

These themes are also illustrated by Mrs Brennan's discussion of a girl who, in her view, differed considerably from other (British) Chinese girls:

> I think (pupil's name) from Hong Kong was quite different to my experience from other Chinese students. Because of her aspirations herself, not just for her family but, she *was allowed to be a person in her own right you know*. I'm not sure whether that's the case with the other girls. I can't be, I didn't know them as well, but it was mainly you know, 'your family needs you to do this or this and *you will do it*'. In (pupil's name)'s case it wasn't that. It was, 'we want you to do as well as you can and here's the money', you know and 'mummy and daddy love you' and it was, in that sense it was much more *Western* (emphasis added).

Mrs Brennan's extract highlights the unconscious privileging of 'Western' notions of individualism and selfhood, which she suggests are not present in mainland Chinese culture ('she was allowed to be a person in her own right' versus 'your family needs you to do this and this, and you will do it'). The notion of Chinese familial duty and demands is juxtaposed with Western family 'love' and choice ('do as well as you can and here's the money'), to create an Eastern-Western cultural dichotomy, in which the 'Other' (non-western) approach is implicitly criticised through a moral discourse of 'love'.

Ran (2001) also found in her research that Chinese parents' high expectations and dedication to their children's learning tended to be interpreted by teachers as 'unnecessarily harsh and undermining of children's confidence' (Ran, 2001, p. 311). As noted by Rattansi (1992) and Alexander (2000), minority ethnic communities that are perceived as being culture-rich (like South Asian and Chinese families) tend to be ambivalently positioned as being both a (positive) source of strength and cohesion and a (negative) source of oppression and restriction of young people.

> On the one hand, the invocation of strong cultural values and traditions are seen as a positive contribution to society, overtly challenging wider social decay, whereas on the other, they are seen as constituting a source of internal oppression for the young.
>
> (Alexander, 2000, p. 5)

Teachers' views of home-school relations

In some respects, teachers suggested that Chinese parents are not a problematic group for schools because they rarely complain and they espouse a congruent high valuing of education. For instance, Chinese parents were described as adopting a 'receptive' attitude to home-school contact, such as parents' evenings, as compared to parents from other ethnic groups:

I know from just anecdotal evidence of parents' evenings, things like that, the parents are very receptive [Interviewer: Right] and they often write things down – so they're clearly very, very bothered about education.   (Mr Cant)

Well I do know they have, you know, a lot of parental support which I see, you know, at the parents' evenings and things like that. You know, the whole family will be there, so we get to the point where it will be more than the mother and father will turn up and you know. … It's quite obvious, obvious to see through the parents' evening that parents are more, they are very interested in what you're saying and any ways how their child can improve. Whereas sometimes when I speak to other parents they are basically nodding their heads, you know watching, looking at their clock, you know? They [Chinese parents] seem to be more interested in how they can support their child and you know obviously improve their academic [achievement].   (Mr Anderson)

As Mr Cant and Mr Anderson's extracts illustrate, this positive attitude is framed in terms of Chinese parents' compliance to the authority of the teacher during these events, as they listen and appear to engage with what the teacher is telling them ('they often write things down', 'they're very interested in what you're saying'). As Walker and Maclure (2005, p. 100) discuss, parents evenings are 'tightly organised, routinised and often hectic occasions … in which "dialogue" between teachers and parents has been found to follow the asymmetrical pattern of "institutional talk"'. This 'instutional talk' is characterised by the 'expert' (the teacher or school) exerting a greater control and command over the nature and form that the interaction takes.

Indeed, when asked, the vast majority of teachers imagined that Chinese parents are happy with their child(ren)'s schooling:

As far as I am aware, the answer is yes there. They're happy with the results, the progress.   (Mr Baxter)

Mr Griffiths similarly assumed that because most British-Chinese pupils continue into his school's sixth form, this represented a 'vote of confidence' by these parents. A few teachers also pointed to instances where this appreciation had been demonstrated in concrete, economic terms, as Chinese families had made gifts of money to the school.

Interestingly I think her dad – I don't know if this is typical of the culture – but dad was so delighted with the school that he made a big donation to the Sixth Form. I don't know you know, I mean we don't normally get donations at all to the Sixth Form so – but it was several hundred pounds, you know.
                    (Mrs Brennan)

I think so, yeah. And they're terribly, they seem very grateful. And we don't have any complaints … one family just gave us £500 they were so pleased with their daughter, yeah. [Interviewer: wow!] You know? That's very atypical. So it's sort of very generous, very supportive, and an acknowledgement that the school perhaps, can do more for their daughter than they could.
                    (Ms Ellis)

As we shall see in Chapter 4, the teachers' overwhelming perception that Chinese parents are satisfied with their children's education was revealed by our data as a misreading. However, teachers also felt that there were various issues with the type of engagement that they received from Chinese parents. In particular, the notion that Chinese parents were offering 'unquestioning' support to the school was problematised and positioned as antithetical to notions of the 'engaged parent'. Furthermore, their under-representation in home-school activities (such as PTAs) was positioned as failing to conform to current notions of the 'participatory parent'.

Thus on one level, Chinese parents' (perceived) 'unquestioning' deference to schools and education professionals was valued as a form of 'support' (and a welcome relief from parents who come 'roaring into school, kicking up a fuss'.[6] However, it was also problematised as a culturally alien practice, an 'almost ... embarrassing kind of humbleness', which teachers tended to feel uncomfortable with:

> I think it is from the parents and the community. I mean I think they, the families have just such a high regard for education, and for teachers. I was thinking about that view as I drove into work this morning 'cos I knew I was meeting with you. But I can't remember, certainly not at Slater School, meeting a family who have challenged us, or been angry with us ... They have a profound respect where, whenever we meet at parents' meetings they just want to thank us for everything we're doing. Wouldn't ever question something they thought we were doing wrong, or if they felt the teaching wasn't up to scratch. It's, you know, it's almost, for some families, especially the more newly arrived families, almost an embarrassing kind of humbleness to the whole system. And I think that's cultural, historically cultural in China, but there is a kind of respect for people that manage education. And that I think is fairly widespread. ... But they do have, you know, this kind of high esteem for education, and would never come roaring into school kicking up a fuss about something we've done [Interviewer: right, yeah.] You know, they really do kind of support us.   (Mrs McCluskey)

It has been noted that, within current education policy, 'Parental involvement in their children's school learning is now generally accepted as being both legitimate and desirable' (Bastiani, 1997, p. 2). This has been reinforced through various official publications, as parents have come to be positioned as 'consumers' (DES 1991, DfE 1994) and 'partners' (DfEE 1998 – see also the 'Excellence in Cities' programme[7]). Chinese parents, however, were described as not fitting this model. In parents' evenings, for example, Chinese parents were described as 'low key' and overly deferential, and this style of interaction was identified as marking them out from other groups of parents (particularly White parents).

> Without exception all of the parents of the Chinese boys that we have been discussing that I've come into contact with have been very low key in their approach to any issue to do with the schooling here. It's almost as if they sort of accept you lot are doing a good job, 'we are happy that our sons are here and having chosen to send our sons here we are accepting classically that you are doing the best job'. It's always been extremely low key.   (Mr Groome)

... when I meet [Chinese] parents they seem to be deferential to teachers, whereas we get other parents from various other backgrounds coming up the school you know wanting to be a lot more quarrelsome. Chinese parents, generally speaking, you know, think that the school is doing the very best they can and their children have got, you know potential and want to do well.

(Mrs Singleton)

From a policy perspective, Chinese parents might be read as not 'doing' home-school relations in the 'right' way – as they appear not to be engaging with and questioning schools. As we will suggest in a later section, this construction mirrors, in some ways, the deficit positioning of British-Chinese pupils in relation to notions of the 'ideal pupil'. However, as Mr Groome also suggests, this perceived veneer of parental satisfaction may, in fact, be hiding other issues, as minority ethnic parents may feel inhibited about voicing their views and may feel compelled to seek solutions on their own:

INTERVIEWER: Is that quite characteristic of most parents or do they stand out?

MR GROOME: No ... they are very distinct in their approach, Chinese parents, very distinct. Certainly the ones I've had contact with. ... I think I've probably got relatively little experience of parents from other ethnic groups but I think that – let's say this: I think your average English family based in [area] or whatever, when they come up here will be a little bit more demanding as it were of what they expect from the school and won't hesitate to actually voice such views. Whereas even if the Chinese or other ethnic families, even if they do have other expectations, it's almost as if they will quietly sort that side of things out by saying, let's provide extra tuition quietly on a Saturday or whatever.

Indeed, research evidence suggests that many Black and minority ethnic parents do not feel listened to or understood by teachers within mainstream schools (Reay and Mirza, 2005). They tend to experience confusion and a lack of meaningful communication with schools (Bhatti, 2000) and report experiencing relations of distrust/mistrust (Crozier, 2005) with staff. Ran describes interactions between Chinese parents and teachers as travelling on 'parallel tracks, seldom making contact' (p. 318) – a situation in which each side cannot 'hear' the other (see Chapter 4 for further discussion).

However, a number of teachers actually felt that Chinese parents were, in some respects, being negligent of their responsibilities to help schools improve by refusing to provide (or witholding) feedback:

INTERVIEWER: Do you think that most Chinese parents are satisfied with their daughter's education?

MR CANT: I've never had a complaint from a Chinese girl, or their parent. ... [but] that's not such a good thing.

INTERVIEWER: Oh right, really?

MR CANT: Well it's, I don't mind the odd complaint because that's people commenting and people saying this isn't quite right, or my music lesson wasn't sorted out effectively, or this isn't, this shouldn't be going on in a maths lesson. That is another way of us improving the school. And whilst in the short term, you know, you're fire fighting, or reacting, and it's frustrating, in the long term you find out what's going on. And you don't get that kind of feedback from Chinese parents.

Teachers generally indicated that, whilst they welcomed and appreciated the respect that families afforded them, perhaps Chinese parents *should* be more 'questioning of the system'. A few suggested that there is a tendency among high achieving ethnic groups (notably Indian and Chinese parents) to place the 'blame' for any problems or under-performance on their children, rather than looking to issues within 'the system' – and that this tendency may reflect their lack of knowledge of the English educational context:

> I mean my interactions with them have always been very respectful [of] teachers and school, yes. I mean they are just very concerned that their children do well. I think they would be more likely to put the blame on their children maybe than the system ... [they are] wanting to help a lot but not quite knowing exactly how to do that. (Ms Platt)

Chinese parents were also criticised for not adhering to a model of active participation in home-school programmes and activities:

> They don't tend to get involved in things like the school association, those sorts of things ... Yeah, they'll come in and say I want to talk about my daughter's education. [Interviewer: Right] They don't, they don't flood in to help with fund raising or anything else. I mean there is a dedicated body of staff [*sic.*] who tend to sort of dedicate themselves to that early on in, you know, when their daughters arrive at the school, and they tend to stay with it until their daughters leave, you know on the parents association and that sort of thing. I'm not that aware of many Chinese, although they're not that significantly represented anyway. (Mr Griffiths)

In other words, Chinese families were positioned as not engaging 'properly', or in the 'right' way with education – i.e. they were not engaging in idealised middle-class ways, as advocated by New Labour policy (Gewirtz, 2001).

As will be noted in Chapter 4, Chinese parents themselves voiced quite different views of their (dis)satisfaction with the education system. It was also notable that it was only Ms Philbin, a teacher of Chinese origin herself, who suggested that Chinese parents might not be entirely satisfied with their children's education (see Chapter 4).

We suggest that these examples are indicative of Crozier and Reay's (2005) argument that, despite policy shifts that emphasise creating partnership and dialogue between parents and schools, power within home-school relations still resides predominantly with the school. Hence current drives and initiatives to improve partnerships between parents and schools 'have little impact on those parents who are disconnected from the school' (Walker and Maclure, 2005, p. 98).

We also suggest that the teachers' concern that Chinese parents fail to challenge them sufficiently might also usefully be read within the context of Walker and Maclure's (2005) empirical research on teacher-parent interactions during parents' evenings. This work revealed how, within these spaces, teachers act consistently as 'experts' who manage down parents' involvements to a minimum. Indeed, Walker and Maclure note that where teachers encounter challenges from parents, they tend to respond defensively and seek to justify their professionalism, rather than engaging with the concern in question. Indeed, parental demands were widely regarded 'as a source of threat and unpredictability' (Walker and Maclure, 2005, p. 103), and parents' requests (e.g. to move their children into a higher ability set or enter them for a higher level examination paper) tended to be futile. This suggests that perhaps teachers might be better understood as reproducing New Labour policy rhetoric around the desirability of parents as 'consumers' and 'active partners', rather than a reflexive desire to promote greater dialogue, accountability and parity within these encounters. As Walker and Maclure note, parents' evenings represent an interface point, 'a location where the norms and practices of the school are potentially challengeable' (2005, p. 103). As such, they suggest, 'it is hardly surprising that schools wanted to police that boundary, while still needing to subscribe to the rhetoric of parental involvement' (ibid.). All parents, Walker and Maclure suggest, are caught in a double bind – they need to show an interest in their children's education and prove themselves responsible in order to have voice and be listened to seriously. Yet teachers may also regard this engagement as a threat, and interpret it as surveillance and/or interfering. However, we suggest that these difficulties may be particularly amplified in the case of minority ethnic parents – who are particularly likely to be assumed to engage in the 'wrong' way.

Teachers' constructions of gender and British-Chinese pupils

Teachers were unanimous in the view that, generally, boys and girls have different learning styles. Views varied, however, as to whether these were seen as resulting from social factors or innate, biological differences (or a combination of the two). In this section we examine teachers' constructions of British-Chinese boys and girls, and the relationship of these to wider contructions of masculinity and femininity and learning.

Teachers' views of British-Chinese boys

In recent years, considerable media and policy attention has been afforded to the notion of 'laddishness' and its potential detrimental impact on boys' achievement (see Francis, 1999). Given the concern of policy makers concerning the possible effects of boys' 'laddish' behaviour on their academic achievement (and our previous research in this area) the notion of 'laddism' provides an interesting and indicative theme around which to further investigations of teachers' constructions of British-Chinese masculinity and learning.

The conception of the 'lad' (as in 'one of the lads') traditionally evokes a young, exclusively male, group, and the hedonistic practices popularly associated with such groups such as: 'having a laugh', objectifying women, alcohol consumption, disruptive behaviour, and pursuit or interest in subjects and pastimes constructed as masculine (e.g sport, etc.) (Francis, 1999). In the past, the term tended to imply working-class White youths (as in the case of Paul Willis' famous study, 1977). But during the 1990s a back-lash against 'political correctness' led to a defiant resurgence of traditional 'laddish' values in the media, typified by the men's magazines *Loaded, Zoo* and *Nuts* and the popular sit-com *Men Behaving Badly*. Thus, the values of 'lads' were appropriated by and popularised for middle-class (and often middle-aged) men, and the term has gained a new prominence in popular and media culture (Francis, 1999).

During the 1990s, policy makers and researchers alike increasingly identified boys' 'laddish' behaviour at school as contributing to their under-performance at GCSE in comparison with girls (eg. Byers, quoted in *The Guardian*, 1998; Pickering, 1997; Younger and Warrington, 1996). 'Laddish' constructions of masculinity have indeed been shown to bear particularly high status for boys among the male peer group (Francis, 2000a; Martino, 1999; Martino and Palotta-Chiarolli, 2003; Skelton, 2003; Younger *et al.*, 2005), and even among female pupils and teachers (Francis, 2000a). The key point in relation to gender and educational achievement is that the 'laddish' construction is seen as 'anti'-academic application, hence having a negative impact on achievement.

This discourse of laddishness was taken up among the teachers we interviewed, with 16 of the 30 teachers feeling that, in general, boys tend to be held back at school by cultures of 'laddishness'. However, when the question was re-framed in relation to British-Chinese boys, only two teachers agreed that British-Chinese boys were as likely to be laddish as any other boys. As we shall now discuss, 12 teachers perceived laddishness to apply to some British-Chinese boys in particular circumstances and 11 teachers felt that laddishness does not apply to British-Chinese boys at all.

Only Mr Griffiths and Ms Battersby felt that British-Chinese boys are affected by laddishness as much as any other boy. Mr Griffiths was rather more tentative in his opinions, however, acknowledging that they were based on the assumption rather than direct experience (he had only taught in a single-sex girls' school). Ms Battersby was of Chinese origin herself, and felt strongly that all boys have a tendency to academic laziness, and hence need more pushing to achieve. It was notable, however, that both these teachers who agreed with the view that British-Chinese boys are as laddish as other boys, drew on a specific notion of laddishness that was framed in terms of educational application and achievement. They did not, for example, associate British-Chinese boys' laddishness with 'anti-social' behaviours, such as drinking, displays of hyper-heterosexuality, and so on.

Chinese laddishness as unusual – the result of ethnic mixing

Twelve teachers felt that laddishness is unusual among British-Chinese boys, and saw it as linked to particular social factors that are external to 'Chinese culture'. The teachers in this category tended to delineate between two types of British-Chinese masculinity – the majority of 'hardworking, diligent, polite' boys (Ms Perkins) who were positioned as 'normal', and a small minority of boys who have 'gone bad', whom schools 'lose to triads'.

'Normal' British-Chinese masculinity was constructed as passive and not highly visible, being 'not as vocal ... not as aggressive' as other boys. British-Chinese boys were not felt to get into as many fights as other boys, and they were described as less likely to play the 'class clown' or to challenge teachers 'to look big'. Instead, teachers suggested that British-Chinese boys were more likely to find alternative means for gaining peer approval, most of which centred around being good at something – such as football, sports or music.

> They're not as vocal as the other boys generally and they're not as aggressive. They don't tend to get themselves into fights ... unless of course they're connected outside of school in that way, then it will come out, and it has come out over the years, I've seen it come out at school. But generally no they're not, I mean they're into being part of the pupil culture and they find route ways into that through the music, through the football, through whatever, but they don't need to be in class challenging teachers to look big or y'know, being the class clown, that sort of thing. It doesn't mean that they're silent in class, they do have their chats, but they're working.
>
> (Ms Perkins)

In this way, 'normal' British-Chinese masculinity was constructed similarly to the 'behavers and achievers' model of South Asian masculinity that has been noted by Gillborn (1990) and Connolly (1998).

These teachers drew a dichotomy between 'good' and 'bad' forms of British-Chinese masculinity – in which 'goodness' is 'normal', and 'badness' is the result of corruption by local peer cultures, notably the influence of Black and White working-class boys (who are positioned as the epitome of 'real' laddishness).

Not only was laddishness seen as unusual in British-Chinese boys, but any manifestations or behaviours that might be identified as laddism among 'normal' boys, tended to be explained away as 'not proper' laddishness. As Ms Bishop explained:

> There are obviously children here who don't fit that mould ... particularly the boys who don't particularly know what they want to do when they leave school and aren't really into education. However, they never go off the rails, so to speak, in the same way that boys of other ethnic groups do, and I think that's a lot to do with their parents ... they never quite slip through our fingers in the same way as maybe some other children do.

Most teachers in this category felt that British-Chinese boys might perform some aspects of popular masculinity as a way of earning peer approval but – unlike some other minority ethnic and/or working-class boys – these performances did not impinge on their academic achievement. For example, Ms Bentley and Ms Perkins both suggested that whilst some British-Chinese boys might 'play up' a bit in class and 'have their chats', they also managed to work hard. This hard work was, however, often hidden and conducted 'under cover', similarly to boys identified in research by Frosh *et al.* (2002):

I think they'd probably keep it under their hats, I think they'd probably keep quite quiet about it.   (Mrs Singleton)

Under-achieving British-Chinese boys were thus positioned as exceptions and were explained away as 'special cases'. However, within this, it became apparent that British-Chinese boys tended to command particularly high teacher expectations, hence some of the examples that teachers gave of their 'under-achievement' tended to be framed differently to other groups of boys. For example, Andrew was constructed by Ms Lynch as 'disruptive' and a 'low achiever'. However, he was in the middle ability set at school and had only just narrowly missed out on being in the top set. Indeed, analysing Andrew's transcript alongside Ms Lynch's, it appeared that much of Andrew's 'disruptive' behaviour could be traced to his annoyance and frustration at missing out on being in the top set. He also expressed anger (acknowledged by Ms Lynch) at being denied additional help with his studies to enable him to try again to progress into the top set. He had overcome some difficult personal circumstances previously, and these seemed not to have been fully acknowledged within assessments of his abilities, achievements and behaviour.

> Well, yeah talking about Andrew again, he is actually very concerned that people know what he can do, he is quite open about what he can't do as well. Like he was very upset that his friend got about one more mark than he did and went up to the top set and he's actually had to stay in set two and this has been a great bone of contention. And he has told me several times, and it's got absolutely nothing to do with me, because he can manage the maths on his own and we obviously can't be everywhere. But no, he has the sense that this is unfair.
>   (Ms Lynch)

A number of other teachers also expressed concern over whether particular British-Chinese boys were achieving their 'whole potential' where their achievement was average or good, rather than outstanding. As we have previously noted:

> Such constructions are interesting because they demonstrate the tightly constrained space afforded to British-Chinese boys within dominant discourse and prompt the question as to whether stereotypical assumptions of high British-Chinese achievement and 'quiet', passive 'normal' British-Chinese masculinity encourage teachers to construct differentially racialised boundaries for boys' laddish behaviours.
>   (Archer and Francis, 2005a, p. 170)

A significant minority (eight) of the teachers associated British-Chinese boys' more extreme performances of laddishness with being 'born and bred' in Britain and, specifically, membership of an urban, ethnically mixed friendship or peer group. In other words, Chinese boys were assumed to be 'naturally' studious and hard working if left to themselves (and/or if recent arrivals in the country), but were seen as somehow 'infected' (Mr Cant) by laddishness where, as Ms Lynch put it, they are 'totally mixed in' and 'can't seek out their own group'.

I mean the Chinese boys generally are diligent, they're studious, generally they want to succeed. But the same could be said of some of the Indian boys. That's quite, or new to the country boys like Kosovan or Albanian boys. When they're new to the country and this is an opportunity that they know they would not have had. They're studious and diligent and, y'know, they go on to be prefects in the same way that the Chinese boys do. Y'know, so, yeah, similar, but also dissimilar, y'know, I mean, the White boys generally aren't studious. They're generally not diligent about their work and will try and get away with not doing their homework, so the Chinese are the opposite of that generally, y'know.

(Ms Perkins)

This form of laddishness was mostly seen as a performance of conformity (the need to act like their peers) that resulted from being born and brought up within a (working-class) British context. For instance, Mr Duckworth explained that a group of four or five Chinese boys sitting together would be 'very studious', whereas 'the most disruptive and unfocused Chinese boys are actually in a group with non-Chinese people, so they're kind of laddish'.

These ethnically mixed 'bad peer groups' were predominantly conceived of as comprising White and Black working-class boys. These peer groups combined the supposed 'worst' aspects of these masculinities, namely a White working-class resistance to, or lack of valuing of, education, and a valorisation of 'bling' and 'the gang thing' associated with Black masculinity:

the peer pressure here with the White working-class community would be that you know, it [education] doesn't matter.   (Mrs Singleton)

These 'nasty' (Mr Duncan) British-Chinese boys were described as members of drug-dealing gangs, and suchlike, although their participation was also assumed to provide a mask for low self-esteem and low academic ability. Hence, laddishness was discursively separated from 'Chineseness' and rendered a product of a classed, gendered and racialised local urban context.

Whilst popular versions of laddishness were widely linked to White and Black working-class masculinities, five teachers identified a distinctive British-Chinese inflection of laddishness. This form of British-Chinese laddish masculinity was seen as based around performances of popular black masculinity, but also expressed through 'triads' and 'martial art type play in the playground'. It was only raised in relation to working-class boys attending inner-London schools in economically deprived areas. As Mr Noakes explained, 'it's very much a Black thing ... but done in a Chinese style'. For instance, these boys were seen as performing aspects of 'Black style' (e.g. wearing baggy trousers, 'bling' jewellery) but added to this a 'martial arts' angle (Mrs McCluskey). Some concerns were expressed that triadism was 'flourishing' (and indeed, a number of boys did report being associated with triads and other gangs, see Chapter Five) – however, it was also acknowledged that boys' performances of triadism varied considerably (e.g. from merely drawing/ graffittiing dragons through to actual membership to participation in organised crime).

It was also notable that even when discussing 'bad' forms of Chinese (triad) masculinity, teachers still maintained a discourse of 'normal' or 'average' British-Chinese masculinity as non-hegemonic and naturally not 'cool':

> I mean at my previous school we were very much aware of Triad activity and things like that, so you know there are other more malign influences going on in their lives without a doubt. ... I mean your average Chinese young lad is probably very very into computer games and it sounds stereotypical, but I see a lot of them drawing.
> (Mrs Singleton)

Indeed, it was interesting that even within teachers' constructions of 'triad' masculinity, British-Chinese boys were still linked to notions of proficiency and ability:

> There's also the oriental tradition of martial arts which presumably is a quite strong influence as well because then you've this kind of *proficiency* at fighting, weapons type interest ... I think it's probably, I think there's more, I think there's probably a bit more emphasis on being *skilled* in some way.
> (Mrs Singleton, emphasis added)

Even these boys' 'violence' was also positioned as tinged with 'humour', as encapsulated in the figure of Jackie Chan, the Hong Kong/Hollywood movie star. In other words, even the most hegemonic forms of Chinese masculinity were given a non-threatening edge that rendered them not 'really' bad.

> I mean this character Jackie Chan, who I think is also, I've not seen any of these things, but kids talk about [it], is as much humour as violence, is that right? ... [he's] a very popular figure, so I imagine that you're probably right to imply that there's a difference in the laddishness.
> (Mrs Singleton)

The absence of laddishness

Over one-third of teachers (11) asserted that laddishness 'is quite noticeably absent on the part of Chinese boys' (Mr Groome). Three key reasons were given for this absence. First, laddishness was positioned as antithetical to (or prevented by) Chinese culture. As noted earlier in this chapter, Chinese culture was popularly constructed as being education-orientated and promoting deference and discipline ('a mentality of hard work', Ms Baldwin). Hence teachers tended to describe British-Chinese boys as nice, quiet, polite and hardworking pupils (the opposition of laddishness). Teachers tended to draw on notions of 'rich' Chinese culture, which was seen as helping boys to resist laddish peer pressure (because they have 'so much more at home to satisfy them', Ms Ellis). As noted earlier, these cultures were also viewed as being strict and prohibiting laddishness, unlike White working-class families, who were viewed as condoning laddishness as 'normal'. However, Tam (1998) argues, such constructions tend to rely on narrow representations of Chinese ethnicity as being 'culture saturated' which, Tam argues, can be read as stereotypical and potentially oppressive.

... and I think, I don't know I mean this is major speculation, but I feel that maybe say going back to Chinese parents, I think that's less so ... if their child is, you know, if their boy is like being laddish, it's like 'well you shouldn't be, do your education'. You know what I mean? Where I sometimes speak to maybe say White English parents and they will near enough say 'oh well you know he's a lad isn't he? You know oh he's only having a laugh' and they don't seem to see the importance or necessity, it's like a great excuse, so. I mean that's more for the working-class parents, but I do notice that some of the minority parents they don't seem to, they don't want to use, they don't want that as an excuse. I usually find that the White working-class parents are quite happy to use that as an excuse.   (Mr Anderson)

You have to bring boys to book over laddishness and their approach. It's far easier to do that with Ben [a British-Chinese boy] because it's almost as if, reminding him of what he should do and what he shouldn't do because it brings back into his mind the way in which he has been taught to behave at home in the past.
                                                                      (Mr Groome)

Second, Chinese masculinity was constructed as inherently feminised and non-hegemonic, and hence not naturally prone to laddishness. In particular, British-Chinese boys were described as being quieter, more restrained, more disciplined, more mature and 'smarter' than boys from other ethnic groups. These qualities of quietness and passivity were also encapsulated by geographies of space and embodiment. For instance, Mr Baxter talked about Chinese boys tending to sit near the back of the class and Mrs Brennan commented on how they don't 'stand out' in class. These 'non-hegemonic' masculinities were explained by teachers in terms of British-Chinese boys' cultural 'independence' – by which teachers meant they did not socialise exclusively within an ethnically homogenous peer group. For instance, Ms Baldwin felt that British-Chinese boys don't seem to contribute to 'the sort of herd mentality that you see in English men'.

No I think they've sort of buck the trend in that really. I think they tend to be sort of quieter, less sort of aggressive ... they tend to be a bit more, they tend to be quite independent and don't tend to sort of, they don't hang around in racial groups like other racial groups do in schools. ... Type of like the Bengali boys tend to hang around in these sort of vertical year groups and so do some sort of, some Black children do too I mean Black African, or Black Caribbean, but you never really see that with Chinese. You know they seem to be more, they're actually sort of more sort of socially independent.   (Mr Hunt)

They just seem to just like the idea of being more mature. [Interviewer: Right, right yes.] I mean the way they dress, they'll mostly dress quite smart whereas maybe other boys will dress quite, like urban style street style type of thing. Whereas I sometimes find that some Chinese kids actually dress more maturely. And I think they just like the idea that they're maybe a little bit better, you know what I mean? [Interviewer: Yeah, yeah.] ... I think a lot of the time their appearance is, can be immaculate you know to compared other children ...

(Mr Anderson)

We would like to flag up how these constructions seem to place British-Chinese masculinity outside of 'normal' youth culture – with boys being described as not into 'urban street style' (Mr Anderson), not 'streetwise' (Mr Baxter) and not 'trend-setting' (Ms Baldwin). Rather, British-Chinese boys are described as being more 'mature' and education-orientated by virtue of their (perceived) 'lack' of popular style and their preference for 'smarter' (rather than fashionable) clothes. Indeed, some teachers felt that these British-Chinese boys enjoyed 'respect, not popularity' among their peers.

Furthermore, it was notable that these constructions had two edges – whilst on the one hand Chinese boys were positioned positively as achieving by virtue of their non-laddish masculinities, on the other hand British-Chinese masculinity was also problematised as producing 'rather quiet' and 'not interactive' pupils (Mr Baxter):

> They don't appear to be quite so loud and I'm thinking loud in all senses, both noise, you know, typical movement, ... or physically, you can either, you can choose the amount of space you take up, just ... But I think their culture says that you shouldn't actually, you should be slightly more, *withheld*. Withdrawn is the wrong word, what's the word I'm looking for? I can't think of the word – quiet about yourself ...but that's not the word ...   (Ms Ogden)

We shall return to this issue at the end of the chapter, where we reflect upon the implications of dominant constructions of the 'ideal' pupil with respect to 'other' pupils and other modes of learning and engagement.

Third, a couple of teachers suggested that instead of being concerned with gaining peer approval, British-Chinese boys prioritised educational success and competition, which increased their engagement and achievement. For instance, Mr Baxter described British-Chinese as 'goal driven' and Mr Anderson positioned them as being more 'mature' (in both their appearance and their attitude) than other boys and being driven by success:

> I think they maybe like the idea of success, you know, and they can witness that in themselves because they compare themselves to their peers, even in younger years.   (Mr Anderson)

In this respect, Mr Anderson suggested that British-Chinese boys are more concerned with competing *academically* with their peers, and so are not interested in performing laddishness (which could hinder their chances of educational success). This construction (of British-Chinese boys as competitive and success-orientated) overlaps and is entangled with the first discourse outlined above, namely that Chinese culture/valuing of education mitigates against laddishness. However, it also presents a slightly different slant, in that it affords boys more agency – rather than framing them as being prohibited by 'Chinese culture' from being laddish. Furthermore, this construction attributes British-Chinese boys with some 'traditionally' masculine traits (of success, competition) which balance the feminised/effeminate constructions of British-Chinese masculinity noted above (some of which are voiced by the same teachers). Interestingly, this construction of British-Chinese masculinity as 'liking the idea of success' evokes a particularly middle-class hegemonic performance of masculinity. It was perhaps no coincidence that the two teachers who voiced this view taught in higher-achieving single-sex boys' schools (an independent, fee-paying boys' school and a long-established state school).

Teachers' views of British-Chinese girls

Whilst we identified how teachers expressed contrasting views of British-Chinese masculinity, it was striking how homogenised teachers' constructions of British-Chinese femininity were. British-Chinese girls were uniformly described as passive, quiet, hardworking and high-achieving pupils and their capacity for 'focused' and 'dedicated' hard work was both eulogised and pathologised. In one sense, they were positioned as 'pure' students who were never 'infected' by anti-education or anti-work attitudes (Mr Cant). However, as we shall now discuss, British-Chinese femininity was also pathologised and infantilised, and girls were likened to educational automatons – being too quiet, too passive and too repressed.

Despite their status as high achieving 'ideal' pupils, a patronising undercurrent could be detected within constructions of British-Chinese girls. For example, they were described as 'little' and 'delightful':

> I did have a delightful little girl who left actually ... she was actually half Chinese and half Japanese – but she had to be top dog she did. ... but actually her little friend, they both started in year seven went right through to year 11 and she was absolutely delightful. ... But no, [name] was the same, she was very hardworking, but she didn't fit the stereotype of being good at maths, I'm afraid, no she didn't. They were from Hong Kong but her brother did, her brother was very good at maths but no [name] wasn't. (Ms Lynch)

On one level, the 'delightful' label might seem positive, but it can also be read as part of an infantilising construction of British-Chinese femininity that speaks down to the girls and their achievements. Ms Lynch was certainly not alone in describing British-Chinese girls in this way – but her position as a member of staff with specific responsibilities for minority ethnic pupil achievement does suggest that there may be scope for encouraging greater reflexivity among practitioners regarding the implications of their commonsense constructions of certain groups of pupil.

British-Chinese girls' capacity for hard work was also pathologised in various teachers' accounts, as they were likened to educational automatons:

> Girls concentrate more but as far as the high achieving is concerned, Chinese girl students I've had, they just, *they would just work until you told them to stop.* (emphasis added) (Ms Lynch)

This notion of a work 'machine' denies girls agency and humanity, and places them outside of discourses around the 'ideal pupil' (as discussed further below). Similarly, British-Chinese girls were widely described as being passive and conformist, and concerns were expressed that they are 'unnecessarily quiet', 'reserved' and 'shy'.

The cause of this 'quiet and submissive' (Mr Purvis) femininity was located within the 'tight', 'close' family structure and Chinese culture – i.e. in the very relations that were also regarded as producing the girls' high achievement. This construction resonates with popular discourses around South Asian femininities, which are similarly positioned as victims of oppressive home relations (see e.g. Brah, 1994; Rattansi, 1992).

Underlying these notions of passivity and educational automatons, were constructions of sexuality. As various feminist academics have noted, discourses of sexuality are often central to constructions of femininities and educational engagement. In particular, working class and 'other' femininities tend to be associated with pathologised hyper-sexualities that operate as markers of their otherness within educational discourses. For instance, White and Black working-class girls are positioned as the 'wrong' sort of pupil by virtue of their association with the performance of hyper(hetero)sexualised femininities (see Mirza, 1992; Skeggs, 1997; Archer *et al.*, 2007).

Whilst hyper(hetero)femininity is equated with working classness and educational under-achievement, controlled sexuality is integral to constructions of the 'good female pupil' and middle-class identities, as encapsulated by Diane Reay's (2001) 'nice girls' and Emma Renold's (2005) 'square girls'. Notions of innocence and chasteness are thus epitomised within the dominant discourse of the 'good' middle-class schoolgirl. However, despite their high academic achievement, British-Chinese femininities were constructed outside of this idealised space. Rather, they were represented as asexual and repressed (as opposed to 'good'/innocent). This distinction was seen as being produced through differential family relations. In particular, whilst Chinese culture and family structures were acknowledged as producing a close 'fit' between British-Chinese femininity and the education system, concerns were also expressed that this relationship could be oppressive/repressive and could result in 'abnormal' young femininities.

This was encapsulated in the feeling, expressed by a number of teachers, that British-Chinese girls lacked 'balance' in their lives. For instance, Mrs Brennan drew attention to one of her pupils who was trying to juggle studying hard, helping out in the family business after school and at weekends and exercising ('working out') at the gym in her spare time. Rather than being seen in a positive light (e.g. as a dedicated pupil and daughter and a healthy individual with a range of roles and interests), Mrs Brennan positioned all of these activities as forms of work (on the mind, body and for the family – through the working body). She thus worried that the girl had no time for 'play' and 'mixing' – which Mrs Brennan considered to be an important feature of 'normal' young femininity. This notion of a lack of play/playfulness on the part of British-Chinese girls was reiterated across the staff interviews – but it was framed in specific, (hetero)sexualised terms, in relation to a popular Western youth practice of 'going out' and engaging in romantic (i.e. innocent, not explicitly sexual) relations with boys. Hence a common concern was detectable, that British-Chinese girls might be problematically repressed within Chinese families. There was also an associated implicit assumption that this social 'mixing' should be with Western peers – as mixing solely within the Chinese community was implicitly assumed to be 'insular' and potentially damaging (e.g. concerns were often expressed regarding

British-Chinese pupils' language skills and their perceived lack of contribution to oral debates in class). It might be noted that rarely, if ever, do teachers express similar concerns about White pupils being ethnically 'insular' (i.e. only mixing with White friends and family) in their leisure time (cf. Archer, 2003).

In some ways, the girl whom Mrs Brennan refers to might be read as exemplifying an idealised femininity – through her dedication to education, her family's needs and to the performance of femininity through care of her body and appearance. And in one respect, Mrs Brennan is exposing the impossibility of this idealised notion of femininity (i.e. she explodes the myth that women can and should 'do it all'). However, Mrs Brennan implicitly values certain (Western) practices (e.g. going out, mixing) over others (e.g. exercise or helping the family) and her example hints at the dangers of this British-Chinese model of femininity. In particular, the 'work ethic', whilst praised, is also positioned as causing overwork and is linked to the notion of a non self-regulating (i.e. unreflexive) identity. In this sense, the example seems to articulate a tension between (Western capitalist) ideals of individualism and reflexive modernity and (what is perceived to be) Chinese collectivist, family-orientated values. The source of this imbalance was attributed to the home and girls' obedience to their parents' desires (for hard work at school and in the family business).

> I would say in general I think the girls have a more obedient attitude to the will of the parents. (Mrs Singleton)

These constructions resound with wider culturalist discourses around 'Asian culture' – which is popularly stereotyped as 'sexist' and 'restrictive' (Archer, 2003b; Brah, 1994; Shain, 2003). British-Chinese girls were positioned outside normal femininity through the ascription of 'asexuality' – although, we would also argue, sexuality constitutes a tight discursive space for *all* girls (Skeggs, 1997; Walkerdine, 2003). Their representation as asexual automatons denies British-Chinese girls agency and humanity (they are accorded no space to be lively, individual or resistant, for example). As such, we suggest that the teachers' constructions might be read as falling within an orientalist discourse that exoticises British-Chinese femininity by virtue of distancing it from 'normal' femininity. In particular, it is distanced from notions of liberal, modern, progressive and hence 'right' femininity – and hence comes to symbolise backward, sexist, other cultures. As Wetherell and Potter (1992) note, this process is integral to the discursive construction and defence of dominant representations of Western societies as liberal and progressive (and hence justified in their hegemony and dominance). Drawing on Brah's (1994, p. 158) critique of how Asian femininity is positioned as exoticised and 'ruthlessly oppressed' within Western discourse, we suggest that British-Chinese femininities are popularly represented as *re*pressed bearers of culture.

As Anthias and Yuval-Davis (1992) discuss, the discursive and symbolic control of women is a key site for the definition and (re)production of the boundaries of ethnic collectivities. Hence anomalies (i.e. girls who did not 'fit the mould') tend to be explained away. For instance, Ms Bentley explained that the British-Chinese girls in her school who were 'not as motivated as the boys' was attributable to 'individual differences'. She effectively de-coupled ethnicity from gender (pointing to the continuance of overall rates of higher achievement among girls) and discursively 'de-racialised' the non-stereotypical girls (to 'individuals'), thus protecting the 'truth' of dominant discourses around British-Chinese femininity.

Conclusion: the discourse of the ideal pupil

Building on the analyses discussed in this chapter, we suggest that, within educational discourse, constructions of 'successful' pupil identity are predicated on a Cartesian dualism (a mind-body split) which is worked out along the lines of class, gender, race and sexuality. We theorise this discourse as operating through the trichotomy shown in Table 3.1 (attributes appear in normal text, inferences regarding pupil identity appear in italics).

Table 3.1 Model trichotomy mapping the discursive production of 'ideal', 'pathologised' and 'demonised' pupils in Western educational discourse

'Ideal' pupil	*Other/pathologised pupil*	*Demonised pupil*
Naturally talented	Diligent/plodding	Naturally unintelligent/ lacking ability
Innovative/initiative	Conformist	Peer-led
'Outside culture'	Culture-bound	Victim of 'bad' culture
Leaders	Followers	Anti-social/Rebels
Enquiring/engaged	Deferent, unquestioning	Problematically challenging and disengaged
Assertive	Unassertive	Aggressive
Independent	Dependent	Ungovernable
Active	Passive	Anomic
'Normal' sexuality	Asexual/oppressed/repressed	Hyper-sexuality
Normal	*Other*	*Other/abnormal*
(White)	*(Asian/Oriental)*	*(Black/White working class)*
(Outside class/middle class)	*(Deserving poor)**	*(Undeserving poor/ underclass)**
(Masculine/masculinised)	*(Feminine/feminised)*	*(Hyper-masculine/Hyper-feminine†)*

* These implied subject positions (regarding the un/deserving poor) reflect the delineation between 'other' and 'demonised' pupils in light of the Bauman (2005) and Mendes (2003) analyses of the processes of dissection of the 'deserving' from the 'undeserving' poor. Within this construction, the blame for failure is disproportionately apportioned to those in the demonised, right-hand column. As Francis (2006) writes in relation to boys' achievement in English neo-liberal policy: 'the poor are subjected to growing public surveillance and those seen as undeserving are subject to increasing coercion and penalties'. That is, within neo-liberal discourse they are rendered 'unacceptable learners' (Youdell, 2004).

† These classifications (of hyper-masculinity and hyper-femininity) represent specifically classed discourses around sexuality, namely the construction of working-class White and Black pupils as hyper(hetero)sexualised (see, e.g. Archer *et al.*, 2007). These are encapsulated in representations of the hyper-heteromasculinities associated with young Black men (see Sewell, 1998) and the 'vulgar', 'tasteless' and 'excessive' (overly and overtly) hyper-heterofemininities associated with White working-class women (Skeggs 1997, 2005; Lawler, 2005) and Black women (e.g. Mama, 1995).

Within this framework, the normalised, ideal pupil thus emerges as male, White, middle class, Western, and so on (see also Francis and Archer, 2005a; Francis and Skelton, 2005). This operates through a splitting and projection of undesirable qualities onto Other groups, which serves to preserve the privileged identity of the ideal pupil. This trichotomy thus provides a way for understanding how minority ethnic success is always-already positioned as 'abnormal'/other and as potentially undesirable – a 'wrong' sort of approach to learning. Furthermore, it also explains how and why minority ethnic and female educational success may be commonly experienced as precarious, such that success, as a subject position, is always under erasure. It also suggests why, as so much research has found, pupils' abilities, achievement and behaviours may be read and interpreted very differently according to the social background and characteristics of the pupil in question (e.g. Walkerdine *et al.*, 2001) – and why these evaluations tend to be 'singularly resistant to influence' (Walker and Maclure, 2005, p. 103).

Drawing on Skeggs' (2004) reading of Bourdieu, we propose that this trichotomy is achieved through 'misrecognition', whereby: (1) 'certain bodies are read through their appearance (and dispositions) as having value/no value' (Skeggs, 2004, p. 169) – as in the case of the centre and right-hand columns – and (2), 'when symbolic capital has been acquired by a successful act of legitimation which itself veils the social processes and structures that are necessary to existence, so is read as natural or individualized personality disposition, a form of cultural essentialism' (Skeggs, 2004, p. 169) – i.e. the solidification of the traits of the ideal pupil as White, male, middle class, etc. in the left-hand column.

As Bourdieu and Wacquant (1992) argue, misrecognition is a technology of power – it ensures that cultural privilege and power is positioned as ascribed (not achieved) and thus justified as natural and legitimate. Value and worth can thus come to be seen as residing naturally with (embodied by) the powerful and privileged – whose power remains hidden (misrecognised). As Skeggs also argues:

> those at the opposite end of the social scale are also misrecognised as having ascribed and essential characteristics. They do not have to achieve immorality or criminality; they have been positioned and fixed by these values. This is another form of misrecognition – ... a hiding of the systems of inscription and classification (which work in the interests of the powerful).
>
> (Skeggs, 2004, p. 4)

The prevalence, power and fixity of the trichotomy within dominant educational discourse thus explains how minority ethnic, working-class and some female pupils may find it 'impossible' to inhabit the 'ideal pupil' identity with any authenticity or in any sustained and permanent way.

4 Minority ethnic parents' views of the British education system

There has been a great deal of commentary on White parents' perceptions of, and engagement with, education – and such involvement has been shown to correlate with children's educational success (Edwards *et al.*, 2000). Our focus in this chapter is on minority ethnic parents' perceptions of, and interaction with, the British education system (about which far less has been said). We shall begin with a brief summary of the body of research regarding (predominantly) White families' engagement with their children's education. We then go on to outline research findings around BME parents' perceptions of and engagement with their children's educational institutions. We then analyse the current policy framework that contextualises these issues at present. Proceeding sections discuss data from our own study to examine Chinese parents' engagement with their children's education.

Research on (White) parents' engagement with their children's schools and learning

Much of this work has centred on the impact of social class on parental engagement. In the 1950s and 1960s 'deficit theorists' maintained that the under-achievement of working-class pupils could be explained by their parents' lack of concern about, or engagement with, their education. This school of ideas was subjected to strong critique. First, by Marxist researchers who argued that the schooling system was deliberately designed to supply and perpetuate the capitalist system and its labour-force demands. In this view it was the education system itself, rather than parents and family life, that perpetuated class inequalities (e.g. Bowles and Gintis, 1976), ensuring that (to paraphrase Willis, 1977) 'working-class kids got working-class jobs'. Studies such as Willis' drew on social interaction perspectives to inject nuance into Marxist materialist accounts of class reproduction in education, showing how constructions of masculinity among schoolboys, and family/community traditions, were implicated in the disengagement of the White working-class 'lads' in his study (Willis, 1977).

Bourdieu's work on capitals and habitus has provided theoretical tools with which to develop a sophisticated analysis of the connected impacts and disjunctions between values of home and school for working-class pupils. As we saw in Chapter 2, Bourdieu maintains that the education system is founded on, and steeped in, middle-class values (see e.g. Bourdieu and Passeron, 1977). Middle-class families have the appropriate material and cultural capital to enable a seamless 'fit' with the education system. That is, their 'taken-for-granted' tacit cultural knowledges and understandings enable them to better understand its values and practices, whilst their economic capital enables them to purchase supplementary support and 'buy' access to the 'best' schools, colleges and universities. Working-class families are faced with a lack of both material and cultural capital in relation to the education system that excludes them from its practices and hampers their ability to relate to, and succeed within it. Bernstein's work suggested that this disjunction or lack of fit is experienced by working-class children at their very entry to schooling due to the different 'speech codes' employed by families from different social classes: the education system invests in and perpetuates middle-class speech practices which in turn positions working-class speech codes as 'wrong' and needing to be re-learnt. Such exclusions and the positioning of working-class practices as 'lacking' inevitably leads to alienation and disaffection from education among working-class pupils (and parents). For example, O'Brien (2003) shows how the working-class Irish girls in her study progressively came to feel that the 'price of educational success' was too high to pursue: 'that the effort required to achieve high academic performance is too gruelling, too lonely, unsociable and stressful' (p. 251).

The othering and exclusion of working-class pupils endemic within the British education system also extends to working-class parents and their experiences of interacting with their children's schools. Working-class parents tend to 'lack' the dominant forms of material and cultural capital that can facilitate smooth and effective interactions with teachers and schools. They may also be judged as not exhibiting an 'appropriate' educational subjectivity, on account of their classed (gendered and racialised) 'other' identities. The work of Reay and colleagues (e.g. Reay, 1998b, 2005; Reay and Lucey, 2003; Crozier and Reay, 2005; Reay and Ball, 1998) highlights the psychic damage visited on working-class parents by their own past negative experiences of being devalued and 'Othered' by the education system and how this can shape their engagement with, or investment in, their own children's education. For example, they may tend to avoid raising their children's hopes and aspirations for fear of these being dashed as their own had been. They may also dislike and/or avoid interactions with teachers and the education system due to their own prior experiences of intimidation, devaluement and alienation (see also Archer and Leathwood, 2003).

Meanwhile, for middle-class children the education system is argued to be far more an extension of home: the values projected within educational institutions, and even the resources available in them, are more likely to be familiar to middle-class than to working-class children (Bourdieu and Passeron, 1977). In this sense schooling is an extension of middle-class habitus; a comfortable and comforting environment. However, this is not to say that middle-class parents constitute a homogenous mass – as the work of Vincent and Ball (2006) illustrates, different sections of the middle class hold different values and practices in relation to education. And yet middle-class parents as a whole do seem to share in experiencing acute anxieties, both in relation to educational choice-making (e.g. choosing schools, colleges) and in terms of reflecting on their own practices in 'working the system' (e.g. Ball, 2003; Vincent and Ball, 2006; Reay, 2005). Despite their anxieties, however, research reminds us that middle-class parents tend to be far more able to use their cultural and material capital to interact effectively with the education system and to maximise the resourcing and hence the achievement of their children (cf. Vincent and Ball, 2006; Lucey and Reay, 2002; Reay, 1998b; Reay *et al.*, 2001). Indeed, the stereotype of the 'pushy middle-class mother' (we read 'middle-class White mother') is commonplace (e.g. Cowan, 2004[1]). Certainly, Ranson *et al.* (2004) found that middle-class parents are the most likely group of parents to come into schools and challenge teachers. Reay (1998b) also found a number of primary teachers (many of whom were themselves of working-class origin) to be highly intimidated by certain middle-class parents who frequently asserted their demands concerning their children's education.

Research on BME parents' engagement with their children's schools and learning

The stereotype of the pushy middle-class (White) mother evokes the issue of gender in home-school relations. It is well-documented that in White families mothers tend to take the primary burden of responsibility in terms of their children's educational progress (which includes engaging with the school). Some fathers in Reay's (1998b) study did provide support, but this was positioned as 'helping out' rather than as carrying central significance. Indeed, Walkerdine and Lucey (1989) analyse the way in which mothers are positioned as guardians not just of their children's education but of their successful production as 'healthy citizens' which, they argue, is grounded within a middle-class model of individualised citizenship. However, as they also highlight, this positioning can generate an intense psychic burden for mothers.

Evidence suggests that for BME groups it also tends to be mothers who carry the primary responsibility in dealing with the school and overseeing their children's progress (see e.g. Reay, 1998b), although this may differ somewhat across groups depending on socio-economic as well as cultural factors. For example, Chinese fathers in our study were clearly often highly invested in ensuring their children's educational achievement, closely monitoring and engaging with their progress apparently in similar ways to mothers. (But the fact that we had fewer fathers than mothers in our study may partially reflect their tendency to be less available to deal with educational issues.) However, as we discuss further in Chapter 6, education policy has tended to position minority ethnic parents as part of the 'problem' of educational under-achievement, presuming that BME parents tend to hold low aspirations and/or expections for their children. This pathologisation of BME parents has been long evident within government reports (e.g. DES, 1981), reflecting US concerns about cultures of deprivation within Black families (see Phoenix 1987, 1988 for a critique). Yet as Crozier (2003, 2005) has found, Black parents often invest considerable financial, emotional and cultural capital in their children's education, engaging in similar practices to those of their White middle-class counterparts. They have also been found to espouse higher aspirations for their children than do teachers (e.g. Archer *et al.*, 2004; Crozier, 2005). Indeed, Crozier (2005) catalogues the concerns which Black parents in her study voiced about institutional racism in schools, highlighting the infantalisation that Black parents often experienced in their interactions with White teachers. These parents spoke of their concern at teachers' apparent low expectations for Black children, alongside teachers' power to decide children's educational fates.

As Phoenix (1987) discusses, mothers in particular have been the targets of pathologising discourses – especially young mothers from working-class and/or minority ethnic backgrounds. Indeed, Crozier (2005) notes, minority ethnic mothers have been targeted and blamed for the apparent under-achievement of their children – even by male critics from their own communities. Reay (1998b) found that in spite of their best efforts, Black mothers in her study tended to feel excluded, or misunderstood, by White teachers. She maintained that in spite of their high valuing of education and their wish to engage with schools, Black mothers tended to be read as having the 'wrong cultural currency' in relation to their children's education and their dealings with educational institutions. Little wonder then that such mothers sought alternative methods of influence and 'voice', for example via dedicated involvement with Black supplementary schooling (Mirza and Reay, 2005). Reay and Mirza (1997) found that such spaces became political both in terms of the alternative curriculum provided and in their facilitation of Black women's shared articulation of concern at aspects of British schooling.

Research by Bhatti (2000) and Crozier (2003, 2005) illustrates the ways in which meaningful communication between schools and minority ethnic parents can be minimal, and/or fraught with suspicion and misunderstanding. Dissonances between the concerns of British teachers and minority ethnic parents, due to distinctive understandings of the nature and purposes of education, are illustrated by Ran's (2001) work. Looking at parent-teacher meetings between Chinese parents and British teachers, Ran discusses how Chinese parents tend to focus on micro issues such as accuracy and achieving 'perfect' scores, whereas (White/English) teachers focus on macro issues, such as approaches to problem solving, and so on. Whereas Chinese parents wanted teachers to point out their child's inadequacies so that they could be made aware of areas needing improvement, the teachers saw their task as being to build pupils' (and parents') confidence by being 'positive' and encouraging. Hence, Ran argues that the teachers and parents were often on 'parallel tracks' in their talk, not actually 'hearing' each other due to their different cultural perspectives.

The policy context

In recent years British education policy has witnessed a heightened interest in parental involvement in schooling (Crozier, 2000; Crozier and Reay, 2005). An onus on parent 'empowerment' has become particularly prominent since the inception of the quasi-market in education – and the subsequent moves towards greater diversity and notional 'choice' in schooling and the positioning of parents (and children) as consumers of education (Stoer and Cortesao, 1999). Hence parents are produced as having 'rights' to become more involved and to express their opinions on the direction of their children's schools. The policy concern with parental involvement has been taken to new levels with the recent controversial government White Paper *Higher Standards, Better Schools for All* (2005), which is being resisted in many parliamentary quarters at the time of writing. Here, the Prime Minister declares his intention to 'put parents in the driving seat for change' (p. 2). For example, it is stated that the school system will be one 'shaped by parents which delivers excellence and equity developing the talents and potential of every child regardless of their background' (ibid., p. 19). It is difficult to see how parents, who tend to be most interested in their own children's progress, and among whom there are many inequalities impacting on their ability to interact with the education system, are best placed to drive a more equitable system. Indeed, we would argue that the values of competition and diversity enshrined within the White Paper undermine this vocational claim. However, as is illustrated by the following quote, parents' envisaged role as 'choice-makers' and consumers is presented as key to the driving up of educational standards:

> If local parents demand better performance from their local schools, improvement there should be. If local choice is inadequate and parents want more options, then a wider range of good-quality education must be made available. If parents want a school to expand to meet demand, it should be allowed to do so quickly and easily. If parents want a new provider to give their school clearer direction and ethos, that should be simple too. And if parents want to open a school, then it should be the job of the local authority to make this happen.
>
> (White Paper 2005, p. 20)

That this is over-optimistic and misleadingly simplistic free-market rhetoric hardly needs pointing out. Not only are the powers and abilities (and expendable time and energy) of most parents vastly over-estimated, but the pragmatic and resource issues are also completely ignored. Jenni Russell refers to such statements in the White Paper as 'the language of the market gone mad, as if schools were no more complex than stalls selling vegetables' (2006, p. 14).

Further, the government clearly hopes that by becoming more engaged, parents will come to develop an appreciation of their children's pedagogic needs, and hence will be better able to support (or police) the school in meeting these needs. As Crozier and Reay (2005) have pointed out, this vision is of course skewed. It relies on an assumption that all parents and pupils in a school will share common goals, needs and interests. But, both ideologically and practically, it is more likely to be middle-class (and probably White) parents (see Vincent and Martin, 2005) who will both share this vision and be able to make their voices 'count'. Furthermore, their mutual concerns with 'standards' and achievement will ensure that schools are driven *in the government's required direction.*

'Other' parents are not completely excluded from the vision. The structural issues that restrict the ability of certain groups of parents to interact effectively with education authorities are not examined in the White Paper, but there is frequent allusion to 'deprived' pupils and families. There is also very vague reference made to 'pupils facing particular challenges, including those from black and minority ethnic groups, disabled children, Looked After Children, and Children with Special

Educational Needs' (p. 44). Why Black and minority ethnic pupils should face particular challenges, and what these might be (given that they are grouped along with pupils experiencing physical, developmental or emotional issues), is not specified. In any case, for parents from 'disadvantaged' or 'deprived' families the White Paper still advocates increased involvement with their children's schooling, albeit on rather different terms. Recognising the access issue raised by the envisaged new parental role, the White Paper describes how local authorities will be empowered to appoint a 'suitably experienced person' to act as a 'Parents' Champion', to 'help parents understand the nature of the problems at their school and the options available to address them' (p. 34). So here we have the prospect of 'an appropriate person' (appropriate to whom?) informing BME/working-class parents *what* their children's problems are and what they should be doing about it. It is hard to imagine that these identified problems might include issues such as institutional racism and racial stereotyping of pupils. These concerns are amplified by the frequent allusions to 'bad' parents that litter the document – underscoring the Othering of those parents who do not 'fit the model'. For example, 'some parents do not take their responsibilities seriously enough, and even question the teacher's right to discipline their child' (p. 11). (This may ring particularly problematically for Black parents, given the highly disproportionate amount of exclusions visited on Black children.) A raft of measures are set out to deal with such 'problem parents' in order to 'force parents to take responsibility for their children's bad behaviour in school' (p. 11).

These measures evoke a two-tier system depending on the 'type' of parent – middle-class White parents will drive schools. 'Other' parents are to be educated via their engagement with schools on how to better support (not challenge!) the school in educating their children. Those who do not engage (in the 'right way') will be forced to do so.[2] As Stoer and Cortesao (1999) observe, in neo-liberal education policy across the EU, attention is given to the 'reconversion' of 'hostile' parents into 'responsible' parents. But for these parents, the unquestioned authority and validity of the education system are taken as a given, rather than open to negotiation.

Clearly, then, this covertly raced and classed discourse of 'parental choice' ignores diversity and structural inequalities and will perpetuate inequity by privileging the interests of White, middle-class parents. Yet there have been few challenges to this perspective. Even among minority ethnic community and support groups, there tends to be an over-simplistic and sometimes over-optimistic view of policies on parent-school interaction. For example, in a piece titled 'Parental support in raising achievement' for the Resource Unit for Supplementary and Mother-tongue Schools' publication *The Bulletin*, Peter Okeye (2005) sets out a whole list of instructions to parents on how best to interact with the school in order to facilitate communication and ensure the child's progress. An indicative paragraph reads:

> Parents are advised to read the information carefully and seek clarification if anything is unclear to them. For example, if a parent does not understand the policy on exclusion, it will be difficult to help a child who is facing exclusion. (p. 4)

Okeye concludes:

> Although schools have a duty to educate children to achieve well and to reach their optimum potential, parents have the ultimate responsibility of supporting both the school and child in order to raise achievement. (p.4)

This view seems odd in a Bulletin serving minority ethnic and refugee communities, many of whose constituents do not have fluent English or extensive experience of the British education system. The notion that such constituents could easily read school documents, and indeed seek clarification 'if anything is unclear to them', completely ignores the issues challenging certain groups, the power differences woven through the home-school interface, and the confidence and assertion required to 'seek clarification'. A deficit view of parents is all too manifest in these quotes, both in the location of responsibility with parents (if BME children are under-achieving, responsibility for action lies primarily with parents), and in the model of 'proper parenting' articulated, which evokes a highly literate, confident, articulate (in English) parent who has the time and resources not just to negotiate understanding of the British education system but to interact with and support it.

Given this rather bleak analysis of the current policy terrain, we turn now to the views of Chinese parents in our study, to investigate their perceptions of the British education system and their levels of engagement with it and with their children's learning.

Chinese parents' constructions of education

Investment in education

It has been suggested that teachers and scholars have traditionally been highly respected in the Chinese community (Taylor, 1987; Pang, 1999), and that Chinese parents' valuing of their children's educational success in Britain is apparent from the stress placed on this issue in their personal testimonies (ECOHP, 1994). Kibria (2002) also notes that Chinese parents in the USA place a strong and distinctive emphasis on the value of education. Like our pupil respondents, *all* the Chinese parents in our study believed that education is important; thus lending further evidence to the suggestion that the Chinese as a group tend to value education highly. Indeed, some seemed flummoxed, or almost shocked at our question 'Do you think that education's important?' For example, Hing replies:

HING: It *is* important, why not?
INTERVIEWER: Why?
HING: Education's not important? Of course it's important! Education at home and at school is very important.
INTERVIEWER: Why do you think that is?
HING: Why? If you don't teach him then how will he succeed?

Another father, Aron, positioned education as absolutely essential to humanity, suggesting that without it we are like animals:

> … Education, because I think for instance animals, like humans, are living things and humans are cleverer than animals because they're educated. If you don't have education then you are like a stray dog, a wild dog, no, no…

Aron's example is particularly poignant given that he is not educated to a high level himself. His equation of education with humanity (and lack of education with bestiality) evokes the psychic implications of the high value placed on education for those who lack it. Like some other parents, Aron went on to stress how his own lack of education has heightened his value of it: 'I'm the first generation in England, I came in 1959, I've been here 40-odd years, I didn't have much opportunity to study, not a good education so I think education is very important'.

This constructed value of education for children – set against parents' own contexts of educational deprivation and hence the wish to provide their children with better educational opportunities – featured strongly in many of the parent interviews. Their transcripts are in places heavy with loss, with hardships evoked by understated hints. TszShun (a mother) explains that 'if you're not educated then the future's very difficult, it's very difficult to survive in this society if you haven't got a good education. Like in the past we had no choice … in Hong Kong'. Parents never dwelt on the hardships in the Hong Kong New Territories that had forced them to seek 'better lives' in Britain (see Parker, 1998a, for discussion), nor the struggle for survival in an unfamiliar and often hostile nation, and the gruelling hard work that this survival had entailed (Parker, 1998a). Yet these experiences were used by parents as examples against which they juxtaposed their aspirations for their children's education. In other words, parents' own lack of education did not in any way decrease their determination for their children to be educated. As Bourdieu (1986) and Bourdieu and Passeron (1977) have discussed, levels of educational participation are often reproduced through generations, hence reproducing inequalities and contributing to the perpetuation of social-class boundaries. Yet these 'working-class' and un(der)educated Chinese parents were passionately committed to providing their children with the opportunities they had lacked in order to foster their children's social mobility.

Indeed, some of the parents who themselves worked in the catering trade, either in restaurants or in takeaways, articulated a desire to protect their children from this lifestyle. This ambition for their children to have an easier life seemed to function as a major driver for the high aspirations towards educational achievement and professional career paths that the vast majority of parents articulated for their children (see Chapter 6 for elaboration).

Parental commitment to education is also evident from the number of children who attended Chinese school[3] at the weekend. Of the 30 parents interviewed, 13 had children currently attending Chinese school, and 16 said their children used to attend when they were younger.[4] In addition to performing an important cultural role (the transmission of Chinese language and 'cultural' values/practices), these schools were valued in terms of their capacity for generating social and educational capital that enabled families to promote their children's educational achievement in mainstream schooling and the (future) workplace. For example, Debbie said that she sent her children to Chinese school because 'It gives them an extra opportunity' and Dolly felt that 'It's just to give them extra language skills which might come in useful'. Chinese school was viewed not only as a means for embedding heritage and culture within the second generation (and connecting British-born offspring with a Chinese 'homeland'), but it was also valued as a resource for (future) use in the diaspora ('It might help her in work in later life', Kin Hong, parent).

Economic capital

Whilst many parents felt they lacked the cultural capital with which to support their children's educational achievement, economic capital was widely mobilised as a means for supporting achievement. Sau Ching was typical in her response, saying 'we already hire a tutor two lessons in one week to help with his homework and everything [...] If he wants to achieve his plans we will definitely help him, because parents have to do that'. Many of the pupil respondents also talked about their similar home tutoring and extra classes, for example Shirley attended a maths master-class at her Chinese church, as did her brother. Parents such as Carmen paid for their children to attend Saturday supplementary schooling and classes, and consequently some British-Chinese children were being schooled six or seven days a week (depending on whether they also attended Chinese school on a Sunday).

The purchasing of additional support occurred (and was prioritised) across the entire sample, irrespective of class backgrounds. Indeed, those pupils in private schooling and who received tutorial support were not from particularly affluent backgrounds, rather their families were investing scarce resources in their education. As one parent put it, 'because I've not been brought up with a good education so we'll try to do anything to give them a good education'. In some cases, familial high aspirations were constantly under threat from the realities of economic disadvantage, as in MayPing's case: 'Because, you know, you have to pay money to go to university like £3,000 [and] I am not really sure if my dad does have that much amount of money, so it really depends'.

Several parents described how they worked additionally hard in the family business to enable their children not to have to help out, to allow them to concentrate on studies. For example, Hong Wah maintained:

> We will try to provide for them, so ... they are not asked to help out with regard to my own business, you know. They've not even been to my shop for a single day ... so they have plenty of time to concentrate.

Indeed, such views appear to be supported by Pang's (1999) research, which found that young people who had had to work in family catering businesses were slightly less likely to achieve their professional aspirations than were those who had not had to help out in the restaurant or takeaway. Parents' fears seemed to arise from their own experience, as several compared their children's and their own upbringings, in which (as Amanda described), their education suffered due to the financial necessity of helping out in the family business.

Economic capital was thus a key resource deployed by parents to support their children's achievement, but it was also used as a negotiating tool, whereby the threat of withdrawal of economic support was used to influence children's decisions or behaviours and to additionally motivate high achievement. For example, Donald's family wanted him to progress to higher education but he worried that 'if I can't, my dad might stop supporting me'. For working-class pupils in inner-city schools, such as James, the motivation not to fail was heightened by the threat of being 'sent back' to China ('he said if I don't learn very good, he said he'd send me back to China with my grandma').

Transmission of the value of education from parents to pupils

Both pupils and parents were found to value education extremely highly. Researchers such as Pang (1999) have argued that the concept of 'family' is extremely important to the Chinese, and the cornerstone of Chinese and British-Chinese culture. Clearly, family is important in most cultures, but the *notion* of 'the importance of family' has been constructed as a particularly Chinese preoccupation (as well as for other minority ethnic groups such as South Asians) in the construction of ethnic boundaries, both on the part of the White majority and by the minority ethnic groups themselves. Some commentators go on to suggest that a Chinese belief in filial piety and respect for one's elders means that Chinese children are more deferent to their parents than are others (Sham and Woodrow, 1998). Parker (1998a, 2000) and Tam (1998) have questioned such notions, arguing that stereotypical views of the Chinese and their 'culture' have been applied to explain their socio-economic positioning in the UK; whereas actually their attitudes are often constructed as a result of, or in reaction to, specifically British structural aspects.

As discussed further in Chapter 6, British-Chinese young people and their parents can, and do, question one another's attitudes and expectations – disrupting any notion of a homogenous cultural approach and challenging Sham and Woodrow's (1998) finding that Chinese pupils 'find it difficult to have an independent opinion since opinions are formed and slavishly followed in a family household from family authority figures' (p. 12). However, the majority of pupils considered family, and their parents' views, to be extremely important and worthy of consideration and/or respect (Francis and Archer, 2005a).

Chinese parents explained how they articulated to their children the value of education and their high educational expectations for them. They also described explicitly 'pushing' their children to succeed. Such practices have been interpreted within racist discourse as evidence that minority ethnic young people (notably Chinese and South Asians in Britain) are 'oppressed by their home culture'. However, extensive evidence shows that parental high expectations and surveillance of children's performance is also usual in middle-class White families, and is a factor in the reproduction of educational success in these families (Reay, 1998b; Walkerdine, Lucey and Melody, 2001; Ball, 2003). Yet White educationalists have often raised concerns about the impact of high expectations or 'pressure' on children from minority ethnic families concerning educational performance, presenting such pressure as oppressive or pathological, while not recognising or problematising similar parental 'pressure' in White middle-class families.

Importantly, we found that even where pupils complained about the pressure they were under from parents, these complaints were often not straightforward: they often acknowledged that parents were doing it 'for their own good', and pupils supported this approach. This finding challenges the positioning of such parental pressure as simply 'oppressive'. Like the Muslim pupils in Archer's (2003) study, the British-Chinese pupils were often also critical of what they perceived as the 'laissez-faire' attitude of parents of their British friends (who were perceived to be 'allowing' their children to under-perform), even while reference to their more relaxed attitudes was sometimes quite wistful! For example, Amy observes several times in her interview that Chinese parents are stricter than English parents, and reports how when she was young she 'was made to sit there until I could recount all my times tables … six years old, yeah'. But despite saying that sometimes this attitude can be 'quite hard', Amy says that 'in the early stages it was quite useful', and affirms Chinese higher expectations as helpful in contrast to (less strict) English parents who 'just tend to let you do whatever you want and try your best' (see Chapter 6 for elaboration).

As well as cultural issues around respect for elders, it may be that verbal encouragement (or pressure) is adopted by some Chinese parents as their only option in terms of encouraging their children in the educational achievement that they value so highly. Those working in the catering industry work long hours, and hence are often not present to help with homework and so on in the evenings, let alone do any of the other activities which constitute educational cultural capital and so-called 'enrichment' activities (Bourdieu, 1990; Bourdieu and Passeron, 1977). As Pang (1999) observes of Chinese parents in the catering industry, 'while they appreciate the importance of education, in practice they are unable to actively encourage their children to focus and devote time to their studies' (p. 49). Moreover, many of these parents are not fluent in English and/or do not possess even basic levels of education necessary to help and advise on schoolwork. This issue was a preoccupation for some of the parent respondents in our study, who clearly felt inadequate and helpless (taking on the shame of the 'bad' parent subject position espoused within the White Paper). SuiHing observes with regret:

> There's a lot of stuff that I can't help her with. My standard of English isn't very good. I can only take on the responsibility of supporting her as much as I can, and to care about her eating and drinking, and to maintain her health! [chuckles] Hoping that she'll have the energy to overcome her difficulties.

Hence for these parents, stress on high expectations in terms of behaviour and achievement at school becomes a particularly necessary disciplinary tool to ensure their children's motivation and achievement, in absence of being able to help in more 'hands-on' ways. It is a strategic response to an acknowledged lack of alternative forms of social capital.

Comparisons with 'back home'

According to Chan (2000), the education system in Hong Kong remains highly selective and competitive, placing 'great emphasis on examinations to select successful pupils ... and, throughout secondary education, youngsters are pushed to secure their place in the tertiary education' (p. 60).

The majority of parents in our study had been educated in Hong Kong, usually in the New Territories.[5] As we note elsewhere (Francis and Archer, 2005a), the education of some of those in our sample had been extremely minimal. But in any case, the sharp contrasts between their experiences as children learning in Hong Kong, or as new immigrants to Britain, and the experiences of their second or third generation offspring, were frequently highlighted. Amanda (mother) reflects on the divergence between her parents' attitude to her education on arrival in Britain and her own approach to her son's learning:

> ...they [parents] thought that you go out to school, you go to school, and what you learn, you should learn, and that's it. But they did not provide you with any back-up or any time ... so really it's up to you. So people who did well, right, is themselves determined: 'I want to have a better job or a better life', so they have to work hard, *really* hard. Apart from coming home and doing your second job. I suppose you had to be very hard-working. Nowadays you know, I don't know how to say it, it's different from my own education and my son's.

Her focus on her 'second job', returning home from school to help out in the take-away, was a common theme for those parents who had been educated (partially) in the UK. There were gendered aspects to these patterns, as Amanda reported how she had been expected to devote time to the family business that her brothers had not; their studies had been prioritised. But for the parents in our sample that worked in catering, a key challenge was to protect their children from such demands and responsibilities. As Amanda reflects in relation to her son's educational progress:

> Yes well he's got no other responsibilities, apart from doing his homework, you know [laughs] he's got no others but for us you know we would have to do a lot of other things when we got home from school.

Parents who had experienced schooling in China and Hong Kong saw even starker contrasts between their own and their children's education. For example, asked how her daughter's education compares to her own, Wing Shan (mother) observes:

WING SHAN: Of course they're lucky. When I studied ...
INTERVIEWER: ... in Hong Kong?
WING SHAN: ... in China when it was the cultural revolution all the schools were closed down, I couldn't study. We all went up the mountains to settle, there's no chance to be educated but now you can study and go to university and study whatever you want.
INTERVIEWER: Where do you think it is more difficult?

WING SHAN: You could say that it is more strenuous studying in China because you have to memorise a lot of stuff but over here you never have dictation, [In China] you'd often have exams and tests, you have two semesters in one year and you have exams twice in each semester.

INTERVIEWER: What do you think of the English education system?

WING SHAN: It's too easy.

Wing Shan's disparagement of the English education system in comparison with the experienced rigours of the Chinese model was a common theme, which we analyse more closely below. Certainly, the education system in Hong Kong, then and now, was positioned as more onerous (and often as more rigorous) than the British system. Debby's comment that there is 'less pressure' from the British system was typical. She explains, 'It's more relaxed here compared to Hong Kong. There's not that much homework.' The amount of homework expected in Hong Kong was commonly noted, and appeared to inform many parents' perceptions of the British system, as we report below. Chinese parents tended to produce the Hong Kong system as very harsh, with copious amounts of study, and very high levels of discipline and achievement demanded. As Yen Wah reflects on her experience of schooling in Hong Kong:

> Teachers don't really care about you; it's up to yourself, you need to study yourself. Here [England] the teachers will pay their undivided attention, if you're not good they'll put you in a special class and if you *are* good then they'll open another special class. I think that the education system here is better than what I used to have.

This view of the Chinese educational model as more demanding than that in Britain was largely supported by the few first generation pupils in our study who had experienced both systems. For example, Ben (pupil) reflects:

BEN: I had like six years education in China so we are used to much harder work so when we come here we feel like the work here is really not hard at all and we can cope with it easily so we don't actually find it that hard or something.

INTERVIEWER: And in Chinese schools do people muck about as much there, or is it much stricter?

BEN: Yes, more discipline I think. The teachers are much more strict and yes, you get in serious trouble for like not much, like if you do the same thing here you probably don't get any punishment at all but there you might get detentions or your parents called into school or something for not really serious things so people behave much better.

There was recognition among the parents that the different models of education between Hong Kong and the UK prioritised different things (reflecting different values). For example, Carmen initially characterises her son's education in Britain as 'spoon-feeding', but expands that there is, 'more guidance and they are trying to coax him to self-direct learning things probably'. And, 'They do let them, how shall

I put it? Give their opinion and have role plays and things like that.' She contrasts these child-centred approaches to her own education in Hong Kong, where 'what the teacher taught us we just write it down, you know, and that's it'. However, it is indicative that when asked what she thinks of the English education system, Carmen responds:

> I don't know, I think I prefer my [Hong Kong] style, I think it has not done me any harm, and I don't mind having a bit of that but I think overall I believe in the old fashioned way, you know chalk and board and that when you calculate you should not use a calculator you should use your brain [laughs]. I think that probably is better.

Parents' levels of satisfaction with, and opinion of, the British education system

Recent research conducted in Scotland found that most of the school senior managers surveyed described their contact with BME parents as 'good' (Arshad *et al.*, 2004). As we saw in Chapter 3, British teachers were under the impression that Chinese parents were extremely content with their children's education in the British system; even highly appreciative. It was notable that it was only really Ms Philbin, a Chinese teacher herself, who suggested that Chinese parents might not be entirely satisfied with their children's education:

> I would say they are very, very concerned. They, oh dear, they have so much high standards for their kids. Sometimes, possibly a bit too much of a high standard sometimes. They are very interested in the children's education and I sometimes feel that they probably are not entirely satisfied with their children's education that they receive in this country. They like to push them even more … the parents that I have spoken to and I've heard from my other previous colleagues as well, they always compare it to oh, you know, 'back in Hong Kong, they do this. They should have completed this work a long, long time ago. Why are they still at this level?' They are surprised at the level of the … they say sometimes, you know, parents say that, 'oh this is quite an easy level for my child – push a bit more to reach a higher level'.

Our findings confirmed her opinion, belying that of other teachers. Only 12 of the 30 parents said that they were, or were 'quite' or 'largely' satisfied with their child's education in England (only five said that they were satisfied without equivocation). A further eight said that it is 'OK' or 'not bad'. And 10 said that they are not satisfied or 'not really' satisfied with their children's education. That one-third were not satisfied, and only five (one in six) parents articulated unequivocal satisfaction, presents a stark contrast with teachers' perception that Chinese parents tend to be extremely pleased with, and even grateful for, the British quality of education.

Similarly, teachers might be surprised to hear the views expressed by parents in our study concerning the British education system itself. Only seven of the 30 parents expressed wholly positive views of it, some of these comparing the British system favourably to that in Hong Kong, which they saw as too strict and exerting too much pressure on pupils. As Suen (mother) observes of the British system, 'They give them [children] a lot of space to manoeuvre, more freedom. It's a lot worse in Hong Kong, it's very hard work'. But twice as many were highly critical – constituting half the sample (15 parents).[6] The strongest narrative to emerge from these parents' responses was that the British education system is insufficiently demanding. It was commonly felt that the system is 'too relaxed', both in terms of the (low) expectations of pupil performance and discipline, and the 'freedom' offered to pupils. The large amount of school holidays was noted by some parents as an aspect supporting this argument, and many parents maintained that pupils are not given enough homework. Kwok Kuen (father)'s response was by no means a-typical:

INTERVIEWER: Ok, so what do you think of the English education system?

KWOK KUEN: English education system? Depends how you see it. I think that Hong Kong education's better.

INTERVIEWER: Oh, why do you think that?

KWOK KUEN: There's more to learn in HK, for instance homework here's not even important.

INTERVIEWER: It's not that strict here?

KWOK KUEN: Yes, yes.

INTERVIEWER: Are you satisfied with your daughter's education?

KWOK KUEN: Me? Of course not.

Wei Ling (a mother) agrees that the British education system is:

Too relaxed. In Hong Kong there's a lot of homework, but here it's very sporadic. After they've done their homework the teachers don't mark it, they just give a general comment, I suspect the teachers don't even check the work. I don't like that. The students won't know where they've gone wrong.

Even Amanda (mother), who was generally supportive of the British system (seeing the Hong Kong system as 'too strict' by contrast), agrees that 'when they're in primary school they should have a bit more homework'.

Some parents identified a discrepancy between the academic demands for GCSE (low) and 'A' level (high). Indeed, two parents maintained that the British education system is too relaxed *until* 'A' level and Higher Education, which are of better quality. Aron (father) explains:

The English education system from primary school, from 6 and below is very relaxed but from A level it's better. It emphasises on higher education, the students from 16 and below are very naughty and just plod along, but after 18 they become really clever.

While the views of many parents were framed by the contrasting Hong Kong model of education (which they constructed as harsher but more rigorous – and hence ultimately as superior to the British system), a few seemed to simply share wider popular perceptions of the British system as having 'dumbed down' in recent years. Hong Wah (father) maintains:

> I think in terms of standards, you know, I do believe that standards have dropped and I mean, if the kids are any good they should find it a lot easier than in our generation … But I think standards of education, I mean GCSEs are not quite the same as the old days, 'O' level, you know.

Several of the parents discussed how the quality of education in Britain differs depending on the school concerned, and that the education on offer is too inconsistent. This may of course particularly reflect the London location of the research, as the 'school access and choice' issue that the controversial White Paper (2005) ostensibly set out to address is recognised to be one particularly affecting London boroughs. As well as complaints concerning lack of consistency in quality across schools, teacher supply was also noted as an issue (again possibly reflecting the London location). Wei Ling (mother) complains:

> I think that there aren't enough teachers. Like last year, in one year they changed teacher four times, and they're all substitute teachers. So hence his English (lessons) have suffered. There are lots of foreign teachers. For instance, when they've just started term and they have a Parents' evening, the teacher that I spoke to didn't even teach my child.

However, parents were mostly reluctant to go into schools and engage directly with teachers over their concerns. Like the minority ethnic parents in other studies, they might be characterised as adopting a non-interventionist approach to their children's schooling (Bhachu, 1985). However, this is perhaps not surprising given that Chinese parents concerns were directed at a macro level (the entire system) rather than the micro level of particular schools or teachers. Furthermore, as noted at the beginning of this chapter, issues such as language fluency and power relations of 'race', class and gender can all render such challenges daunting and/or unfeasible for minority ethnic parents. However, this 'non-interventionist' approach does render such parents vulnerable to critique (as abnormal others) by normalising and dominant discourses. For instance, Gibson's US research with Punjabi Sikh families records:

> Few of the parents … ever visited the schools unless expressly requested to attend because their child was having a problem. Nor did they volunteer for any of the myriad activities that seem to be the mainstay of public elementary schools in middle class neighborhoods in this country today (p. 177).

Perceptions of their children as students

Asked whether they saw their children as good students, in keeping with these children's generally high levels of educational attainment, few of the parents were very dissatisfied with their children's approach and/or performance. Some were highly satisfied and proud of their children. Debby (mother) felt that her daughter is a good pupil because, 'She is very hard working. She does what she has to do. She would work hard to learn'. And Lai Wah (mother) asserts that her daughter is a good student as she 'does what she has to do and listens to the teachers, and if she needs to improve herself she will'. These were among the most affirming accounts – there was little hyperbole among the parents, rather a tendency for pragmatic and somewhat cautious responses. Carmen's is typical:

INTERVIEWER: Ok and do you think that your son is a good pupil?
CARMEN: Sorry?
INTERVIEWER: Is he a good pupil? Is he a good student?
CARMEN: Umm, at the moment yes [laughs] and if his homework doesn't go hay-
wire, he's alright you know, he's still not at the rebellious stage yet and I hope
that he'll keep that way.

A few of the parents' answers seemed to conform more to the stereotype of Chinese parents as highly demanding and hard to satisfy that was perpetuated by a few of the teachers in our study. For example, asked whether he thinks his son (who has won prizes for Science) is a good student, Aron (father) replies, 'Umm, OK, passable. His school report is quite good'. Amanda (mother) agreed of her son's studentship, that he is 'reasonable … average', explaining that he is a 'very laid-back person', and 'if he was more hard-working and put more effort and time and thought into his work, I think he would do better'. (Her son had won prizes for maths and went on to gain seven A and A* grades at GCSE.) It is hard to tell whether such responses do reflect unusually high expectations, or whether there is a cultural aspect at play reflecting a performative tendency to 'talk down' success (in the expectation that others will challenge them, with a resulting public emphasis on the actual success/achievement which seems to characterise collective constructions of 'face'). Certainly, Shun Hei (father)'s response defies popular Western stereotypes concerning the 'pushy' oriental parent:

INTERVIEWER: Is your child a good student?
SHUN HEI: [laughs] This is a very difficult question! What's good and what's no
good?! As long as he produces results at school and he can keep up with the
learning then that's satisfactory. We can't pressure him that much. If you put too
much pressure on him then you might affect his self-confidence. For instance, in
Hong Kong, as soon as the results come out for 'A' levels, then they think stupid
things and do stupid things when they don't achieve the grades they want.[7]

Perceptions of teacher attitudes

As we discuss elsewhere in this book, many of the pupils felt that teachers held particular stereotypes of Chinese pupils, which entailed implications for their expectations of these pupils. Specifically, some pupils felt that teachers tended to expect Chinese pupils to be clever and hard-working, an expectation which these pupils felt exerted an unfair pressure on them. Further, it seemed that a few teachers perceived 'imperfect' behaviour more harshly in British-Chinese pupils than in their peers from other ethnic groups, due to these higher expectations applied to Chinese pupils (see Archer and Francis, 2005a; Francis and Archer, 2005b). When parents were asked whether teachers have particular views of Chinese pupils, many affirmed that teachers held high expectations due to their perceptions of Chinese pupils as innately clever and/or particularly diligent. However, in contrast to pupils (see Chapter 7 for further discussion), parents tended not to see such perceptions as problematic, often affirming such readings themselves. For example, Pui Keung (father) responds as follows:

> Let me give you an example, in one of the parents' evenings, I spoke to the French teacher and she said that 'You shouldn't need to worry too much about (daughter's name)', that's my daughter's name, she said that 'She's done quite good in her French, and another thing is your race – you're Chinese and generally speaking Chinese people seem to do well in education, [chuckles].

Rather than positioning the teacher's comment as offensive (being both racist, and stunningly dismissive), Pui Keung agrees, 'I think in Chinese family, how shall I put it, we are very conscious, we know that education is important so we will tell our child … encourage them to do well in school. So I think that is what she [teacher] is trying to say.' Pui Keung's example of the French teacher's statement is interesting because it shows how the 'Chinese value of education' is a racialised discourse, used by the White population to position 'the Chinese' in a particular way. We would argue that it is part of the wider discourse that positions the Chinese as diligent and conformist (Chau and Yu, 2001; Parker, 1998a). Yet the Chinese respondents appeared to be drawing on this narrative to fashion a positive construction of 'Chineseness'. Hence another father (Aron) speculates that teachers might have high expectations of Chinese pupils because, 'I hear from people that Chinese students compared to English students are a lot better, because compared to English kids they are not so naughty. Chinese kids concentrate more'. Lai Shan observes that teachers are bound to be interested in clever pupils, suggesting that Chinese pupils may be 'a little bit' cleverer, 'for instance in maths'. Hence Lai Wah concludes that 'because Chinese pupils have better grades I think they [teachers] like them better'. As Carmen explains, she sees education as important because of her Chinese culture: 'Because of culture: I was brought up in believing that if you've got a good education then it's better than money [laughs]. I will always have this in my mind'. Pupils also affirmed this view (see Chapter 5). A construction of attributes in racialised boundaries is evident in these responses; a Chinese 'we' who value education positioned against an English (White) Other who do not.

As we discuss further in Chapter 6 and elsewhere (Francis and Archer, 2005a) the notion of high value of education as a feature of Chinese culture (see Taylor, 1987; Parker, 1998a; Pang, 1999) was acknowledged and articulated with pride by many of the parents. We argue that a discourse of 'Chinese valuing of education', constructing high valuing and prioritisation of education as something distinctive and essential to Chinese culture, was being drawn on by Chinese parents and pupils to construct a diasporic cultural boundary for the first and second-generation Chinese in Britain (Parker, 1998a).

Parents' constructions of Chinese people as inherently intelligent and/or as valuing education especially highly fits with the dominant discourse within teachers' talk (identified in Chapter 3) which reifies Chinese children as pure and virtuous, but in danger of corruption or contamination by non-Chinese 'others' (see Francis and Archer, 2005c; Song, 1997). Kwok Keun illustrates this narrative in his reflection on teacher expectations of British-Chinese pupils, when he says: 'For instance normally we [Chinese parents] would rather them [children] have contact with Indians rather than Blacks because Indians are more hard-working than black people'. Perhaps unsurprisingly in light of his own racist statement he concludes with regard to teachers, 'Prejudice, I think it's worldwide. There must be more or less'.

Debby (mother) refuted this view that teachers might be 'prejudiced' against Chinese pupils, but other parents were more sceptical. For example, Diana (mother) maintains that:

> I think that English the teachers give grades more leniently to English students but they're stricter to Chinese. You have to be very, very good and if it's very difficult to find a mistake then they'll give you a good grade.

Wei Ling (mother) concurs that 'they are a little biased towards the English students'. Shun Hei (father) muses that, 'There must be a little bit of prejudice of course, this is inevitable, from teachers and from schools', but conversely asserts that, 'As teachers they shouldn't have prejudice, whether Chinese, English or Black. A true teacher should treat every pupil the same and be expect the same success for each of them'. However, like the American Punjabi Sikh parents in Gibson's (1988) research, parents rarely attributed blame to schools or teachers with regard to their children's experiences of racial stereotyping.

Interestingly though, only one parent demonstrated awareness of the Westernised lens through which her son's behaviour was surveyed and evaluated by teachers (Archer and Francis, 2005a; Francis and Archer, 2005b). Carmen (mother) reflects:

> I have a feeling – the feeling he gives me, that they tend to think that being Oriental or being Chinese, sort of, umm, respect and they tend to want him to be more upfront and participate more in class rather than keep quiet and absorb all the knowledge.

Hence Carmen recognises the way in which her son's behaviour is constructed and interpreted through Enlightenment and Orientalist lenses as deferent and 'passive', and how such subdued learner behaviour is in turn constructed as inappropriate within a Western model that valorises learning by (active, assertive) questioning. It is important to note the imperialist psychic violence that this imposition entails – the construction of one's or one's child's learning approach as 'not correct' (see Walkerdine, 1988), and as Other, inadequate, essentially different, out of place.

Conclusion

It was noticeable that Chinese parents largely did not share the concerns reported by Black parents concerning the pernicious stereotypes and low expectations applied to their children by White teachers. A few Chinese parents felt there might be some discrimination, and favouritism of White children, but by and large their concern was that children generally were not being fully stretched by (what they saw as) undemanding English schools. There was little or no general concern that low expectations were being applied to their children as a group. This reflects the generally very high achievement of British-Chinese pupils in the British education system, a different pattern to the experiences and educational outcomes for many other minority ethnic groups. It also (relatedly) reflects the 'positive' stereotypes of Chinese ability which parents often recognised as applied to their children by White teachers. While these stereotypes were often experienced by pupils as offensive, constraining and damaging (see Chapter 7 for discussion), parents often appreciated the teacher perceptions as 'supporting what we already know' (in keeping with the discourse of Chinese 'valuing of education'). Clearly, the application of such seemingly 'positive' stereotypes to their children within the British education system predicates a very different discursive environment to teacher–parent interaction as compared with parents from other minority ethnic groups who may suspect teachers of applying racist low expectations to their children.

In terms of facilitating this high achievement, Chinese pupils and parents appear to work together, collectively drawing on the discourse of 'Chinese valuing of education'. This discourse was central to the formation of a diasporic collective habitus in which educational achievement becomes something that 'people like us' do, irrespective of current 'social class'. Together with the deployment of economic capital, these practices formed a strategic counterbalance to Chinese families' 'lack' of cultural and educational capital (see Archer and Francis, 2006).

To extend and invert Skeggs' theorisation of the (re)production of privilege, we would also suggest that many Chinese parents maintained their own economic and social 'fixity' in order to facilitate their children's social mobility via educational achievement. This was manifested through processes of migration to Britain (for their children's education and employment) and – for many non-professional parents – their own involvement in long, hard and unsociable forms of work (such as the Chinese catering trade). Both working-class and middle-class families prioritised economic capital to support their children's learning (whether this took the form of paying for private schooling, tutors or avoiding the necessity for children to help out the family businesses). It also provided a motivational and aspirational impetus for their children to succeed. In other words, families operated as resources to facilitate their children's social mobility.

However, it was also clear that pupils and their families were struggling on an uneven playing field, inflected by inequalities of class and 'race'. They were thus required to negotiate a range of difficulties and injustices throughout their engagements with the education system which produced particular psychic consequences for pupils and parents.

As Skeggs argues, access to economic capital alone does not guarantee access to privilege and power, and mobility (and control over mobility) 'both reflect and reinforce power' because 'mobility is a resource to which not everyone has an equal relationship' (Skeggs, 2004, p. 49). Thus for minority ethnic groups, access to economic capital (and indeed forms of social capital) does not necessarily entail access to symbolic capital. Indeed, pupils and parents were well aware of the limiting effects of racism upon their success and future ambitions and the use of safe or known routes provided at least one potential means for negotiating these hazards. They also displayed psychic unease and concerns over the fragility of their children's educational achievement – encapsulated in the notion of always wanting or needing more and higher attainment.

Aside from the issue of educational achievement, the Chinese parents' perspectives illustrates how BME parents' expectations of education are informed by their own experiences, and by the educational philosophy dominant in their country of origin (Ran, 2001). Yet these differing experiences and expectations are often not recognised or understood by teachers, with the result that even when they do communicate, White teachers and BME parents may be talking 'on parallel tracks' (to quote Ran). We have also seen, again, how the application of an unarticulated Western epistemological model of education and the 'proper' learner can 'Other' even high achieving minority ethnic pupils and their parents' educational interests.

We would argue that there is an important scope for developing better modes of communication and interaction between parents and schools, which are based upon a critical examination of power relations. As Cummins (1986, p. 26) argues 'When educators involve minority parents as partners in their children's education, parents appear to develop a sense of efficacy that communicates itself to children, with positive academic consequences'.

5 Young people's educational identities

Research conducted within the fields of sociology and the sociology of education has shed valuable light on the ways in which young people construct racialised identities (e.g. Alexander, 1996, 2000; Back 1996; Brah and Minhas, 1986; Dwyer, 2000; Hopkins, 2004; Nayak, 2001; Parker, 1998a; Song, 1997, 1999) – and specifically, BME young people's experiences of racialised identities within the context of education or schooling (e.g. Ahmad, 2001; Archer, 2003; Basit, 1997a, 1997b; Connolly, 1998, 1998; Dewan, 2005; Frosh et al., 2002; Haw, 1996; Mirza, 1992; Sewell, 1997; Shain, 2003; Youdell, 2003). Particular attention has also been given to the ways in which BME pupils construct their identities linguistically, in complex hybridised fashions (e.g. Cummins, 2000; Rampton, 1995; Wei, 1994). Alongside the attention that has been paid to young people's identity self-constructions, insightful critiques have also been produced of institutional and policy constructions of BME pupils as learners, and of the impacts of such positionings on 'race' and achievement (e.g. Gillborn, 1990, 2005; Gillborn and Youdell, 2000; Hewitt, 1996; Wright, 1987a).

Within the educational literature, considerable attention has been paid to the notion of 'learner identities', with critical approaches highlighting how learning (across the lifecourse) is a cultural – not merely a cognitive – process that is intricately tied up with issues of identity and social context (e.g. Avis, 1996; Lave and Wenger, 1992). It has also been argued that people's approaches to learning and their learning identities and experiences change over time and across context, and hence might be better conceptualised as 'learning careers' (Bloomer and Hodkinson, 2000, p. 585). In particular, it has been argued that 'learner identities' are strongly inflected by issues of 'race', class and gender (e.g. Renold, 2001; Youdell, 2003).

However, on the whole, relatively scant consideration has been paid to BME pupils' *own* constructions of themselves as learners and their learning preferences and identities. In this chapter, we aim to bring a critical approach to bear upon an analysis of the learner identities of higher achieving, British-Chinese pupils and their engagement with schooling, examining these pupils' own accounts of their preferences and presentations of self as learners within the British education system. In so doing, we illustrate how ethnicity and gender (and the discursive resources available as a result of these positionings) can impact on learner identities.

Given that there has, in any case, been so little educational research on British-Chinese experiences, it comes as no surprise that there is scant documentation concerning their preferences for, and approaches to, learning – or indeed about their perceptions of themselves as learners. However, one of the few recent educational research projects to have focused on Chinese experiences in the British Education system studied these very issues (Woodrow *et al.*, 2001). Taking a largely psychological approach to their analysis the researchers noted distinctive features about pupils of Chinese origin's learning preferences and perceptions that distinguished them from their White-British classmates. For example, they found British-Chinese pupils have a preference for rote-learning and memorisation of facts, and for competitive and individualist approaches to learning. Woodrow and Sham (2001) note what they refer to as Chinese pupils' 'passivity' and diligence in class. They also found Chinese pupils four times more likely than their White counterparts to think the most important part of a teacher's job is providing them with enough facts to pass an exam (63 per cent). Very few (0.7 per cent) thought a teacher's job entails making lessons interesting and enjoyable. However, as we shall explain later in more detail, Woodrow and Sham read these findings as indicative of an 'unwholesome' approach to learning – a view which we seek to refute.

In this chapter we want to explore British-Chinese pupils' constructions of learning, and particularly to contribute an analysis in terms of gender and social class. We focus on British-Chinese pupils' favourite and least favourite subjects, their constructions of themselves as learners and their approaches to learning – all of which we analyse in relation to constructions of masculinity and femininity. We then take a detailed look at the young people's views on 'race', class, gender and achievement through the lens of the 'laddishness' debate. We explore the meanings and implications of British-Chinese boys' and girls' accounts of British-Chinese boys' positioning in relation to this debate, teasing out what such constructions and performances can tell us about the ways in which 'race' and gender mediate discourses around educational achievement and the 'ideal pupil'.

British-Chinese pupils' choices of favourite and least favourite subject

We asked pupils about their favourite and least favourite subjects at school. The British-Chinese pupils' explanations for their favourites were usually that these subjects are interesting, fun, easy, or the teacher particularly engaging. Table 5.1 sets out their favourite subjects, ranked according to the number of choices, and divided according to gender.[1]

Several things are striking about these results. The first is the clear preference for maths, which is the most popular subject among British-Chinese girls, as well as boys (although proportionally more so for boys, among whom nearly two-thirds have identified it as a favourite subject). Maths has traditionally been constructed as masculine (Boaler, 1997; Mendick, 2006; Walkerdine, 1988, 1989); and has in the West traditionally been less enjoyed by girls (Mendick, 2006; Spender, 1982; Whitehead, 1996), although evidence suggests that more girls engage a preference for maths than was the case in the past (Wikeley and Stables, 1999; Francis, 2000b; Francis *et al.*, 2003). The second noticeable trend is a general liking for traditionally

Table 5.1   British-Chinese pupils' favourite subjects, placed in order of preference

Subject	No. of girls' choices	Subject	No. of boys' choices
Maths	16	Maths	19
Art	12	Science	13
Science	10	Art	7
IT	6	IT	6
English	4	Graphics	5
Geography	4	English	4
History	4	Business Studies	3
Biology	3	Music	3
Design Technology	3	PE	3
French	3	Biology	1
PE	3	Chemistry	1
Business Studies	2	Chinese	1
Chemistry	2	Design Technology	1
Graphics	2	French	1
Drama	1	Geography	1
Languages	1	Manufacturing	1
Music	1	Media Studies	1
Physics	1		
Textiles	1		

masculine subjects among both British-Chinese girls and boys (see Harding, 1991; Thomas, 1990; Francis, 2000b; and Paechter, 2000, for a discussion of the gendered history and epistemology of curriculum subjects). We can see from Table 5.1 that British-Chinese girls and boys share the same four favourite subjects, albeit science and art switch places between second and third favourite in boys' and girls' preferences. Science features prominently in their choices, as do 'technical' subjects such as graphics, design technology and IT. Art is a common choice among both boys and girls, and English is also represented on the lists. However, compare the choices of favourites with a mixed ethnicity sample of 100 London pupils in the same age-group,[2] drawn from a previous study of gender and learning (Francis, 2000b). Table 5.2 represents the top four subject choices of all groups.

Even keeping in mind that many pupils chose more than one subject, and that there are proportionally fewer boys in the British-Chinese study sample than in the ethnically diverse study, there are some clear, profound differences here. For example, the very low rating for English among British-Chinese girls and boys in comparison with other groups of pupils. It should not be assumed that this is explained by British-Chinese having English as a second language, as for a vast majority English

Table 5.2   Comparison of favourite subjects of British-Chinese pupils and of mixed-ethnicity sample

Subject	British-Chinese girls	Other girls	British-Chinese boys	Other boys
	(N: 48)	*(N: 50)*	*(N: 32)*	*(N: 50)*
English	4	29	4	24
Maths	16	20	19	17
Science*	16	11	15	16
Art	12	15	7	10
IT	6	7	6	8
Drama	1	14	0	7
PE	3	5	3	15

*all science subjects included

is their primary language, albeit not necessarily the one they learnt first (many spoke Cantonese, Hakka or Putonghua with their parents). Maths stands out as a particular favourite of British-Chinese boys: where less than half of pupils in the other groups rated maths a favourite, nearly two-thirds of British-Chinese boys chose it.[3] (British-Chinese girls and boys were also less likely to list maths and science as a *least* favourite subject than were their counterparts in the mixed-ethnicity groups[4]) Both British-Chinese girls and boys are more likely to rate science as a favourite than are other groups. There is proportional similarity in the ratings for art and for IT between groups, but there are clear dissonances concerning the interaction between gender and ethnicity in relation to both drama and PE. In the case of drama, British-Chinese of both genders are less likely to choose drama as a favourite than are their mixed-ethnicity group counterparts, but this difference is particularly striking among the girls. Conversely, there is a striking difference between boys' ratings for PE, with far fewer British-Chinese boys rating this as a favourite subject than the boys in the mixed-ethnicity group.

These latter findings, coupled with the general trend for British-Chinese girls to favour science/technical subjects rather than (gender-stereotypical) arts/humanities subjects, illustrate the way in which ethnicity interweaves with gender in pupils' constructions of subject preference. We do not read these distinctive preferences as reflecting trends of inherent differences in interest and aptitude. And while it is tempting to see, for example, a Chinese preference for maths, and less enthusiasm for physical (PE) and 'extrovert' subjects (drama), as indicative of cultural background, we are interested in the ways in which discourses underpinning subject preference may be more available/constrained for particular ethnic groups. Hence their preferences may reflect discourses produced by their 'cultural' perspective and the interaction with/positioning of these by the dominant Western discourses sustaining the British educational system. A preference for maths appears to be an example of the cultural impact on discursive and social resources, as a particular approach to maths in Chinese families (and consequent preference for maths among young Chinese) has been noted elsewhere (Ran, 2001; Woodrow and Sham, 2001), and was referred to by some of the pupils themselves. Yet there were also examples of how the British curriculum may take a 'Eurocentric' stance which does not always accommodate cultural difference, and may therefore constrain Chinese pupils' opportunities and preferences. For example, asked why she had identified Religious Education (RE) as her least favourite subject, ChingChing (Butcher Comprehensive School) replies, "Cos I think I don't have that cultural background'. The interviewer asks,

INTERVIEWER: Aren't they meant to look at all sorts of different religions and cultures, or does that not happen?
CHINGCHING: Yeah, it doesn't, no.
INTERVIEWER: Ah, OK.
CHINGCHING: They learn Christian, that's it.

And asked why she does not enjoy Media Studies, Mary explains:

'Cos it's mostly about TV, like chat show, and I don't really watch English TV, 'cos my family, my Mum and my Dad kinda can't speak English so they watch like Chinese channel, so I have to watch it as well.

But whatever the cause, it is interesting that their curriculum subject preferences position Chinese girls – sometimes seen from a Western perspective as 'traditionally' feminine in their apparent self-effacing 'quietness' – as masculine, in their comparative preference for maths and science (a finding that will no doubt be welcomed due to current education policy concerns with the national and international under-representation of women in Science, Engineering and Technology (SET) fields[5]). Similarly, while British-Chinese boys' heavy preference for these masculinised subjects can be read as investing them with masculinity in a Western gender order, their tendency to dislike PE renders them out-of-step with one of the key Western markers of popular masculinity – sporting enthusiasm and prowess (Connolly, 1998; Martino, 1999; Francis, 2000b; Jackson, 2006). We discuss British-Chinese constructions of masculinity in the context of British classrooms in more detail later in this chapter.

British-Chinese pupils' constructions of themselves as pupils

Asked 'Do you think you are a good pupil?', a very high proportion of British-Chinese pupils gave a positive response. 70 per cent (56) pupils (39 of the 48 girls, and 17 of the 32 boys) said that they consider themselves good pupils. Only four pupils (three girls and one boy) did *not* see themselves as a good pupil (a further 10 pupils argued that they were 'average' pupils, and another 10 pupils were equivocal or did not answer clearly). This is a very different picture to that presented by Francis' previous research findings with an ethnically diverse sample of middle and high achieving pupils, discussed earlier (Francis, 2000b). In that sample only 16 out of 50 girls and 13 out of 50 boys answered 'yes' when asked if they are good pupils. And 11 girls, and 13 boys said 'no', they were not good pupils (the rest replied either that they were unsure, or that they were average).

Clearly, these positive responses from British-Chinese respondents included pupils from all social classes: this is an important point given that we might usually expect some working-class pupils to be less educationally engaged/enfranchised than their middle-class counterparts. For instance, Reay (1998, 2001) discusses how education is often experienced by working-class learners as a process of 'losing yourself', 'never being sure' – and coming to see oneself as a 'nothing' (Reay and Wiliam, 1999). Our findings – that British-Chinese pupils of all social classes are more likely than other pupils to see themselves as 'good pupils' – appear to affirm our previous findings that British-Chinese pupils are particularly educationally oriented and place high currency on the value of education as a specific element within their (relational) British-Chinese identities (Francis and Archer, 2005a; Archer and Francis, 2006). One teacher speculated on this complex interweaving of social class and 'race' on achievement, observing:

> Our theory is that it's more linked with class than it is with race in some ways. But then I have to say I think Chinese community defeat that logic because they are mostly working class. I mean a lot of the families are working in the catering trade. We see that when UCAS forms go across our desk, I mean you obviously see restaurant worker on the forms of students. But they do have, you know, this kind of high esteem for education.   (Mrs McCluskey)

As we discuss elsewhere (Archer and Francis, 2006), this example serves to highlight how current accounts of social class – both 'culturalist' and materialist readings – tend to be formulated with reference to White populations and do not necessarily map straightforwardly onto BME or British-Chinese trajectories (see also Chapter 6).

Furthermore, that such a high number of British-Chinese pupils (but particularly working-class young people) in our study positioned themselves as 'good pupils', and such a low number responded that they are *not* good pupils, evokes a relatively high level of confidence and self-affirmation among our sample in relation to their position as students. This lends support to Chan's (2000) finding that British-Chinese pupils have high self-esteem generally in relation to education – higher than that of both their White British and Hong Kong Chinese counterparts. This raises an interesting point as to whether, and how, particular cultural discourses play a role in generating resilience and a sense of self-affirmation in relation to the construction and maintenance of learner identities in particular times and spaces.

It is notable that the level of self-assurance indicated by the particularly high proportion of British-Chinese girls who asserted that they are 'good pupils', jars strikingly with the construction of British-Chinese girls by teachers. As outlined in Chapter 3, we found that British-Chinese girls were overwhelmingly represented by their teachers as passive and 'unnecessarily quiet', as well as hardworking and high-achieving. As with South Asian girls (see Brah, 1994), British-Chinese girls were often positioned as victims of an 'oppressive' and 'restricted' home life, which was assumed to result in their lack of voice in the classroom. Hence the apparent silence, obedience and diligence of British-Chinese girls is constructed by their teachers as reflecting their lack of assertion and lack of confidence as a result of their 'repression'. In fact, many of our female pupil respondents presented themselves as behaving very differently to this model (maintaining for example that they were 'loud-mouths' in class, 'can't stop talking', did not take learning seriously, and so on). Indeed, when pressed about particular girls, some teachers did sometimes concede that there are 'exceptions' to their generalised construction of British-Chinese girls' classroom behaviour. However, it is also interesting to reflect that the sorts of behaviours which teachers are reading as evidence of British-Chinese timorousness are actually constructed/produced by British-Chinese girls in a deliberate positioning of themselves as 'good pupils', which they cite as contributing to their educational self-affirmation. For example, Chui reflects in relation to her classroom behaviour:

> School work, I do my homework. I've never actually been in school detention before and that's since Year Seven up til now … And yeah, I think I've been a very good example to the school I think, yeah.

One or two pupil respondents conveyed an awareness of the potential dissonance between their own views of themselves as an ideal pupil and that of their teachers/non-Chinese peers. Helen, for instance, claimed to be a 'good pupil' but when asked whether there were any respects in which she is not, she replied:

> I'm generally quite good but I think I need to be more confident in speaking in class. Ask more questions and kind of contribute more to the class sometimes. Because I like, because I mainly like work individually, I like working by myself. So I need to improve on that.

Certainly, she identifies some of the concerns expressed by Sham and Woodrow (1998) who brand British-Chinese pupils 'passive', 'deferent' and 'conformist' (Sham and Woodrow, 1998; Woodrow and Sham, 2001). In their opinion, British-Chinese pupils 'find it hard to form an independent opinion since opinions are slavishly formed in a Chinese household from family authority figures' (Woodrow and Sham, 2001).[6] These attitudes are problematised by Sham and Woodrow for providing 'little impetus for growth and change' (Sham and Woodrow, 1998; Woodrow and Sham, 2001). Clearly, we would not support such negative and pathologised readings of British-Chinese pupils (although we would also like to emphasise here that we are not seeking to glorify 'non-traditional' presentations either). However, they do serve a purpose in that they highlight a dominant Western model of learning and education – albeit one which often goes unanalysed and unarticulated (e.g. valorising and normalising the questioning, challenging pupil). Clearly, many British-Chinese pupils are being negatively positioned in relation to this European model, and will be found wanting in spite of their achievement because – to borrow from Walkerdine's analysis of girls' approaches to maths – they are not seen to be learning 'in the right way' (Walkerdine, 1988).

Approaches to learning

Asked whether education is important, it was notable that *all* 80 of our pupil respondents said that it is, again reinforcing (and often utilising) the discourse of 'Chinese valuing of education' (Francis and Archer, 2005a). When invited to talk about their own approaches to learning, many of our respondents presented an approach in keeping with the stereotype of Chinese pupils as highly applied, conscientious and diligent. For example, Kate observes, 'I don't talk to people that much and I concentrate on lessons'. George explains, 'I try and complete everything within a certain time, by the deadline and I try and do it well so basically I try my best'. Helen agrees, 'I think when say work is really difficult, I still kind of put a lot of effort into it. And I believe that if you put a lot of effort into it you like get rewards at the end. So I just, even if it's difficult I still kind of pay attention'. As Benton (1998) discusses, British-Chinese young people may be more likely to envisage educational success as achievable via 'hard work', whereas their White peers may be more likely to subscribe to notions of success as determined by 'innate ability/intelligence'.

Yet, other pupils said that they were far less conscientious, and more representative of attitudes Westerners see as typical of (White-British) teenagers in relation to schoolwork. Grace describes her approach to her schoolwork as: 'Talks too much, got a big mouth. Rude all the time and call out in lessons all the time, which is stupid'. Hong says that he is 'lazy' elaborating, 'I do try but when you're lying down in your bed you're not really too bothered to get up but I do try to get up and do my work'. Phil equivocates that his approach 'Depends on the mood really. It's like if I'm annoyed I won't do any work. Like if I'm in a chirpy mood I'll be doing the work'. Others agreed that their approach depended on their mood and whether or not they could 'be arsed' (as Donna puts it), or whether the lesson concerned is 'boring'. Many pupils shared Judith's approach of 'usually I leave everything till last minute' (although some also specified that they always succeed in completing work, even if in a rushed form, or with little effort put in). Generally, we found plenty of evidence to confound dominant stereotypes of British-Chinese pupils as silenced and/or 'abnormal' – although as we discuss further, towards the end of the chapter, such constructions do give us pause to reflect on the (Western) values and assumptions underlying dominant constructions of 'normal adolescence'.[7]

'Race', gender and achievement: British-Chinese pupils' views on the 'laddism and achievement' debate

As discussed in Chapter Three, policy concerns about 'race', gender, social class and achievement have coalesced around the notion of 'laddishness'. In particular, high profile debates have arisen regarding how, and whether, laddishness impacts negatively on the learner identities and engagement of boys (and more recently girls, see Jackson, 2006). Attention has been given to particular racialised forms of 'laddishness' (Archer, 2003; Archer and Yamashita, 2003), recording how the term is sometimes applied by pupils themselves to multi-ethnic groups in discussion of laddism (Francis, 1999). In the following discussion, we seek to explore how a particular minority ethnic group of pupils, the British-Chinese, conceive of 'laddish behaviour', and how they construct their gendered selves in relation to this.

General perceptions concerning the extent of 'laddish behaviour' in school

Two-thirds of pupils in Francis' (1999) study with young people from diverse ethnic groups agreed with the view of policy makers that boys' 'laddish behaviour' is impeding their school achievement. The responses of British-Chinese pupils in our study affirm the prior findings, with a majority of British-Chinese pupils supporting this view in relation to all boys. Indeed, British-Chinese pupils were more likely to support this view than were those in the previous ethnically diverse sample (although as with respondents in the former study, many of the British-Chinese pupils tempered their responses by pointing out that it is only the case for some boys, rather than all boys). Like pupils from other ethnic groups, British-Chinese pupils seemed for the most part to have a common understanding of the notion of 'laddish' behaviour as projected by policy makers, and were not surprised at the perception that such behaviour is impacting on the achievement of some boys. Although as we shall see, the pupils' perceptions of behaviours *constituting* 'laddish' conduct transpired to be somewhat diverse and differentiated from the views of policy makers and teachers.

The four key narratives drawn on by the British-Chinese pupils to explain boys' apparently laddish behaviour reflected those used most frequently by pupils in the earlier study (see Francis, 1999, for discussion). A narrative of 'the greater maturity of girls' emerged particularly frequently, and was exclusively present in British-Chinese *girls'* explanations. The narrative that there are 'distractions/boys are more easily distracted' was also drawn on. As in the first study, football was singled out as a particular distraction for boys. A narrative of 'pressure from, or the need to impress friends' positioned laddish behaviour as the result of peer pressure. The closely related narrative of 'wishing to appear "hard" or "macho"' was also evident in many of the students' explanations for such behaviour.

Hence the British-Chinese pupils' responses concerning the notion of laddish behaviour broadly reflected those of the ethnically diverse sample. However, when asked whether the argument that boys' 'laddish' behaviour is affecting their achievement is applicable to British-Chinese boys, some quite different discourses began to emerge.

Constructions of British-Chinese boys' masculinity and 'laddism'

Constructions of British-Chinese boys as engaging in 'laddish' behaviour

A substantial majority of pupils considered that some British-Chinese boys can and do behave in 'laddish' ways. Twice as many of the boys said the argument about laddish behaviour and achievement does apply to British-Chinese boys than did those who said British-Chinese boys do not behave in 'laddish' ways. Also, 22 girls agreed that British-Chinese boys can be laddish, while 13 said they are not. As LaiFong (Albert Square School) agrees, 'Yes 'cos I know a lot of Chinese boys that have that sense of like if you do your work then it's not cool'. These results are important, given our finding that teachers tend to perceive British-Chinese boys as non-laddish, obedient, 'good pupils' (Archer and Francis, 2005a). As we discussed in Chapter 3, a majority of teachers presented a dichotomous view of British-Chinese boys: the vast majority are seen as diligent and obedient, and as not expressing 'laddish' behaviours, except in a small minority of cases where 'bad' Chinese boys (often 'infected' by Anglo and African-Caribbean working-class boys) are frequently associated with Triadism (Archer and Francis, 2005a). There did not appear to be any middle ground in this construction of 'good' and 'bad' British-Chinese boys. Yet British-Chinese pupils were, in contrast, tending to argue that British-Chinese boys can and do behave in 'laddish' ways.

Explanations for British-Chinese boys' 'laddish' behaviour

Some of the pupils who argued that British-Chinese boys display laddish behaviour drew on a discourse of inherent gender differences to explain this. Hence LaiFong muses, 'I guess it's natural for them to act that way'. This discourse presents all boys as simply expressing their biological programming. This discourse of 'natural'/ biological maleness was felt to over-ride ethnic and cultural boundaries. Another discourse which was drawn on to present all boys as the same was that of racial equality. For example, Harry says that laddishness applies equally to Chinese boys because, 'I don't think that race really matters about that, it's just being male really'. HoiLing constructs a slightly different angle, maintaining that there will always be a few 'bad apples' within any culture:

INTERVIEWER: This idea of sort of laddishness and messing about, or being hard, or macho, or whatever, do you think it applies equally to Chinese boys or not?

HOILING: Well most of the boys I know are quite intelligent and they do well in school, but there's always like the bad ones who, they've got a group and they act hard. So there's always, in any culture, there's the good ones who study hard, and then there's the bad ones who like mess about and everything, and don't pay attention.

This notion of laddish British-Chinese boys as 'bad apples' clearly positions laddish behaviour as highly negative, and rather reflects the view of teachers that such behaviour is only evident in a small minority of British-Chinese cases (Archer and Francis, 2005a). For example, Alice says that the view of laddish behaviour and learning is only true of 'some Chinese boys'. She elaborates, '[it] depends on their families, I mean there are quite a few families who are really – they are well disciplined. But then you get Chinese families who are more free with their children, they're the trouble makers'. HeiHei speaks glumly about the descent into laddishness of some of his peers from primary school:

INTERVIEWER: Some people are saying that boys are under-achieving at school 'cos of their laddish attitude. What do you think about that, do you think that's true or not true?

HEIHEI: It depends on the person, who they hang around with. I hang about with like all the boffins, all the clever people, ... the mad boys, there's some that hang around with them and they get into really bad habits and they really change. I got some Chinese friends who were at primary school and we used to be like quite clever and then, now they've like really changed a lot. They're not ... the same person that I used to know but every Chinese people expect their sons to be really good and don't be a disgrace to the family.

So although many of the British-Chinese pupils positioned the laddish behaviour of some British-Chinese boys as 'natural' and relatively harmless, some pupils constructed such behaviour as highly deviant and pernicious, and as 'going against culture' (Archer, 2003). The pupils tended to position such 'laddish' British-Chinese boys as having been influenced by 'other' boys, hence positioning laddish behaviour as *unnatural*, rather than natural, for Chinese boys. So rather than being seen as reflecting inherent tendencies, the 'going bad' was viewed as the result of corrupting Western culture and the product of families who are 'too free'. This construction of 'liberal' (Westernised) families directly challenges dominant Western constructions of oppressive/repressive minority ethnic families (e.g. Chinese, 'Asian'), suggesting that a Western model can be 'disgraceful' and educationally counterproductive. When asked whether notions of laddish behaviour apply equally to Chinese boys, Ruth reflects,

RUTH: Maybe for some, but there's a lot of our parents are like, 'oh, you get a good education and achieve more in life' so the parents probably encourage them more.
INTERVIEWER: Right and do you think, do you think Chinese boys, sort of, try not to, do they muck about as much or do they not muck about as much?
RUTH: They can be influenced by other people as well, so.

Hence Chinese families are positioned as encouraging their offspring 'more' than do other sorts of family, although Chinese boys can fall under the corrupting influence of 'others' (non-Chinese) students, who are positioned as a distraction. 'English' [White[8]] boys were frequently constructed as 'laddish' and 'a bad influence', and 'Black boys' were occasionally mentioned in this light too. Chui of Albert Square School alludes to the 'rude boy' culture in his inner-city school as an example of laddish behaviour, and observes, 'you get quite a lot of rude boys and stuff like that but usually like Black people are usually like rude boys'. Hong (Albert Square School) refers to some British-Chinese boys who adopt a 'Black attitude' to being cool – supporting observations by researchers such as Hewitt (1996) and Archer (2003) and Archer and Yamashita (2003) that boys from various ethnic backgrounds can perform particular stylised forms of 'Black masculinity' (termed 'cool pose' by Majors and Billson 1992) to gain 'cool' status.

As Ruth's response (above) suggests, non-Chinese families, and 'English' families in particular, were constructed by British-Chinese pupils as less disciplined, and less concerned about their children's education than Chinese families (see also Francis and Archer, 2005a). Hence Ying of Fowler School says that 'some' Chinese boys adopt laddish behaviours:

> Especially the ones that have grown up in England. Yeah, because like a lot of my Chinese friends, they've grown up in China, so their attitude to work is quite serious. They take work really seriously. And all their grades are like '*wow*'.

Asked why those growing up in China have a more serious attitude, Ying explains that, 'basic education in China is taken very seriously', and compares this attitude to the English one: 'here I don't think primary education is taken that seriously, you just sort of like, you know, stroll your way through primary school, yeah'. Indeed, her frequent use of the word 'seriously' to describe Chinese attitudes to education suggests the 'unsaid' of English frivolousness in this regard.

Chinese families were presented as playing a pivotal role in aiding and expecting high educational achievement. This was felt by some of the pupils to result in British-Chinese boys being less likely than others to display laddish behaviour. Maggie maintains this point, saying, 'it's all about family influence, and family, Asian families do push like their, like, children really hard'. ChingChing agrees that Chinese boys are not laddish because 'they get pressure from their parents' and hence 'they feel [more] under pressure than British boys, I think'. Here the attitudes of Chinese parents are being directly contrasted with those of White parents. Kitty agrees that British-Chinese boys do not usually behave in laddish ways at school because 'The family just wants them to grow a bit harder and achieve the best'. She observes that 'English families are, like, not as strict. And they just you know grow freely'. Archer (2003) discusses a similar construction of White British families as frivolous and irresponsible among South Asian Muslim youths. Whereas Kitty's positioning of English families as laissez-faire might be seen as ambivalent, her moral opinion is revealed in her statement that 'other' boys' (poorer) behaviour arises because 'the family doesn't care about them much or something'. Like British-South Asian Muslim pupils, British-Chinese pupils often constructed White families' apparent lack of concern for their children's education as resulting from a general lack of care (Archer, 2003). This positioning radically contests the Western discourse of 'oppressive home culture' often articulated by White educationalists in concerns about the 'pressure' exerted by Asian parents on their offspring regarding their educational performance.

The view of laddism as a Western 'disease', and of 'good' British-Chinese boys as being influenced or coaxed into such behaviour by 'bad' White and Black boys, was shared by some of the parents. As we discussed in Chapter 3, it was also evident in the talk of teachers, some of whom actually used the word 'infected' when describing how Chinese boys are influenced in laddish behaviour by boys from other ethnic groups. Song (1997) observes that second-generation offspring who show unwillingness to conform to the wishes of Chinese parents or the needs of the family as a whole are positioned as Westernised (with traits such as selfishness and laziness being constructed as 'Western' or 'English'). In this sense, Chinese culture/ethos is presented as a civilising discourse, a construction which may be used by Chinese in Britain to challenge Western racist discourses which present other (including Chinese) cultures as problematic or pathological. So in this construction (perpetuated both by [mainly non-Chinese] teachers and by Chinese pupils and parents), Chinese pupils are positioned as good or 'pure', but open to infection by Westernised others.

Despite the apparently 'positive' positioning of Chinese pupils that is agreed between the proponents of this discourse, we might warn that it relies upon fixed, homogenous, idealised and essentialised representations of both Chinese pupils and 'western' pupils. Furthermore, there was also some evidence that this notion of the Chinese value of education and British-Chinese boys' application was somewhat idealised and not always borne out in practice, even by its proponents. For example, Phil draws on the discourse of 'Chinese value of education' (see Francis and Archer, 2005a) to maintain that British-Chinese boys tend to be less laddish than other boys, 'Well from my experience, Chinese people grow up and it's like education and hard work gets you through life'. Asked why this might be, he explains, 'Eastern countries, they're more based on hard work and education'. However, later in his interview when talking about some of his British-Chinese peers, Phil says,

PHIL: Because from my experience I've known quite a lot of people who like, they don't give you know, two fingers about school really. And they go out, they have fun, you know. They join this, they join that. There's quite a lot of things, but not exactly the laddish way as they call it. It's like a lot different. But there is an alternative version really.
INTERVIEWER: So when you're saying they join this, they join that, are you talking about gangs?
PHIL: Gangs and everything, yeah. Because I've known a few. So.

In this extract, Phil's earlier reification of 'Chinese value of education' contrasts with his discussion of his own lived localised experiences which involve gangs, truancy and other behaviour which might be conceived as 'laddish' aspects of masculinity. (Although Phil himself differentiates between 'laddish' behaviours and the values and performances of Chinese gangs, illustrating both the subtleties and differentials in constructions of high status masculinity according to 'race' and other factors, and the different readings of such performances according to one's subjectivity.)

Constructions of British-Chinese boys as not 'laddish'

Only just over one-quarter of the pupils (22) thought that British-Chinese boys are *not* laddish, although an additional eight pupils specifically argued that they are less laddish than are other boys. In some pupils' responses laddishness seemed to be conflated or equated with low academic ability – British-Chinese pupils were presented as clever, and hence automatically *not* laddish:

Well there's only a few of us [Chinese boys] in our year that but I'd say, actually most of them are pretty clever. They're all, see I'm probably not the smartest one of them, they're all like Set One and stuff, I'm close Set Two, especially in English, but yes they don't really hang out with that kind of [laddish] group anyway. (Paul)

The views of pupils that claimed British-Chinese boys are not laddish mainly built on the themes discussed above, maintaining that laddish behaviour is the province of 'other' boys, and that this is because British-Chinese boys prioritise their education more than do boys from other ethnic groups. Again, the notion of family expectation and discipline was stressed in relation to this prioritisation of education and apparent eschewal of laddism. Hence British-Chinese boys were presented as valuing education more highly than other boys, and prioritising their educational achievement over the opinions of their non-Chinese peers. Man explains, 'we don't go out to impress. We like to be ourselves'. He says there is 'more pride' in Chinese families about education and future prospects. Bridget affirms this view, and observes the role that family competition and 'face' can play in these performances:

> I think the parents, Chinese parents encourage boys to work really hard. They give them like tuition and stuff like that and well there aren't many – compared to like English or other, there aren't many Chinese boys that think they're hard or [laddish], because they're all hard working. The ones that I know they are all hard working so because everyone, their Mums are like 'oh my son's got A's' and I think they've got competition and pressure and things like that.

In these pupils' responses, laddishness and hard work are positioned as binary opposites and educational achievement is justified as sufficient validation in itself for British-Chinese boys' identities. Unlike other boys, they are positioned as less interested in the status afforded by being 'cool' and resistance to education. Indeed, a few specifically aligned themselves with 'boffins', apparently without concern (cf. Frosh *et al.*, 2002). Shirley says of British-Chinese boys, 'they think it's good to be hard working and I think it is too. It's good on them, it's good on us [Chinese generally]'. Hence Shirley positions the apparent diligence of British-Chinese boys as a beneficial point of pride for the whole Chinese community, providing an indication that such educational performance among British-Chinese boys may be validated by some of their Chinese peers.

Is there a specific Chinese version of laddism?

Of those pupils who argued that British-Chinese boys can express laddish behaviour, respondents were fairly evenly divided in their opinions as to whether or not there is a specifically Chinese form of laddism. A slight majority argued that the type of laddish behaviour exhibited by British-Chinese boys is the same as their peers in other ethnic groups. Their responses, where developed, tended to articulate the narrative of equality, and sometimes that of racial equality. For example, asked whether there are different versions of laddishness between boys from different ethnic groups, MaiLai (Beale High) replies, 'No I don't think that culture and what skin colour you are makes a difference really'. Hence this narrative is used to discursively position all boys as the same.

However, seven boys and 10 girls maintained that British-Chinese laddism differs somewhat in expression. (A further three pupils said it depends on the circumstances.)

Several of these pupils maintained that there is a particular 'look' which identifies 'laddish' British-Chinese boys, and which differs from the fashion style adopted by 'lads' from other cultures. The bleached hair sported by many of our more fashion-conscious male interviewees was identified by several respondents as a marker of the 'laddish' British-Chinese boy. But more than this, a number of respondents observed that 'laddish' British-Chinese boys are highly fashion/designer-wear conscious, and impress through their clothes. Ying reflects:

> I think that like Chinese boys they dress, or sometimes, like the cool ones, like I walk down the street and I see a Chinese, I'll [be] like, 'wow'. I think that sort of person, those sort of Chinese boys, they dress like, they're like really in to fashion. [Interviewer: Right.] They're like, they know how to dress themselves, and they like take notice of like what's like in and what's out and stuff.

Judith differentiates between the dress sense of Chinese and other 'lads', saying of the former, 'he's [got] dyed hair and he wears all these chains and this and that, but I don't know. And like a White person'll be a load of like boots, wearing all these hoodies and stuff like that.'[9] Judith maintains that this laddish Chinese 'look' is influenced by Hong Kong movies: 'if you like watching Chinese films, yeah, like all these Triads or whatever like that, they're all like sort of look the same … I guess we all try copy them'. And Rebecca links such fashion style with a 'cool' attitude:

> Chinese boys they think they're cool, they just tend to sit around by themselves and then all the girls just come following and they just sit there looking cool and that's it, and dye their hair golden or something. That's what Chinese boys are like.

Other pupils maintained that 'laddish' British-Chinese boys tend to have specific interests or pursuits that differ from other 'lads'. Nintendo games, 'mucking around with like electronics', and Martial Arts were pastimes that pupils identified as differentiating the British-Chinese 'lad'. Mary maintains that some of her male friends 'hardly go to school, they only go to college like one day in the term'. She explains that these boys skive off school and go on the internet throughout the night, and that this behaviour is not known about by their parents – who have to leave them unsupervised due to the demands of the catering trade. She concludes that, 'Chinese people they won't really mess in class, but in their life outside of school [they] might be'. Mary's suggestion that British-Chinese lads resist or perform masculinity in ways that do not directly disrupt the classroom was a theme developed in other pupils' ideas about Chinese 'lads'. It was often implied that British-Chinese manifestations of 'laddish behaviour' comprised a *mild* version of laddism. Hence (although directly contradicting Mary), Alice maintains, 'they don't really play truant or anything like that, they're just, mucking around'. HoiLing reflects, 'I think that the Black sort of group [of lads] would be more harder and be more like involved in punch-ups, and things like, than the Chinese ones'. And Hui describes laddish British-Chinese boys, but finishes by emphasising that they are not 'really bad' (because such behaviours are just part of the boys' performances of masculinity):

I know a few boys with their hair dyed. They can't really be bothered with their education. They think it's like it's not our place, they can just work in their parents', I don't know, shop or something like that. They kind of act hard so no one can, you know, I don't know, insult them or something but they're kind of like soft at heart if you really get to know them.

A rather different idea implied by a couple of pupils is that British-Chinese boys perform laddish masculinity via their educational credentials, and that this differentiates them from other 'lads'. Helen maintains that sometimes British-Chinese boys 'kind of impress with their intelligence if you get what I mean, like with grades and everything. Like "oh I got a high mark for this" and stuff like that', whereas 'other boys' are more physically competitive. In this way Helen also perpetuates a gendered and 'raced' construction of the Cartesian mind/body split, locating 'mind' with 'Chinese'. Man suggests the root of such attitudes comes from the family, as a Chinese version of laddishness comes from 'being respected by your families and your grandparents and things like that'. As we have seen, academic achievement and kudos is seen by most theorists of the field as antithetical with Western conceptions of laddism; which is exactly why it is suggested that laddish behaviour undermines academic achievement. On the other hand, as several researchers have identified, academic competition and pride in achievement can be a way of delineating other powerful versions of masculinity. For example, the White, middle-class 'Real Englishmen' in Mac an Ghaill's study (1994) constructed their masculinity via academic competition and disparagement of under-achievement. Francis (2000a) suggests that such methods of masculinity construction may be particularly open to/ utilised by boys who construct themselves as learning-oriented (rather than 'laddish'), and this would tie in with the dominant construction of 'Chinese value of education' among the British-Chinese (Francis and Archer, 2005a).

Doing 'lad' in school: British-Chinese boys' performances

It would appear then, that a majority of British-Chinese pupils constructed British-Chinese boys' expressions of 'laddism' as less frequent, and often as less 'hard' or extreme, than those of boys from other ethnic groups. That being said, given the stereotyping of Chinese as uniformly diligent, deferent and conformist, it seems important to note that we observed clear examples of 'laddish' performances among our interview respondents. We discuss a couple of these cases briefly here to illustrate the point, and to illuminate the diversity of such expressions.

Donald (of Evans High) is a highly self-confident boy who wears fashionable clothes. He stands out in the sample because he had moved to Britain only quite recently from Hong Kong – yet he has fluent English with hardly a trace of an accent, and constructs himself as 'British'. He surprised the interviewer by claiming that he acts tough in front of his mates, and messes about in class 'all the time'. He maintains that he has 'loads of friends' at the (largely working-class) school as a result. But Donald is also a high-achiever, and prioritises this achievement (to the point of showing off). This achievement is maintained, Donald was proud to point out, despite his habit of truancy (Donald was on truancy reports). According to Donald, 'It's like I bunked the first three weeks and I study for the last three weeks – that'll give me a good grade'. So Donald encapsulated the masculinised construction of 'effortless achievement' (Bourdieu and Passeron, 1977), winning his academic credentials in spite of his non-conformist and laddish behaviours, and hence able to construct his credentials as a bolster to his construction of masculinity. Yet, as we shall relay in Chapter 7, Donald's awkward positioning in the school's racial peer dynamics was very clear, and appeared to us to contribute to his construction of masculinity. Attempts to 'fit in' with his racist White friends may have contributed to the particular manifestation of his 'laddish' persona, and his (negative) relational construction of other East Asians. His responses suggest a high psychic cost borne from his positioning in the particular race and gender discourses at work in his (school) location.

Hong, of Albert Square School, had bleached hair and a diamond-style stud earring. He hung round with a group of British-Chinese boys (including Phil, discussed below) who dressed similarly and were constructed by the contact teacher as charming rogues with a penchant for cheek and truancy – typical 'laddish' behaviour. In his interview, Hong complained that 'me and my Chinese friends all get picked on' by teachers. Asked what for, Hong maintains, 'Mostly uniform and just in class as well. I don't know why'. The interview continues,

INTERVIEWER: And you think more so than for other students?
HONG: Well, the Black people as well, they just get it as bad so.
INTERVIEWER: So are you, ethnic minority students generally, or just Black and Chinese?
HONG: Yeah, mostly Black and Chinese.
INTERVIEWER: Why do you think that is?
HONG: Because I think it's the attitude that we show them that we don't really care anyway.

Hong argues that some Chinese pupils at the school do not experience this problem, but that he and his group of British-Chinese friends 'hang around with Black people', and get picked on by teachers as a result. Asked whether he thinks this is due to racial discrimination on the part of teachers, or to he and his friends 'not fitting in with the school ethos', Hong replies, 'a bit of both'. As we observed earlier, we found that both teachers and some British-Chinese pupils saw 'laddish' British-Chinese boys as having been 'contaminated' by (working-class) White and Black boys, and this identification is what Hong is problematising. Teachers appeared to construct such laddish British-Chinese boys as 'really bad' in contrast to their 'good' peers (Archer and Francis, 2005a), and it may be that Hong and his peers find themselves on the 'thin end' of this teacher construction.

An aspect of 'bad' Chinese manifestations of laddism for teachers was Triadism. Parker (2000) and Tam (1998) both maintain that Triad activity is vastly over-emphasised and hyped in the Western media, often providing a moral panic at particular socio-historic junctures (e.g. concerning immigration) – a view with which we would concur. However, we would also argue that Tradiism remains an unremarkable, low-level feature of some inner-city areas where Chinese businesses are highly concentrated. Our fieldwork period coincided with a periodic upsurge in violent Triad activity: between late April – early June 2002 we heard weekly news (partly in the local media and partly from contacts working in London's China Town) of attacks on the restaurants and gambling dens owned by the '14-K' Triad gang, by the 'WoSangWo' gang, as the WoSangWo sought to re-establish a footing in London's China Town. Such activity is no longer exclusively Chinese: some of the 'foot-soldiers' or 'little-brothers' involved in these raids were reported to be African-Caribbean and White teenaged boys. Anecdotal reports also indicate that Vietnamese are increasingly represented. Triadism is highly glamorised in the Hong Kong film industry (much as Italian gangsterism is in Hollywood), and arguably Triad 'secret societies' represent the ultimate masculine environment – competitive, disciplinarian and hierarchical, with values of 'hardness', risk, male-bonding, bravery, ruthlessness and respect. Such values might be appealing to and/or employed responsively by disenfranchised young men who feel marginalised in educational institutions that reflect White, middle-class values. British-Chinese boys tend to be positioned as 'good', hardworking boys by teachers (and sometimes by other pupils), with the associations of femininity that this construction involves. Conversely, associations with Triadism offer the appeal of a more powerful masculinity. However, as noted below, such identities may also not be a straightforward matter of choice, reflecting some boys' structurally risky social locations.

Little wonder then that 'gangs' were mentioned by a number of our respondents, either as a marker of 'laddish' British-Chinese boys, or simply as a feature of their own lives. For example, after establishing mutual knowledge of particular restaurants and personnel in China Town with the interviewer, Hong cautiously mentions his older brother's Triad allegiance. Phil (who is part of Hong's peer group and sports a similar bleached hair-style) says that laddish Chinese boys join gangs, and HoiLing reflects that Chinese boys 'like to see themselves as a gangster, they think it's cool. Here, I don't know, I don't know, there are a few like triads and everything, where there's like really dangerous Chinese blokes'. Sammi argues that British-Chinese boys will work hard at school irrespective of any Triadism, explaining, 'because I've got some friends that are in Triads but they're not that horrible though, they still do their work'. (This statement again raises the theme of British-Chinese boys being 'laddish' but still focused on their education, hence re-inventing the notion of the 'lad'.) Yet it was Phil's interview that particularly illuminated the pressure and temptation for boys to join gangs, Triad or otherwise.

Having discussed gangs, Phil explains that the values of Triads are very different to Western notions of 'laddish' behaviour. He then goes on to articulate the appeal of power and status derived from being a triad, which is shared with the high-status masculinity ascribed to laddish boys. He describes British-Chinese boys who are linked to particular 'gangs'[10],

> Well all I can say, it's like they would walk around schools with their head high. And like anyone that's a slight sting to them, they will go, 'You know, you'd

better watch yourself, next time I see you', blah, blah, blah, all stuff like 'we're going to, if you …' get like all their friends like kind of thing.

Similarly to work conducted with other young men (e.g. Alexander, 1996, 2000; Westwood, 1990; Archer and Yamashita, 2003), Phil's description of his local area combined themes of space, place, ownership, belonging and safety/danger, which were played out within specific racialised, gendered and classed boundaries. For example, he suggested that in his local area of South London 'it's mainly Black people and my people who like run the area'. Territoriality – and the demarcation of particular areas into gendered (masculine) and racialised spaces – has been identified as a characteristic feature of the performance of urban young masculinities. It constitutes a terrain of local geographies of 'risk'/'safety' and belonging (known) versus othering/unknown, within and against which masculinity is enacted and contested. Hence particular performances of masculinity (e.g. powerful, 'head high' as Phil describes) can be maintained and validated within particular ('our') spaces ('my area' – see Phil's extract below) – with boys' territorial claims on such spaces offering a sense of protection, safety and/or affirmation. Elaborating about 'laddishness', Phil says:

PHIL: It's like if I was walking down a Black neighbourhood, yeah, I would get picked on, it's obvious, yeah. If I was … I would get picked on yeah. But if they walked in our neighbourhoods, well the … it's like everyone, because like when I first moved here I was a child, right. Everyone else was a child. So I sort of grew up with them. So like they know that, you're generally safe, whatever, so you don't do anything. But if like the lads you know, will walk through my neighbourhood, they will get picked on straightaway.

INERVIEWER: When you say… 'I walk down a Black neighbourhood or whatever, I'd get picked on, it's obvious'. I mean is it obvious?

PHIL: It's obvious.

INTERVIEWER: And because you're Chinese and that's wrong, or because you're just someone not from that area?

PHIL: It's sort of like because I've grown up with them, they all know me, so it's alright.

INTERVIEWER: Can you walk round there?

PHIL: Yeah, in my area. But if go to other areas right, that don't know me, they will look at me strangely. And after that, when no-one's looking they will come up to me, you know, and start trouble, whatever.

The 'hardness hierarchy' (Skelton, 2001) of performed young masculinity, and the real consequences in terms of fear, intimidation, physical restriction and violence are clearly revealed in Phil's matter-of-fact description of this territorial policing of the local geography (Westwood, 1990). In response, the interviewer reflects:

INTERVIEWER: And I mean in that case, the whole sort of status thing, it must be very tempting to – if like Chinese gangs, Triads, or whatever offer boys, Chinese boys a way of being safe, being hard and the sort of security in a group and so on, they must be very appealing.

PHIL: No. If it were appealing, it's like because some people I know, they don't want to join like this, they [Triad members] will actually more or less force, because they [Triads] will intimidate them. Like they put them in a room basically, and about four big guys will say you know, 'Join', 'Join The Family' as they call it. And like if you say 'no' they will say, they won't do anything, they'll just, you're pretty much forced in, but when you're in right, yeah, it feels like you would enjoy it. … if you find a way out you wouldn't go out because like you felt you know, 'I can walk around safe. I'm part of this and I'm part of that, you going to start trouble?', ra, ra, ra.

INTERVIEWER: It's kind of a pride thing, and a security thing that it offers.

PHIL: Yeah.

Phil's response is somewhat contradictory in that he initially rejects the 'temptation' of Triadism as a means for ensuring a high status masculinity, as well as protection, arguing that people are forced to join rather than choosing to. But the latter part of his statement affirms the feeling of security and status that such membership can bring. We suggest that his ambivalence provides an important challenge to any potential romanticisation of 'hard' young male cultures – reminding us that they can entail complex power relations of violence and coercion, as well as camaraderie and belonging. Phil is clear that such constructions are gendered. Asked whether the issues are similar for girls, he muses:

> But like well with this area they [girls] don't have to join gangs and everything. They have their little group of friends, right. And I'm not … but boys like, they will sort it out with their fists, yeah. But girls right, they would sort of like you know, bitch, they would bitch each other. Like they don't use their fists, because like you know, this is the way like. It's the way it works you know, in South London. Like the boys with you know, fists, you know, girls just bitch. Unless it gets to a point where they have to use their fists.

Hence Phil presents a stereotypical dichotomy where boys engage in physical conflict and girls in verbal conflict. He maintains that the issues of territory that he has been discussing do not apply to girls as they do to boys. This construction reflects perceptions of the public sphere as a male domain, but particularly the policing of territories as a male concern. Hence racialised masculinity is being performed through the negotiation of territorial boundaries.

'Theorising British-Chinese laddishness'

Our arguments can be further illustrated if we take the case of 'laddishness' in relation to the British-Chinese. Let us unpick some of the closely woven discourses of race and gender emerging in the talk of pupils and teachers, and consider what traits are inferred or contained by the discursive constructions of: (a) the 'lad'; and (b) the 'Chinese pupil'. We suggest that the following traits construct these subjects, and

Table 5.3 Discursive constructions of 'the lad' and 'the British-Chinese pupil'

Lad	British-Chinese
'having a laugh'	serious
hedonistic	stoical
disruptive/irresponsible	responsible
rebellious	(conformist)
camaraderie/peer led	(independent)
actively heterosexual	(asexual)
young/youthful	mature
hard	(soft/weak)
cool	uncool/geeks
not achieving	achieving
focused on non-educational subjects and pastimes	focused on education
low value on education	high value on education
lazy	hardworking
(masculine)	(feminine)
(active)	(passive)

that they are in many instances oppositional (brackets denote where an opposition is implied in Western discourse, rather than actually articulated by the respondents in our study). (See Table 5.3.)

Clearly, masculinity is located in the 'lad', and as the Chinese construction is functioning as a binary opposite it is consigned to the feminine (this 'othering' is compounded by the femininity of many of the traits stereotyped as 'Chinese'). While 'extreme' versions of laddism are seen as worrying by educationalists, 'laddish' behaviour tends to be seen as 'natural' in boys (Epstein *et al.*, 1998), and is often condoned and colluded with by teachers (Francis, 2000a) – although as noted by Francis and Skelton (2005), laddishness is also being increasingly problematised and medicalised in contemporary educational policy. How, then, does the above discursive configuration impact on British-Chinese constructions of masculinity? The boys' constructions of masculinity are constituted through discourses of 'race'/ethnicity (and as we have written elsewhere, constructions of ethnic identities are inseparable from/constituted via gendered discourses (Archer, 2003)). Hence it may be that the quality of rebelliousness in the face of authority (as manifested in dominant constructions of laddish behaviour in the classroom) is less central to Chinese constructions of masculinity than is the case in popular Western constructions. And perhaps within the discourse of 'Chinese value of education', constructions of masculinity via academic competition may be particularly available to British-Chinese boys, facilitating achievement. However, such constructions of masculinity are undermined by the Westernised, racialised discursive positioning of British-Chinese boys by their teachers via the discourses of 'Chinese value of education' and 'the good Chinese pupil' as diligent, passive, deferent, and achieving via hard work rather than natural flair (see Chapter 3). Hence the traits constructed in the discourses of 'Chinese value of education' and 'the good Chinese pupil' are consigned to the feminine, and consequently position British-Chinese boys as 'not proper boys' in Western readings.

As noted in the preceding sections, some British-Chinese boys appeared to be resisting dominant constructions of 'the British-Chinese pupil' through their performances of 'hard'/'cool' 'laddish' identities. However, the dichotomy helps us to understand these performances are destined to remain only 'locally hegemonic' (Archer, 2003) – since they cannot transcend their embodied locations and hence may not achieve the mobility of some other boys' performances (i.e. the 'authenticity' of their performances may be more open to challenge within a dominant gaze).

Conclusion: reflections on British-Chinese and Western constructions of education

So what has this chapter shown us about British-Chinese youths' perceptions of their approaches to learning, and of the impact of constructions of gender and ethnicity on these?

We have explored how British-Chinese pupils' constructions and preferences differ somewhat from other pupils in that:

- They tend to prefer different curriculum subjects compared with ethnically diverse sample groups.
- They are particularly likely to see themselves as 'good pupils', and as educationally applied.

These constructions are gendered (e.g. British-Chinese girls were more likely than boys to see themselves as 'good pupils'), as well as 'raced' (e.g. British-Chinese girls are more likely than others to enjoy non-gender traditional curriculum subjects).

Their constructions of issues around masculinity and learning are somewhat distinctive in that:

- They are particularly likely to support the view that 'laddish' behaviour is detrimental to the educational achievement of some boys.
- A substantial majority of the respondents maintained that some British-Chinese boys behave in 'laddish' ways: this contrasts with the views of (mainly non-Chinese) teachers, among whom a large proportion thought that British-Chinese boys are never 'laddish' (Archer and Francis, 2005a). Hence it seems that British-Chinese pupils themselves construct Chinese boys as more (or at least more often) 'laddish' than do their teachers.
- While teachers tended to construct 'laddish' Chinese boys as 'really bad', British-Chinese pupils themselves tended to construct such laddism as a particularly *mild* version in comparison to manifestations of laddish behaviour expressed in other ethnic groups.

What are the implications? Besides confirming previous findings concerning the British-Chinese investment in a discourse of 'Chinese valuing of education', and the powerful impact of this discourse on their educational practices and outcomes (see Francis and Archer, 2005a), this emerging picture might be read as stereotypically presenting the British-Chinese as 'odd' and 'other'. For example, their association as 'good pupils' may confirm stereotypical views of the Chinese as unhealthily diligent, obedient and conformist (see e.g. Woodrow and Sham, 2001). The discourses of 'Chinese value of education' and of 'the good Chinese pupil' were drawn on extensively by both pupils and teachers. They were used by both groups to position British-Chinese pupils as outstandingly diligent and high-achieving. British-Chinese pupils tended to construct greater behavioural diversity among their British-Chinese peers than did teachers, as some teachers appeared to apply an Orientalist (Said, 1978) view of the Chinese as a homogeneous mass uniformly conforming to industrious Eastern values and tyrannous family expectations. We have also argued that British-Chinese pupils and parents use the discourse of 'Chinese value of education' with pride to perpetuate the construction of themselves as high-achievers, and as being 'true to culture' by respecting and valuing education (see Francis and Archer, 2005a, 2005b). The British-Chinese pupils' tendency for distinct curriculum preferences might position them as 'different', and pathological in their disregard for 'British' constructions of 'normal' masculinity and femininity in the school environment. So should we be anxious that we are supporting an Orientalist view of the Chinese as Other? Should we be analysing distinctiveness according to ethnicity at all?

One of our intentions in conceiving our original research project was to examine factors which might be contributing to the high achievement of the British-Chinese as a group within the British education system. We do not seek to shy away from or 'hide' difference in an effort to homogenise ethnic groups. However, we are keen to avoid the reification of such expressions of difference as essential to (fixed) 'cultures': our data demonstrates extensive diversity in responses and attitudes to educational issues among the British-Chinese pupils, as we hope to have illustrated throughout the book. Gender, class, locality, place of family origin and so on, all impact here as well as do individual differences among respondents.

We also maintain, however, that British-Chinese pupils tend to draw on specific discourses in order to construct distinct, racialised identities in relation to other cultures (Francis and Archer, 2005a). Hence particular discourses around education are mobilised to construct and delineate a specifically British-Chinese identity and production of 'Chineseness' (see Song, 1997). Homi Bhabha (2001) reflects on such diasporic positions:

> In-between spaces provide the terrain for elaborating strategies of selfhood – that initiate new signs of identity, and innovative sites of collaboration, and contestation, in the act of defining the idea of society itself. It is in the emergence of the interstices – the overlap and displacement of domains of difference – that the intersubjective and collective experiences of nationness, community interest or cultural value are negotiated (pp. 136–7).

In the case of British-Chinese pupils and parents, we the found the discourse of 'Chinese value of education' to be a primary tool in this fashioning of 'nationness'. Within this outlook on education, there are clearly other narratives and practices which need to be teased out (such as 'Chinese ability at maths' and the practices associated with this discourse). However, it does appear to be the case that the British-Chinese belief in education as an expression of their 'Chineseness' and also as a method for 'bettering oneself', positions British-Chinese pupils of all social classes (and is utilised by the pupils to position themselves) as educationally committed. It may not be surprising, then, that the practices resulting from this discourse result in behaviours and constructions which are relatively particular to British-Chinese pupils. For example, their listing fewer curriculum subjects that they dislike in comparison to other pupils, their generally 'good' and applied behaviour in the eyes of teachers and themselves, and their positioning of themselves as 'good' pupils. These practices, and the general valuing of education as a provider of intrinsic and extrinsic benefits, clearly provide discursive and behavioural foundations for their (generally) high educational achievement.

What is of more concern from a social justice perspective is the way in which these 'good' behaviours and high achievement remain problematised and sometimes pathologised by educationalists. As we have already seen, we found that many teachers saw British-Chinese pupils as 'too good' to be 'ideal' pupils. As we noted in our proposed trichotomy, a Western (middle-class, masculine) model expects pupils to be questioning, and for pupils to achieve through natural talent: achievement through diligence and obedience is disparaged as 'plodding' (Bourdieu and Passeron, 1977; Stanworth, 1981; Clarricoates, 1987). It is this model which has traditionally pathologised the learning approaches of girls in relation to boys; their apparent conformity and diligence perceived as lack by educationalists, irrespective of achievement (Clarricoates, 1987; Walkerdine, 1988; Skelton and Francis, 2003). In the case of British-Chinese pupils, the (stereotyped) classroom behaviours of both girls and boys are constructed as feminine (diligent, quiet, deferent, conformist), and hence as 'not quite right'.

We want to radically challenge and unmask this hidden, 'raced' model of 'the right way of learning' which, while demanding obedience, hard work and application, only rewards these attributes if they are expressed in the 'right' ways (e.g. 'active' learning by questioning) and by the 'right' bodies (White, male, middle class).

We hope to have demonstrated the diversity not just of British-Chinese responses to our questions on 'laddism' and school achievement, but also of the boys' personal performances of masculinity. Our findings concerning British-Chinese interpretations and performances of laddism demonstrate the ways in which 'race' and gender mediate discourses around gender and achievement and the construction of the ideal pupil. British-Chinese constructions of education and of appropriate masculine behaviour may facilitate the educational achievement of British-Chinese schoolboys, but this achievement may itself be problematised by raced, classed and gendered notions about the 'correct' ways to learn and achieve in a British context. We suggest that work needs to be done to interrogate the 'unsaids' of the British educational model, and to examine these in relation to diverse approaches, in order to ensure that BME pupils (and indeed White girls and White working-class boys) are not unduly problematised.

6   Linking identities, aspirations and achievement

In this chapter we bring together, and contrast, analyses of the data from teachers, parents and pupils in order to explore their constructions of British-Chinese pupils' aspirations and the link between aspirations and achievement. We begin by introducing the education policy context, and key current government conceptualisations of the issues concerning minority ethnic families and aspirations. We then move on to consider the views of teachers, parents and pupils in turn. In doing so, we highlight links and lacunae between the different viewpoints. In particular, we develop an understanding of the importance of 'safe'/'known' routes and how these are employed within families as a device for facilitating the chances of social mobility and 'success'.

Educational policy and minority ethnic pupils' aspirations

There are frequent references to 'aspirations' within UK education policy documents (see e.g. DfES 2005, 2004, 2003). Indeed, the 2005 Paper *Higher Standards, Better Schools for All*, acknowledges of the 2004 White Paper that 'More than anything it is a White Paper about aspiration' (2005, p. 7). Within these policy texts, 'aspirations' are closely linked with achievement and performance. In particular, it is assumed that 'low' aspirations among pupils and parents corrolate with low academic achievement. For instance, in his foreword to the DfES five-year strategy for children and learners, Charles Clarke (the then Secretary of State for Education) refers to 'a national scandal of low aspiration and poor performance' (DfES, 2004, p. 3). This 'scandal' of low aspirations has been largely framed as the result of poverty ('We need to break the link between poverty and low aspiration once and for all' (DfES 2005, p. 18)) – but it has also been linked with minority ethnic groups:

> There is a way to go before every child, regardless of their ethnicity, has an equal chance of reaching their potential.
>
> (2005, para. 4.30)

Indeed, both working-class and minority ethnic pupils have been targeted for having low aspirations which, the policy argues, require 'raising' or 'stretching'. For instance, the 2005 strategy paper explains:

> our 'Aiming High' programme, focused on stretching the aspirations and achievement of Black and minority ethnic groups, has begun to tackle deep seated underachievement ...
>
> (2005, para. 4.4)

These discussions about minority ethnic aspirations have addressed the role of both pupils and parents. The 2005 strategy paper, for example, posits that the school choice agenda might be used to raise the interest and aspirations of parents. More explicitly, the 2003 Aiming High consultation document (the strategy aimed specifically at raising minority ethnic achievement) states:

> Where parents have high levels of education and/or high aspirations for their children, this can be a strong factor in promoting high levels of achievement among pupils, both from minority ethnic backgrounds and across the wider population.
>
> The involvement of parents [footnote in original: All references to parents in this section also equally apply to other carers and guardians.] and the wider community is vital to establishing firm foundations in the early years and to raising aspirations and expectations through the child's education.
>
> (2003, para. 2.32)

As such extracts illustrate, policy discussions around aspiration and achievement are predominantly framed in individualistic terms (that is, aspirations are understood to be personal choices) and are overwhelmingly discussed in terms of pupils and parents. Very little consideration is given to the role that teacher aspirations and/or wider structural factors might play in shaping pupils' aspirations and achievement. One exception is a paragraph in the 2003 Aiming High consultation document, which does acknowledge that teacher expectations can also play an important contributory role to shaping (and depressing) minority ethnic young people's aspirations:

> Sometimes teachers or parents expect too little from young people. They think that they won't be able to get good exam results or aspire to go into further education or to college. Sometimes those low expectations relate to racist stereotypes. Such stereotyping then tends to reinforce a cycle of underachievement. This is not just a problem for those perceived as low achievers either. Many students get average results, when they could do much better. Unless we expect more from young people, whatever their ethnic background, they will expect too little of themselves.
>
> (2003, para. 2.23)

However, the overwhelming thrust of policy discourse in relation to 'raising' aspirations and achievement remains firmly grounded within a discourse of individualisation (termed 'personalisation'). This approach places the primary responsibility for action (and hence 'blame' for low aspirations/achievement) with pupils and parents, rather than focusing on teachers, schools and policies:

> Personalisation is the key to tackling the persistent achievement gaps between different social and ethnic groups. It means a tailored education for every child and young person, that gives them strength in the basics, stretches their aspirations, and builds their life chances. It will create opportunity for every child, regardless of their background.
>
> (2005, para. 4.1)

In this chapter we provide a critique to dominant policy approaches as we take a detailed look at teachers', parents' and pupils' constructions of aspirations and the link between aspirations and minority ethnic achievement.

Teachers' views of minority ethnic pupils' aspirations

As we discussed in Chapter 3, various researchers have highlighted the importance of teacher expectations to minority ethnic pupils' achievement. Research indicates that teachers tend to express lower expectations of the abilities and aspirations of minority ethnic pupils, but particularly Asian (especially Muslim) and Black pupils. For instance, Muslim girls in Parker-Jenkins *et al.*'s (1997) study complained that teachers did not hold high enough expectations of them. They felt that staff expected Asian/Muslim girls to get married rather than pursue careers, and so paid them less attention. This resulted in the girls feeling 'left behind' and not receiving adequate careers advice or support. Similarly, the Muslim 'gang' girls in Shain's (2003) study also reported receiving little or no encouragement with regard to their careers aspirations and future plans. Indeed, Basit (1997a, 1997b) argues that even when some Asian pupils explicitly hold and state 'higher' aspirations, some staff may judge them to be unrealistic.

Young Black women have also been found to complain that teachers hold lower expectations of their abilities and do not consider them destined for university. For instance, Archer *et al.* (2003) found evidence of ambitious young Black Caribbean women being dissuaded by their teachers from applying to university. As Mirza (1992) discusses in her classic study of young Black women and schooling, many Black girls are forced to negotiate 'back door routes' through the education system in order to achieve their ambitions. The impact of racism on the aspirations of young Asian/Muslim and Black boys has also been documented (see Archer, 2003; Mac an Ghaill, 1988; Sewell, 1997). All these studies have demonstrated how lower teacher expectations regarding the achievement and aspirations of minority ethnic pupils can feed into under-performance and negative school experiences. But what happens in the case of 'achieving' and 'aspirational' minority ethnic pupils?

Across the board, teachers in our study recognised that British-Chinese pupils expressed 'high' aspirations, aiming to enter higher education and 'professional' jobs:

> They tend to be professional … the professions, law, accountancy, medicine … that kind of thing.   (Mr Cant)

> Of all the ones that I've spoken to, over the years and at Wellard High School, want to go on to do some sort of higher education, regardless of where they come from. Regardless of what their parents are doing in this country, they all want to go on to do a University Degree, as a kind of minimum.   (Ms Ogden)

Several teachers likened British-Chinese pupils with Indian pupils in this respect, suggesting that the higher achievement of both these minority ethnic groups is linked in some way to their higher aspirations. As noted in Chapter 3, high achievement and aspirations were viewed as being the product of a cultural valuing of education:

> I think that what comes across is that there is ambition, there is always ambition. The few girls I have known, they are never going to settle for low status jobs. I mean it is a family thing isn't it? It is similar to the Indian girls, I have taught lots of Indian girls in the past and there is the ambition and the status to be something, to be a doctor, to be a lawyer or to be a businessman or to make money, you know. So it will come through in kind of an altruistic job or else one where there is high money. Again there is a danger of stereotyping but I do think it is there. It is a cultural thing from the home where education is valued and education is seen as highly important and I think that is why they succeed and I think that is why Indian kids succeed as well.   (Ms Naismith)

The source of these pupils' high aspirations was widely perceived to derive from their families' desires for social mobility and 'bettering themselves' (Ms Baldwin). In this way pupils' aspirations were understood as being closely linked to parental aspiration. In other words, these pupils' aspirations were not seen to be a 'personal', individual choice, but formed part of a family project of social mobility and 'escape' from poverty:

> Yeah, I think, I think they do aspire to educational goals and I think they want to get their turn at the professions … Yeah, I think they're going to, I think you know to enter the professions, you know, engineering, computing, law, I think that's what their parents, you know, quite a few of them do have things like take-aways and whatever, and I get the impression that their parents don't want them to be working in a take-away on the New Kent Road, you know, its sort of like, you know … you know what I mean, they want them to … [inaudible] Yeah, in the kids, and also, I get the idea that as well as entering the professions, that they're using this as a starting-off point, they don't want to stay in these sort of estates round [area], you know? I think the geographic mobility is part and parcel of it, you know, whereas I don't know if some of the other groups, sometimes have got that. They see academic mobility or moving up the class

system as also a geographical mobility – to get out of this area and move out to Bromley or Kent, or something like that, I think there's a lot of that involved.

(Mr Duncan)

When asked what sort of aspirations they thought British-Chinese pupils held, teachers were remarkably unified in their responses. Only nine career paths were identified, the most popular of which was medicine (see Figure 6.1, the number of teachers citing each aspiration is given in brackets).

As we shall discuss later in the section on pupils' aspirations (see Figure 6.2), this represented a much narrower range of aspirations than those expressed by pupils themselves. Whilst medicine was similarly identified by pupils as the most popular aspiration, teachers seemed to under-estimate British-Chinese pupils' interest in law, business and arts/humanities (e.g. 'because the [Chinese] families work on fairly low-level heated debate, we don't generally see a student with clear Chinese background necessarily going in to law' Mrs McCluskey).

Despite respecting and admiring pupils' 'high' aspirations, some staff expressed concern that these pupils' professional aspirations were 'narrow' and 'stereotypical':

[I] Can't say much about the girls' aspirations, other than that they tend to be aiming for a narrow range of professional jobs. (Ms Hall)

It's probably unusual to come across somebody who has very different aspirations. I think, you know, the thing is to be successful and go on to higher education.

(Mrs Barlow)

Whilst most staff felt that pupils were continuing to express 'stereotypical' aspirations to a relatively narrow range of occuptions, a few felt that the pattern is slowly changing over time and successive generations. For instance, Mrs McCluskey commented:

I think it's moving away from the kind of stereotypical aspirations, which I would have said, certainly from my experience in London in previous years, would typically have been science and maths. …. I do think we are noticing a lessening of that through the generations. And it's much more normal to see students with Chinese roots stepping outside of that stereotypical pattern.

Medicine (11)

Sciences (6)

IT/technology (5)

Law (4)

Engineering (3)/Pharmacy (3)

Accounting (2)

Art/design (1)/Business (1)

Figure 6.1 Teachers' constructions of British-Chinese pupils' occupational aspirations

However, she also hinted at an issue of intergenerational differences of opinion between pupils and parents with regard to deviation from stereotypical routes:

> I think that is becoming an increasing issue, where the girl maybe doesn't want to do what the family stereotypically feel they should do – which is often medicine or work with pharmacy, or any of those skills.

Later in this chapter, we discuss pupils' and parents' use of 'stereotypical' career pathways and aspirations and suggest alternative ways of understanding these patterns of 'known' routes. But here, we would like to focus on the teachers' references to the perceived extent of congruence or 'clash' between pupils and parents in relation to their occupational aspirations. Various teachers framed the perceived 'stereotypical' nature of pupils' aspirations as resulting from the 'tight' family structure discussed in Chapter 3. Hence pupils' aspirations were viewed as 'bound by their parents' guidelines' and 'following their parents' sort of trends and thinking':

> I think they are more bound by their parents' guidelines [inaudible] they don't tend to rebel against the dictates of their parents. I remember one or two I've had in the past who seem to have had quite strict parents – there didn't seem to be any rebellious ones. (Ms Baldwin)

> Most of them have very professional aspirations … Most, most of them want to move onto higher education and also get well paid, probably also well respected jobs … certainly following their parents' sort of trends and thinking. But no, no conflict that I know of. (Ms Greene)

> Well the conversations I've had with the students that I've taught have been quite positive really, they seem themselves going into professional careers. And that's kind of, they still have that kind of pressure from home, that they wanna go into sort of careers, such as, you know a legal one, or an accountancy one.… – they're quite traditional careers as well. (Mr Noakes)

Indeed, this conformity was described as marking British-Chinese pupils out from Asian pupils:

> Well again, I don't know of any sort of clash between parental views and their own wishes. Sometimes you do hear kids talking about that, 'oh, I've got to choose this because –', but again, that comes from the Asian background I've heard that, not from the Chinese. (Mr Griffiths)

As discussed elsewhere (e.g. Archer, 2001, 2003), 'Asian' pupils are commonly associated with notions of generational 'culture clash' within popular discourse – and such assumptions can be understood as forming part of wider discourses of cultural pathology. However, the exclusion of British-Chinese pupils from such constructions does not necessarily mean that they are viewed more positively. Indeed, a number of teachers expressed a degree of suspicion as to whether the apparent public congruence between pupils and parents in their views was 'really' true. For instance, Mr. Noakes wondered 'Whether the kids accept that, I mean as far as I know, they do accept those aspirations, to be their own, but it seems to me there is some sub-conflict there'.

Similaly Mr. Baxter and Ms. Platt were unsure as to whether the apparent 'united front' presented by parents and pupils was just a surface appearance:

> You know, if it's something like medicine, then all of them, mother, father, son, they're all asking the same questions about the future and they appear to want the same things, but as I say, I don't know really what goes on.   (Mr Baxter)

> On the surface they seem to go along with what their parents want but I don't know how much, how deep down that goes. If that's just sort of being good or if it's, there's more you know, there's a sort of different idea below the surface.
>
> (Ms Platt)

There was a sense among these teachers that they were unable to get 'below the surface' with British-Chinese pupils and their parents to understand 'really what goes on'. This may well be symptomatic of the lack of 'real' communication in home-school relations experienced by both teachers (Chapter 3) and parents (Chapter 4) – a situation that Ran (2001) describes as parents and schools travelling on 'parallel tracks'. However, it is also interesting to consider whether teachers would be asking similar questions if, for instance, a White middle-class boy and his parents were expressing the same professional aspirations and presenting a similarly united front. This is particularly relevant in light of the range of critiques (see e.g. Archer, 2003) that have been made of popular and social psychological accounts of minority ethnic identity development, which assume that second and third generation minority ethnic youth must inevitably and 'naturally' conflict with their parents' views. However, as we shall now discuss, the suspicions of some staff that there might be a wider range of views within families regarding children's aspirations than is apparent to most teachers, was borne out to an extent in the interviews with parents and pupils.

Parents' views on childrens' aspirations

Across the board, parents said that they aspired for their children to go to university and enter a professional career.

> University. And be able to get a reasonable, secure job and umm, be able to provide for themselves   (Hong Wah)

> This generation of Chinese people all want their children to go to university.
>
> (Aron)

> I'd like him to carry on studying, to go to college and to university.   (SiuChun)

> Err, what do I expect? To do something professional.   (Wei Ling)

These aspirations for higher education were universally expressed by parents, and were considered so 'natural' and taken-for-granted that some parents expressed surprise that the British-Chinese interviewer (Sau-Wah Lam) would even be asking them about it:

> Of course! All parents want their kids to [go to university].   (Po Kei)

Of course I want her to go to a good university, and to find a better job.

(Lai Shan)

The strength and 'everydayness' of these views are even more striking when we consider that in the 1980s progression into UK higher education was relatively rare within the Chinese community (Taylor, 1987). The fact that currently over 90 per cent of British-Chinese students progress to University stands as testament to the dedication and persistence of them and their families and their remarkable achievements within a relatively short space of time.

Beyond this aspiration for higher education, parents tended not to nominate particular careers, suggesting instead that the precise occupational route would be their child's choice. However, as suggested by Hing and Shun Hei, below, among those few parents who did indicate preferred careers, medicine, accountancy, law and IT were all named. Parents' preferences for this tight range of routes were framed primarily in terms of the financial security they offered, and the opportunity for progression and respectability.

> Be best if she could find a job as a Doctor or accountant but then she can't become a Doctor because she doesn't like Chemistry. I want her to study accountancy. [Interviewer: accountant?] The society needs accountants and it can be a widely sought after profession … if she's had higher education then you can do any job unless you are very picky and say you have to have a particular job, then that might be very difficult. As long as you are willing to work then I don't think it is difficult to find a job. (Wing Shan)

As already noted, later in this chapter we will discuss ways in which we might read and understand these constructions of 'safe' routes. However, we feel it is worthwhile noting here how parents' aspirations for their children to go to university and enter professional careers were often framed within a discourse of respectability and financial security, encapsulated in the notion of a 'decent' job and the achievement of social mobility:

> Well, I hope that he will carry on and go to Unversity … err … get a decent job, and erm as long as he's happy and he's doing some decent things, I'm happy.
> (Carmen)

> I'd like him to go to university [Interviewer: university] and to find a good job but the main thing is not to learn bad things. … because as a parent of course you want him to find a better job. Of course I want him to study medicine maybe, or things like that but that doesn't mean that he would like that [Interviewer: yes] – reality and aspirations are different. (Hing)

> In the past I've joked with him to go into accountancy, but if he can't, he can go into IT. But if he can't get into both then [I joke] 'you can go into the kitchen'! [both laugh]. He says 'No way!' [Interviewer: So he definitely wouldn't?] No parent would want their child to do this job. Obviously unless that was the last resort.
> (Shun Hei)

As these extracts illustrate, the notion of a 'decent' job was not solely constructed in terms of financial or social status – it was also linked to a broader discourse of morality ('doing ... decent things', Carmen, and avoiding 'bad things', Hing). This emphasis upon morality might be read as an example of parents regarding social mobility as a means for escaping the risks and dangers of life within deprived urban areas. It might also be read as part of wider discursive constructions of social class, which as Sayer (2005) argues, are often framed as moral discourses. Indeed, Lai Wah confided her hope that her daughter would succeed in becoming a professional so that she would be able to avoid 'common jobs' (see also discussions around 'respectability', gender and social class by Skeggs, 1997; Lawler, 1999).

Parents were asked about the extent to which their aspirations for their children matched their children's own plans and views. As noted in the preceding section, teachers tended to perceive a 'united front' and high degree of congruence between parents and pupils' aspirations. Parents, however, differed somewhat in their responses. A few parents indicated that their aspirations meshed with their children's, but the majority (18) felt there were substantial differences, belying the idea that Chinese pupils simply echo or follow their parents' wishes in their educational choices and progression. Among those parents who felt that their views were similar to those of their children, the level of agreement was framed at a fairly general level – i.e. 'to do well' and to 'go to university', rather than in terms of the specifics of what subjects to study or what occupation to go into.

> Mmm, I would say so yes I think we have the same aims, I'm sure she wants to do well.
>
> (Pui Keung)

> I don't think I know what his aspirations are because his interests in what subject or what occupation, I don't know yet ... I've got a lot of confidence that he'll go to university. I've got a lot of confidence that he'll go to university.   (Diana)

Ping, however, suggested that the current level of agreement between herself and her daughters was largely due to their age, and hence might change, particularly as er younger daughter got older and developed her own ideas:

> Um, at the moment because she's quite young, umm, you know, I give my opinion and she accepts it at the present ... quite similar at the moment because she's quite young yet.
>
> (Ping)

On the whole, most parents suggested that their own views differed considerably from those of their children. This contrasts with teachers' assumptions of congruence and their discourses around the 'strict' and 'tight knit' family. Parents commonly explained the differences between the views of themselves and their children as due to a generation gap and because their children were 'born here' and hence held more 'Westernised' views than themselves. But it was interesting that parents also drew on 'Western' discourses of the child as an individual in their accounts:

> I don't think they would be ... he has his path and we have ... and our ages are different, there's a generation gap so the way we think is different, it's difficult to be aligned.
>
> (Aron)

> Views? They're not the same [Interviewer: why?] because as adults we have our own way of thinking and children have their dreams … our views are very different.
> (SiuChun)

On further probing it appeared that the differences that parents alluded to focused on specific choices of future occupation and/or lifestyle, rather than the issue of whether or not to go to university.

YUEN YEE: I think they're not. It's the generation, they're different now…

INTERVIEWER: There's a generation gap. Do you think she'll want to go to university and get a job?

YUEN YEE Yeah

INTERVIEWER: You think she will? Do you still think that you have different views about the future?

YUEN YEE: [sighs]

INTERVIEWER: You don't have the same views?

YUEN YEE: No.

> Aspirations? Are they the same? The same thoughts? [Interviewer: yes] of course they're not [Interviewer: they're not the same? Why?] They want to study what they are interested in for instance art, but obviously as a parent you don't want them to (sighs) … it's up to them. I wouldn't force them to do anything, it's up to them.
> (TszShun)

The issue of differing aspirations between parents and children was predominantly framed as an inevitable generational issue – an acknowledgement that 'times are changing' and/or are different within the contemporary British context, as opposed to 'how things were' in China/Hong Kong. Suen's response was typical:

INTERVIEWER: Ok, do you and your son have the same views of the future?

SUEN: Of course not! [laughs] Because they were brought up here and I was brought up in Hong Kong. When we studied we were taught Chinese morals and it's different from what they learn here.

Changing lifestyles and family roles were discussed particularly in relation to daughters and a wistful regret at this disjuncture imbued many of the parents' comments. For instance Wing Shan and SuiHing both agreed that their daughters shared similar views with regard to going to university, but felt their aspirations differed with respect to how their daughters live their adult lives:

> Yes there is [a difference]. Before children would live with their parents in the future but now there is no chance of that so I won't force her to live with me. I live by myself and she'll live with whoever. The most important thing is that she has a good job and have a good family, I don't mind.
> (Wing Shan)

In [our] thinking there's obviously a gap. Err, a generation gap. I try my hardest to bridge that gap, because she's still young, but even basic things such as the way she chooses to dress and her appearance are different to what I choose. You can't force her by saying 'You can't wear this and you can't wear that', so I grit my teeth and bear it. I have to bear it [laughs]. But she doesn't realise that. There is definitely some generation gap. Nowadays it's different.   (SuiHing)

There appeared to be a gender difference within parents' answers, as none of the 14 parents with sons felt that they shared similar views and aspirations, and 12 asserted that there was a clear discrepancy (two parents were unsure). In contrast, six parents said there was a difference between the views of themselves and their daughters whereas the other parents felt that their daughters' views and aspirations for the future mirrored their own expectations (one parent was unsure).

As Anthias and Yuval-Davis (1992) argue, gender is central to constructions of ethnicity, and women tend to be positioned as 'cultural carriers' – that is, bearers and enacters of traditions – within ethnic collectivities. The maintenance and performance of culture is thus popularly positioned as the particular responsibility and duty of women, rather than men. There was a general concensus among parents, however, that changing traditions in relation to marriage (notably women delaying marriage and motherhood in order to have careers and the rise in cohabitation rather than marriage) were not a key concern. Indeed, many parents agreed that they would prefer for their children/daughters to prioritise their careers first and leave 'settling down' (marriage and children) until later (a view that was reiterated by pupils). In this way, Chinese parents' constructions appeared to coalesce with a dominant middle-class White (heteronormative) aspirational model of career and lifestyle for their children.

Err, well [laughs] it would be nice for them to have a family and get married but I don't know. I mean things change these days [laughs].   (Dolly)

In contrast, parents did seem more concerned when they felt that their children's different aspirations were 'lower' than they (as parents) would like:

Aspirations? Very different. I think that my son's aspirations are very different and not that high [Interviewer: but your's are (high)?] [laughs]. The way I think and their views are very different. We came from Hong Kong and they were born here.   (Kwok Kuen)

However, as we shall discuss in the next section with pupils, some of these concerns might be interpreted as due to parents' relative unfamiliarity with a broad range of career paths and their anxiety to safeguard, as far as possible, their children's chances of success through the promotion of 'known', 'safe' routes.

Many of the parents described being caught in a difficult position, whereby they strove to support their children's academic achievement and aspirations in whatever way they could, whilst also walking a tightrope in trying to ensure that they did not 'pressure' their children too much.

INTERVIEWER: Ah, ok, do you think that the way that you think and the way your daughter thinks about the future, are there any differences?

WEI LING: Yes, there are (.) ways of thinking. Mm, for instance, me, I don't want her to do a tough job, because I'm pushing hard for her now. She hasn't made her mind up on what to do, she's only at secondary school, but I mean, she hasn't chosen her subjects yet, but she makes out that we're already putting pressure on her. She has asked 'mummy, what subject should I choose?', I've told her to look and see what kind of job she wants to do in the future to give her a goal. But she feels that I'm putting pressure on her. Do you understand what I'm saying? ... Yes, her goal is to go to university. What job she wants to get I don't know, but she definitely wants to go to university.

Such tensions illustrate the anxiety and desire of parents to protect their children from the harsh and painful experiences they themselves endured as immigrants. This may also explain the levels of surveillance and control that many parents took for granted in relation to their children's educational progress. When asked what they thought their children would do if they did not achieve the expected educational outcomes, several parents surmised that they would 'make them return to study'. For example, Amanda reflected that if her son decided he did not want to go to university, her acceptance would depend on the situation: 'If he's got a good reason then we might ... go along with it, but if he hasn't got a good reason then no, that will be the end of it, "You're going to Uni", you know'.

Some parents contrasted the values of duty and responsibility to elders that were ascendant in their own upbringings, to their children's greater emphasis on 'freedom' of choice and expression.

I don't think they'll be too similar [Interviewer: Not the same as yours? What differences?] Err, they were born here so they don't have the same way of thinking as us, they want freedom and they want to pursue their own interests. Not like when my mother said 'get a good job' – the most important thing was her interest.

(Lai Shan)

These parents also suggested that whilst they themselves had grown up within a context in which the authority of parental aspirations and 'pressuring' children to follow particular routes was a normal occurrence, they felt it was inappropriate and 'old fashioned' in the current time and cultural context:

Yeah, but for me, you know, I will just keep calm and when the time comes we will have a discussion but I will not force my ... I just want him to do what he's comfortable with and what he's good at and ... umm (.) well, I think it's up to him really. Perhaps I could guide him and give him some alternative ideas or ... but I haven't, I don't really sort of [laughs] how do I put it? I'm not of a very old fashioned way, of like 'you have to do that' or pressurise him. I just think that if he can't achieve that then we will think of alternative ways that he can branch out or diversify.

(Carmen)

'Um, now the mothers do not force them. It's very natural, if they do they do, if they don't then they don't. It's not to say that just because a mother wants him to do this then he'll do it. He might not want to follow his mother's wishes. [Interviewer: are they the same?] you can't say that they're the same, every individual has their own thougths. I have to do what a mother has to do and he does what he does, if he succeeds then of course I want him to succeed ... he has his own plans so I can't help him, it just depends what direction he wants to follow.   (Po Kei)

A number of parents voiced a discourse of 'difference as natural', in which the notion of individual differences was employed to explain different aspirations between parents and children as a natural feature of human life. Shun Hei, for instance, invoked a famous Chinese saying – that even your own ten fingers differ from one another – to explain the naturalness and inevitability of parents and children holding different career aspirations:

Any parent wants their children to carry on studying. ... But if he has [different] aspirations then I shan't hinder him. It's very natural instinct [Interviewer: OK, do you and your child have the same aspirations?] There are discrepancies. They have their hopes, and we've got out hopes. You've got ten fingers, each different sizes. You can't have the same aims, it's very natural.   (Shun Hei)

'Because (.) umm everyone is different. Because you are thinking that maybe this is what they want and ... what they do but just let them free and let them do what they want.   (Nina)

Alongside these constructions of differences as 'natural', several parents emphasised that their children's aspirations were 'beyond my control'. These parents consistently articulated 'free choice' discourses typically associated with Western models of individual agency and democracy. For example, Carmen says that 'when the time comes' to discuss her son's future with him, 'we will have a discussion, but I will not force my ... what I want him to be on him, I just want him to do what he's comfortable with and what he's good at'. And Kwok Kuen and Kin Hong (both fathers) comment:

It's difficult to say, everybody wants their child to study but you can't necessarily make it happen. For instance, my eldest has already gone off with someone, my second one has gone to university.   (Kwok Kuen)

If she can't achieve her plans then it's her own problem. It's out of my control because for instance, her homework she has to do it but I can't push her, let her grow, let her develop herself ... that's up to her, that's her choice. I can't tell her what to do. She's grown up now so it's her own choice. Even as a parent you can't say to them 'you can't do this, you can't do that' it just depends what job suits them.   (Kin Hong)

These extracts would appear to contrast sharply with popular Western stereotypical assumptions regarding the privileging of conformity within Chinese cultures and societies. Shun Hei's extract is also particularly interesting because his defence of individual differences is rooted firmly within a Chinese cultural discourse and thus resists being read as a case of assimilation or taking up of 'Western' discourses. Thus, we would argue, these parental discourses actively challenge popular culturalist discourses (like those found within some of the teacher interviews) because they confound notions of a cultural binary in which 'Western' is equated with individualism and freedom of choice and 'Chinese' is equated with conformity and authoritarian will of the parents over children. They appear to also challenge teachers' assumptions about the 'strictness' and controlling nature of Chinese families over their children.

British-Chinese pupils' aspirations

In line with the wishes of their parents and the expectations of their teachers, it was striking that all of the 80 British-Chinese pupils who took part in the study said that they wanted to go to university. A number also explicitly talked about wanting to pursue postgraduate studies (e.g. at Masters level). The vast majority of pupils aspired to professional careers, irrespective of their own social class backgrounds. However, as we shall discuss further below, it was notable that pupils identified a diverse range of careers (far broader than teachers or parents acknowledged), which included a considerable emphasis upon Arts and Humanities. A sizeable number of young people (N=19) also held no specific aspirations and were deferring making any decisions about their future careers until after university.

Figure 6.2 details the pupils' stated aspirations. Note that some pupils expressed more than one aspiration, hence the numbers add up to over 80.

Medical, para-medical and medical-related (17)	Medicine/doctor (12) Pharmacy (2) Psychologist (2) Vet (1)
Arts/Humanities/Creative (17)	Fashion/designer (6) Architect (5) Journalist/Writer (4) Comedian (1) Advertising (1)
Science, enginering/technology and IT (14)	IT/computers/tech (7) Scientist (4) Thermal dynamics/mech. engineer (2) Technical (car) design (1)
Law (11)	
Financial (8)	Accountant/finance/banking (8);
Business (6)	
Vocational/'practical'(4)	Childcare (2) Swimmer (1) Make-up artist (1)
Other (1)	Lecturer (1)
Deferred/'wait and see until after uni.' (19)	

Figure 6.2   British-Chinese pupils' occupational aspirations

Across the sample, pupils described how talking about their aspirations and 'the future' was a normal part of everyday family life.

> My parents are like every time I come home …[they'll] come and sit down next to me and start talking about, you know, what university you should go to, and like what job you should do.
>
> (Ying)

This, we would suggest, indicates how an aspirational model that involves planning (as opposed to leaving things to fate or chance) forms an important dimension of contemporary British-Chinese diasporic habitus. The practice of planning, resourcing and strategising for the future has been identified as an important component within White middle-class families' educational practices to reproduce social privilege (Ball, 2003; Vincent and Ball, 2006). Likewise, we would argue that the practices here constitute a strategic and effective strategy for promoting success with British-Chinese working-class and middle-class families. However, it is also important to note that Chinese families' engagement with their children's education is enacted within different social relations of power and thus may be additionally sensitive to the management of risk and wider structural inequalities. Furthermore, it is notable that this engagement and planning takes place primarily within the home, rather than at the interface with schools, as might be found more in the case of White middle-class families.

'Hot' and 'cold' influences on aspirations

Ball and Vincent (1998) suggest that there is an important classed dimension to the types of information that families privilege and draw on when making choices and decisions about schooling. In particular, they argue that working-class families tend to base their choices on 'hot', interpersonal, 'grapevine' knowledge, whereas the middle classes are more adept at using 'cold', official sources (e.g. prospectuses, league tables and so on). This finding has also been borne out in relation to choosing further education (e.g. Ball *et al.*, 2000) and higher education (e.g. Archer *et al.*, 2003) and in relation to the formation of aspirations (Archer *et al.*, 2005). Ball *et al.* (2002) identify similar processes between middle-class minority ethnic students (who are identified as 'embedded' choosers) and working-class minority ethnic students (who are termed 'contingent' choosers).

The British-Chinese pupils in our study seemed to fall outside of this model, however, in terms of the sources drawn on in the formulation of their aspirations. Very few – even those from more 'middle-class' backgrounds (i.e. whose parents were in professional careers) seemed to make use of 'cold' knowledge. For instance, only five pupils said that the school (including advice from teachers, careers education, careers advisers and work experience) had played any role in helping to shape or inform their aspirations. Helen stood out for having made use of 'cold knowledge' and having found it useful – although she was one of the pupils from a 'working-class' background:

Well last year we started these little work projects, and about work experience and stuff like that. And we got these booklets. And I was just reading through and like it's got lots of stuff about them. And I thought it sounded interesting because it had all the stuff that I enjoy doing at school as well … We haven't actually like had proper like sit down talks about it. But I think they just want like what I enjoy. They don't force me to do anything I don't want to do. So I think kind of it's alright really.

(Helen)

The media might be ambivalently classified as combining elements of both 'hot' and 'cold' knowledge – but it was particularly important in shaping the aspirations of pupils from working-class backgrounds. Television was identified by a group of seven working-class girls as inspiring their future ambitions.[1] For instance, Mayping suggested that TV programmes had given her the idea of becoming a doctor – which she also regarded as a way of becoming able to help her family out further (her dad was unable to work, her mum worked in a take-away):

I don't know, I just watch the programmes on TV and I just see doctors helping people and I am just like … helping my dad which is rather cool, I don't know what you would call him and plus he is quite old and he has got problems and I just want to help people.

(Mayping)

Soaps and popular programmes featuring the lives of aspirational, middle-class professionals (e.g. *ThirtySomething*, Hui and *Ally McBeal*, Susan) were named as particular sources of ideas.

INTERVIEWER: Where did your ideas for what you want to do in the future come from, how do you get your ideas?
NANCY: TV. [Interviewer: TV?] Yeah. I saw some interesting programmes on like working as a doctor.
INTERVIEWER: Oh right which sort of programme?
NANCY: Soaps, like … .

However, whilst programmes such as the US series Ally McBeal might be read as espousing a 'Western', 'middle-class', materialist and individualist discourse of personal career development, the British-Chinese girls argued that the main motivation underpinning their professional aspirations was to 'help others'. This vocational concern has been shown by Francis (2000b) to be shared with girls from diverse ethnic groups as a key aspect in their career preferences, and as a facet in their performances of femininity. The girls also indicated that they drew on forms of media alongside TV, such as popular books and novels, films and newspapers. In particular, several girls cited the Chinese or Hong Kong media as a direct influence on their aspirations (e.g. '… TV and like, you know, newspaper, from Hong Kong', Susan). Sally and Bridget, for instance, both aspired to be psychologists:

I saw it on TV. I watch quite a lot of Chinese films to improve, because I only can speak Chinese, I can't really write because I haven't got the time, so I watch a lot of Chinese films and there's a some psychologist, I don't know, characters, and I just find it really interesting. ... It's like helping, sort of, children, like, family problems.   (Sally)

I just like helping people. [The idea is from] TV and oh books. I read books and like there's so many people with problems and I feel like helping them all ... I don't know anyone that's done psychology.   (Bridget)

These girls' engagement with the media enabled them to develop aspirations for a broader range of jobs than they had experience of, or access to, within their immediate environments. In other words, they were able to translate their consumption of the media into a form of cultural capital that could aid their future social mobility. Laura, for instance, recounted how reading books and watching TV had given her the idea to follow a career in forensic science – a far cry from her father's job as a bus driver:

Probably from books. When I was younger I used to read a lot of books of science and stuff so I got really interested and [Interviewer: How did you get the idea of forensic science?] TV probably.   (Laura)

In contrast, boys from working-class backgrounds were more likely to draw upon their own personal interests and aptitudes as a potential source of their future aspirations. For instance, seven pupils suggested that their ambitions were based purely upon personal interest (e.g. 'I just like it'), of whom Nick and HeiHei were typical. Nick extrapolated the idea of scientist as a career from his enjoyment of maths and science at school and HeiHei aspired to be a car designer due to his interest in drawing, cars and his desire for 'challenging' work beyond his parents' take-away:

INTERVIEWER: And where did your ideas for your future plans come from?
NICK: Mostly what I like. Yeah, maths is really good, yeah. Well it's because everything in maths and science, they're just everything together. So that's why I like it, so that's being a scientist.

Basically I just wanna find a job where it suits me, I wanna become a designer, like design like cars or something really mechanical, you use your brain, something really hard, like challenging, like ... inside ... that's really hard, you have to be really clever to get into that role then to work for like teams and stuff, companies. ... Basically, since I was about, as a young kid, a young child I was being, I've been like so interested in drawings and start moving on to that harder stuff and into like technical stuff like cars. [I'm interested] about how things work, and how like things in the world, your real world, that goes and just – [I] like wanna be a designer then and basically just wanna be like it.   (HeiHei)

Whilst the working-class British-Chinese pupils cited above were finding ways to circumvent their potential lack of cultural capital in relation to the area of aspirations, it was also notable that those pupils who advocated deferring their career decisions until after university ('wait and see') were almost uniformly from 'working-class' backgrounds. This group of pupils contained an equal balance of boys and girls, but they predominantly comprised pupils whose parents worked within the catering trade. The use of a 'wait and see' discourse has been noted among working-class, urban pupils from ethnically diverse backgrounds in other research (Archer *et al.*, 2005) as a strategy that both arises from, and is designed to negotiate, 'risk', uncertainty and a lack of educational and cultural capital. In this respect, these British-Chinese pupils can be understood as facing similar inequalities and challenges to other groups of urban, working-class pupils. However, the crucial difference is that the British-Chinese pupils in our study were extending the 'pass bar' to University degree level, whereas the ethnically diverse sample of urban pupils in Archer *et al.*'s project were deferring their choices until after their GCSE results.

In contrast to research conducted with more ethnically diverse groups, British-Chinese pupils appeared not to make such extensive use of information from peers. For example, only one pupil (Edith) said that her ideas and aspirations were shaped by her friends ('Well [because] my friends think that I look like a business woman, you know'). Furthermore, Edith also emphasised that her family were an important influence, who wanted her to pursue a professional career.

For the overwhelming majority of pupils, the family acted as the main source of inspiration, motivation and advice – indeed, over half (52) of the 80 pupils explicitly named family members as the main source of their future plans. This immediate, 'hot' interpersonal knowledge was valued across class groupings (cf. being identified as a predominantly 'working-class' model by Ball and Vincent, 1998). Indeed, pupils (and their families) aspired to broadly similar (professional) routes, irrespective of their class backgrounds. A classed difference was revealed, however, in terms of whether pupils were effectively 'following in the footsteps' of a relation (pupils from professional backgrounds) or whether they were being encouraged into a new, socially mobile route that was not yet experienced within the family ('working-class' pupils).[2]

'Known' routes and 'safe' routes

Across the board, pupils indicated that their parents were an important source of encouragement and motivation and whilst (as discussed by the parents themselves) going to university was framed as a non-negotiable option, the majority of young people emphasised that, beyond this, they had a 'choice' regarding their aspirations for future careers:

> My parents don't really push to say you have to do this, so it's really my choice … Yeah, well I have, well I'm not allowed to like to stop education. I have to go to university, but I want to, so it's OK.   (Elizabeth)

As evidenced in Figure 6.2, it was striking that, in general, pupils and parents aspired to similar types of professional career, despite many parents' perceptions of differences of opinion between themselves and their children. For instance, the aspirations of pupils from more 'middle-class' families tended to closely mirror their parents' and close relatives' careers:

My dad would probably be pleased cause he's an architect.   (Paul)

[It] comes from because my auntie was doing banking, was doing banking, and I think the salary's quite good. ... and you don't have to work really, really hard.

(Chingching)

These family members' knowledge and experience of different professional careers was exchanged as a form of cultural capital that was built into the fabric of the family's 'normal' and 'thinkable' horizons of choice. The preference for 'known' routes was framed within notions of safety and risk ('just a steady kind of stable job', Maggie). That is, 'known' routes were used as a strategy for guaranteeing success and protecting against downward mobility. The chance of success within known routes is increased because families possess relevant social and cultural capital with which to facilitate their children's entry and progression into these professions:

My parents are involved in it ... My parents would like me to get into a financial business I think because we talk about it quite often. Yes, and my parents have like loads of links to loads of businesses and stuff, so.   (Ben)

Some pupils from working-class family backgrounds were also able to draw on the experiences of relatives from within their wider familial and community networks and/or older siblings who had managed to access professional careers. Where these links existed, pupils were aiming to follow within these 'known', 'safe' routes:

I enjoy doing maths and like, when you enjoy something, you do it better ... And we've got accounting also from my big sister, she also does accounting, and since my sister's doing accounting, yeah, I thought, I said to her, 'what's accounting?' She goes, 'just doing maths and a bit of business and your income too – that's no limit', so I thought 'ok then, I might as well be one'. And my Mum, and she come to me and say 'oh do accounting'.   (David)

My auntie told me how she used to be an accountant so I just [got it] from her. ... She's very modern and she's not married to like a Chinese man so she's, she influences me a lot 'cos she's just individual.   (LaiFong)

As we shall discuss further in Chapter 7, the importance of 'known' routes and pathways into these professions is underlined when we consider the context of multiple inequalities within which British-Chinese pupils and their families are located. Certainly, many parents and children were aware that their likelihood of success in the labour market was tempered by racism, hence 'known' routes constituted a strategic tool for navigating inequalities and achieving social mobilty.

These issues were also illustrated where there were instances of disagreement within families over children's aspirations. As noted earlier in this chapter, teachers tended to perceive most families as presenting a 'united front', whereas parents suggested that disagreements over aspirations were commonplace. The young people in the study tended to echo the views of the parental sample, namely they all agreed (without exception) that they aspired to go to university, but a number also experienced differences of opinion with their parents concerning the exact jobs that they hoped to pursue. These disagreements arose over deviation from known/safe routes.

Approximately one-eighth of the sample of young people said that their parents disagreed with their aspirations. Within this, the three professions of medicine, law and accountancy were all consistently identified as their parents' preferred routes (with science and computing also featuring). The young people indicated that their parents preferred these occupations due to their association with high pay and high status:

> 'Cos its [a] good job, good pay, like that, you get looked up at and everything … it's because it's high or something. It's high in jobs and that – prospective. Yeah, she wants me to do well, so, get a well paid job.   (Donna)

There was also an explicit recognition that jobs falling outside of 'safe'/'known' routes would be more difficult for British-Chinese young people to access and progress in. For instance, Wai's parents worried that design would be more of a struggle and would require gaining entry to a 'really, really good university' in order to be successful, as compared to being a doctor.

> I don't know, well 'cos like if I, say if I wanna be a designer and I have to, before I … good job, I have to like work very hard, like study very hard maybe it's harder than if I wanna be a doctor because if I wanna be a doctor I can go to like university … But if I wanna be a designer I have to really get into the really, really good university. It might be hard.   (Wai)

Similarly, MaiLai's family warned her that she would find it more difficult to secure a job as a designer than a doctor ('They say you can't get a job if you do designing'). The perceived barriers to finding work in fields such as design were highlighted particularly poignantly in the case of Alice, whose own mother worked as a designer, but who was warning Alice away from this career due to her own experiences of racism:

ALICE: I would like to be a designer. But because my mum's a designer herself, she thinks that it's not a good job. She'd rather me do something else … My mum wants me to be lawyer. That's really not my type of job. And she says either a lawyer or an accountant. But I'm a bit iffy, I don't think that's going to happen.
INTERVIEWER: Why those ones? Are they –
ALICE: I don't know, they're just really typical Chinese jobs. [Interviewer: Right] And she says you can earn a lot of money out of it …
INTERVIEWER: Do you think anything would stop you becoming a, a designer?
ALICE: My parents, obviously. I guess the media, because you know you don't really see famous Chinese people. Especially in this country, most jobs are like for the English people. My mum said if you're going to be something like that you've got to move on, either go back to Hong Kong or go to America where it's more multi-cultural.… Yeah, my mum says if I do want to become a designer she won't pay for my university fees. That's how strongly she feels about it. And it's really upsetting because she gets all her friends to tell me that it's not a good job

and I should do something else. I think it's petty. It's something that I'd love to do but I can't.

INTERVIEWER: Do you think she'd come round, or –?

ALICE: No, my mum is a strong minded person. She won't change her mind.

INTERVIEWER: What do you reckon you'll do then?

ALICE: Probably choose [to be] a lawyer or an accountant, unfortunately. I don't know, hopefully I'd be able to design, hopefully. ... I've always watched my mum doing her work. I just like watching her. I don't know, it's just really fun how she makes these real different materials, different designs and everything. ... And I've always drawn from an early age ... if I do become an accountant or a lawyer then hopefully I'll be successful in that, but try and do like designer stuff as part-time or something, and not give that up. 'Cos I'll work hard in whatever job I'll get, hopefully.

Alice's extract highlights the complexity of issues that British-Chinese young people and their families may have to negotiate. The strength of Alice's mother's wish to channel her daughter into a 'safer' and less risky occupation is underlined by her threat of withdrawal of financial support ('if I do want to become a designer she won't pay for my university fees') and by her mobilisation of friends and colleagues to join in persuading Alice to choose another route ('she gets all her friends to tell me that it's not a good job and I should do something else'). Alice and her mother are both aware of how racisms within society are blocking their chances of success ('you know you don't really see famous Chinese people – especially in this country, most jobs are like for the English people') and this requires both mother and daughter to engage in considerable psychic work to reconcile (and in Alice's case, to subjugate) her interests and desires in the face of this reality.

This issue of obtaining social mobility and/or protecting against downward mobility were also the point of conflict between Dorothy and her parents. Dorothy came from a working-class family (her parents worked in a fish-and-chip shop) and wanted to pursue a career in childcare. Her aspirations derived from her immediate experience and 'hot knowledge' of having young cousins and babysitting for neighbours ('I don't know, I just love children. All my cousins are really little and like my next door, my nan's next-door neighbour's got loads of kids and everything so I look after them'). In this sense, her aspirations follow a 'classic' pattern noted among many working-class young women (see Osgood *et al.*, 2006). However, Dorothy's parents wanted her to become a lawyer or an accountant in order to achieve upward mobility and 'respectability'.

These examples also enable us to contextualise Sally's account, in which Sally explains how her parents are concerned by her aspiration to become a psychologist (a relatively 'unknown' and 'untested' route) and are pushing her to be a doctor instead, as a 'better' option. Parents' distrust of such routes was amplified in the case of 'exotic' and less obviously structured career pathways. For instance, Alistair dreamt of becoming a DJ ('I want to be a DJ as well, but my mum really doesn't like that sort of stuff') and HoiLing explained that her family would 'hate' her to study philosophy or literature due to the assumption that these areas are difficult to succeed in and do not offer high salaries. However, as noted below, a number of pupils concurred with their parents' views:

> Yeah, they'd hate it if to do like philosophy or something like that, or where you study literature or something. Because they want a job where I could earn a lot of money. And they expect that of me. And I feel that it would kind of disappoint them if I didn't, if I didn't like work and everything, and I didn't get the professional job. (HoiLing)

> Well I make most of the decisions myself but I'm kind of pushed to certain things by my family. [Interviewer: What sort of things do they favour?] I don't know, they encourage me to do the law side of things but, it's not so much a problem with me but I guess if I'd like to do something like, what I'd consider the less conventional things like Art or something like that, it would probably upset. But with me it doesn't really apply that much. I like doing what I'm doing. (Eddie)

The fostering of aspirations through social capital and diasporic familial habitus

As the preceding sections have demonstrated, British-Chinese pupils tend to exhibit high aspirations to progress into higher education and predominantly professional careers. But what generates and drives these high aspirations? We have already outlined in Chapter 4 how minority ethnic and/or working-class parents may be disadvantaged and limited in the support which they can offer their children's education due to lacking dominant forms of cultural capital and 'taken-for-granted' knowledges of the system. And we discussed how parents found other ways to support their children's achievement by making economic investments in their children's education, conveying a high valuing of education and providing explicit encouragement to succeed – points which are all reiterated by pupils as supporting educational success (Chapter 5). Now we would like to turn our attention to two specific drivers of high aspirations, as identified by parents, pupils and, to a lesser extent, teachers.

The first factor which respondents drew attention to is the role of social capital[3] – particularly social competition between and within British-Chinese families – as a practice that encourages high aspirations.:

> [My parents] know other people who might do like exceptionally well, and they say 'oh but their child is doing really well and you should be doing just as well' and I'm like '[but] that's them and this is me' and they'll be like 'oh but –' … they just see a few Chinese people [doing well] and think all Chinese should be like that. (Carly, pupil)

Chinese forms of social competition existed within familial and community networks, which were felt to promote and encourage educational achievement through concerns with 'face'. This operated through the competitive maintenance of collective Chinese family honour via the fulfilling of family expectations ('It's like a competition', HeiHei), in which educational achievement functioned as a key currency:

> My parents ... like to make comparisons with ... other Chinese people ... They expect me to be better than other people and if I don't, then they'll continuously start nagging at me to do better ... I think it's like [Chinese] culture and everything ... they look at like their Chinese ... friends and ... they're like 'well she should be like [them], we should make our daughters do well'.
>
> (HoiLing, pupil)

Social competition functioned as a source of motivation to high academic achievement and was internalised by pupils, such that personal achievement (or failure) was viewed in collective terms ('Well, I don't like disappointing people', Barbara). Similarly, Sammi described the interconnection between personal and family pride:

> Because I've got my cousins that go to university and I think they're well good, clever, to go to university. So I think, I should be one of the clever people and go to university. I'm proud of them so I want to be proud of myself. And I want people to be proud of me as well.

Social competition also heightened motivation for social mobility regarding school choice/entry, university entry and achievement and subsequent job market/occupational achievement. As Frances put it, 'my auntie and her son are always like [in] competition on what school you got into'. Similarly, Mary outlined the extent of educational and occupational competition:

> 'Cos when you like, talk to my aunties and uncles they always talk about education, what grades their child gets and what university their child goes to.

HoiLing explains, 'they just expect me to do really well, and sort of make comparisons with like other Chinese people, and be like "oh, why can't you be like her and get as good grades as her?" And they like telling their friends, "oh, my daughter's a lawyer", or something professional'. This competitive element was reported by British-Chinese pupils as motivating achievement (see also Woodrow and Sham, 2001):

> Being clever for the Chinese is a good thing, secondly, is that many Chinese people like when the, if someone is cleverer than the other the other person will try to improve him or herself, you know to get like better grades than the other person like. It's like a competition, it's like getting better than her, Alison. Later on in the year, she's been like revising at a thousand more than me, she's gonna get more than me and for the Chinese this is a good way of learning and it's really good and that's why we study more.
>
> (HeiHei)

As indicated by HeiHei's extract above, this discourse of social competition was not only enacted within Chinese families and communities, but was also used to draw discursive boundaries between ethnic groups by both parents and pupils. For instance HoiLing suggested that her parents expected her to achieve better 'than like other groups of people' and she compared a White familial discourse of 'doing your best' with a Chinese discourse of 'being the best'. Similarly, Sarah reflected 'like my thought is different from other English people. Traditionally we think that education is a really, really important part of our life'.

Ms Tilsley (a British-Chinese teacher) recognised the role that 'face' can play in driving high aspirations and achievement, although she also warned that too much competition might provoke tensions:

> There's a lot of competition, you know, to outdo each other between parents, so that might be a bit of hindrance, if for them [the children] they're always being compared to other pupils.... I mean, I think it can, it can go both ways, it can sort of like motivate you and make you do better, but then you can, it can kind of hinder. Well it depends on the child really, it can hinder them, you know [if] they're sick and tired of hearing about so and so's daughter.

However, pupils were mostly in agreement that social competition was 'good' and was ultimately in their own best interests:

> The pressure from my parents. They do, like I feel that Chinese parents, they do pressure the children to do better, and they expect their child to do, to get a professional job in later life. But I think they also expect their children to do better in their … than like other groups of people.... In some respects I want to like do really well in order to prove to them and show them, but sometimes they pressure me too much, when I'm just like well, 'I don't want to do it and you can't force me'. And so it's, but I think when my parents pressure me, it like pressures me in to doing well. So I think it's better for me rather than if they didn't pressure me and let me do my own stuff, then maybe I would be lazy and not do as much.   (HoiLing)

The second element that we have identified as encouraging high aspirations and achievement is, what we have termed, the British-Chinese diasporic habitus. This is a specifically aspirational habitus, in 'valuing of education' and high aspirations were constructed in specifically racialised cultural terms, and were positioned as defining features of 'Chineseness' – or more specifically, the British-Chinese diasporic experience. In other words, educational achievement, valuing education and high aspirations were constructed as 'something that we do'. For example, Carmen (a parent) described '[the] culture I was brought up in, believing that if you've got a good education then it's better than money [laughs] I will always have this in my mind'. Hong Wah, another parent, also described education as 'a way of life really'. These parental discourses reflected not so much the reality of parents' own upbringings (many of whom had engaged in relatively little, if any, compulsory schooling), but rather a discourse of Chinese aspirational diasporic identity within the British context. It was also cited as one of the core reasons underpinning migration (to enable children to get educated).[4]

Drawing on a Bourdieuian analysis, this discouse might be understood as part of the British-Chinese collective habitus. It contains aspects of the past and present (namely histories and experiences of migration and economic/social hardship) that motivate current behaviours and values (high aspirations) and shape/constrain the range of possibilities that can be perceived and considered of by parents and pupils (e.g. in terms of known/safe routes or 'risky' aspirations). The role of past family hardships and lack of education provided a key impetus for children's current/future achievement and engagement with schooling, encapsulated in the notion of families 'always wanting' education in the past but having 'no choice' (TszShun). Another parent (Aron) explained, 'I'm the first generation in England, I came in 1959, I've been here 40-odd years, I didn't have much opportunity to study, not a good education so I think education is very important'. These aspirational narratives were passed on to, and internalised by, their children, as Sally (Slater School for Girls) recounts:

> Because when I was young my parents told me about them, always wanting to have education but they didn't have money to go to school. So, my parents said that it's really important that you put your education first.

Some parents even appeared to use classed discourses against themselves – denigrating their own lack of educational qualifications – in order to both motivate and better position their children. One of the parents, Aron, asserted 'if you don't have education then you are like a stray dog, a wild dog'.

Working-class Chinese parental and pupil narratives were flavoured by a strong (classed and racialised) preoccupation with 'the future' (see Francis and Archer, 2005a), in which the aim was to 'escape' from the family's current (working-class) positions in the Chinese catering or laundry trade. For example, Pui Keung felt 'it's a tough occupation isn't it? You work unsocial hours, long hours, you don't have a social life' and SinNing stated 'I don't want her to do a tough job'. Shun Hei similarly argued:

> I'm working in the kitchen; do I expect my son to work in the kitchen? Of course not. I hope he makes his own developments. If he's got good aspirations I'll obviously support him … No parent would want their child to do this job. Obviously unless that was the last resort.

The importance of mobility through education was also recognised by pupils, such as Laura who said 'My dad is a bus driver, and my mum's a housewife. The jobs aren't really quite good, that's why they push me so hard'. This marks a contrast with many White working-class families who, research indicates, may value 'holding on' and 'not getting above your station' (e.g. Lawler, 1999; Archer and Leathwood, 2003), and who are less likely to 'plan ahead' (e.g. Reay and Ball, 1997). In this respect, family ambition to social mobility might be read as a form of capital, a resource that families construct, employ and deploy to promote achievement.

There was a parallel discourse among the professional/middle-class Chinese respondents that revealed a concern not to 'fall back' in occupational terms to the catering trade. These accounts mirror those in Song's (1997) research with British-Chinese young people who similarly talked about how 'wanting more' was grounded within central narratives of migrant hardship which 'make you grab a little bit more'.

It was notable across class boundaries that British-Chinese families were adopting what has been identified as a 'White middle-class' habitus approach to their children's aspirations and education, namely treating the child as a family project (Vincent and Ball, 2006). Ideas about future options seemed to be embedded within families, often constituting a topic of joint discussion from an early age:

> My parents are like every time I come home … [they'll] come and sit down next to me and start talking about, you know, what university you should go to, and like what job you should do. (Ying, pupil)

> You hear it [when they're] talking on the phone … kind of overhear. (Nora)

> Yeah, they sort of used to ask me a lot when I was younger like 'what do you want to do?' 'cos it's a good idea to know what you want to do at an early age and I was like 'I've got no idea at all', and they said 'what are you good at?' and I said like science and stuff and they said you could do medicine. (Carly)

However, despite the apparent success of this British-Chinese aspirational habitus in promoting educational achievement, the data also hinted at potential problems and issues arising. In particular, there appeared to be various psychic costs associated with 'success', and the constant need to re-achieve and re-perform this success. Thus, some pupils (but particularly girls), doubted their abilities, despite being high achievers. Barbara, for instance, felt she must be doing 'really badly' at school (despite being reassured to the contrary by her teachers) because her marks were lower than her brother's (which were 'all brilliant'). The sense of 'never feeling good enough' has been identified as a classed discourse in which social mobility is experienced as inauthentic or fragile (see e.g. Mahony and Zmroczek, 1997) due to what might be termed the 'hidden injuries' of class (Sennett and Cobb, 1977).

Some parents also seemed equally nervous or uneasy about their children's educational success – displaying an ever-present anxiety that success was not yet secured and thus requires constant vigilance and effort. For example, one father suggested that his daughter did not have a sufficiently high IQ despite winning various prizes at school in the past. Kwok Kuen similarly expressed this restlessness for 'wanting more':

INTERVIEWER: Are you satisfied with your daughter's education?
KWOK KUEN: Me? Of course not.
INTERVIEWER: Why do you think it should be better?
KWOK KUEN: It should be better, but she doesn't have any drive. Her heart's divided.

A mother, Wei Ling, also described starting the aspirational process with her daughter at a relatively young age, but worried about where the limits of acceptable and productive pushing and encouragement might lie:

> For instance, me, I don't want her to do a tough job, because I'm pushing hard for her now, she hasn't made her mind up on what to do, she's only at secondary

school, but I mean, she hasn't chosen her subjects yet, but she makes out that we're already putting pressure on her. She has asked 'mummy, what subject should I choose?', I've told her to look and see what kind of job she wants to do in the future to give her a goal. But she feels that I'm putting pressure on her. Do you understand what I'm saying?

Conclusion

In this chapter we have outlined and contrasted what teachers, parents and pupils have to say about the aspirations of British-Chinese young people. We began by introducing how recent education policy texts treat the aspirations of minority ethnic pupils and their parents as potentially problematic (as being 'too low') and therefore constituting a site for intervention. We then moved on to explore the views of teachers, noting that whilst teachers recognised British-Chinese pupils as holding high aspirations (and these aspirations formed part of a family project of social mobility), they also expressed some concern that these aspirations might be rather 'narrow'. We highlighted how both parents and teachers actually expressed a narrower range of aspirations than pupils themselves, with both adult groups underestimating British-Chinese pupils' interest in creative, arts and humanities careers. We also explored issues of 'disagreement' over aspirations from the perspectives of both parents and pupils. These instances were seen as arising from concerns over whether children were following (or not) 'safe' and 'known' occupational routes. We traced some of the ways in which classed, racialised and gendered inequalities can impact on the aspirations of British-Chinese pupils and their families, and how these work together to constrain the range of choices and options that are known or 'thinkable' within families. The preference for safe/known routes was thus theorised as both arising from, and being a strategic response to, British-Chinese families' experiences of living and negotiating their way within complex structures of power and inequality. In other words, the preference for (and following of) 'known' routes provided a strategic means for achieving social mobility and navigating through racial, gender and class inequalities.

We also discussed how the framing of talk about children's aspirations and future plans as an 'everyday' activity within families can be understood as part of the construction of diasporic habitus that prioritises social mobility. In this respect, family ambition to social mobility might be read as a form of capital in itself – a resource that families construct, employ and deploy.

However, we feel it important to flag up at this point that aspirations must be treated with care in that they do not equate with, or translate straightforwardly into jobs. That is, whilst the young people's aspirations seemed to be having a positive impact on their educational achievement and motivation to succeed (and were helping them to make strategic, timely decisions regarding their futures), they cannot be assumed as evidence that their success is guaranteed. For instance, as Pang (1999) notes, young Chinese adults in the British labour market (e.g. those in professional/ white collar jobs) still encounter unequal pay differentials and 'glass ceilings' (blocked promotion to senior levels). Indeed, Pang draws attention to how there is a bimodal distribution of Chinese adults within the employment market (younger generations work either in professional/white collar jobs or in the catering sector, with little variation between the two), which she argues highlights how 'the younger generations of Chinese in Britain are still circumscribed in their choice of employment ... [and] racism and discrimination are barriers towards the integration of Chinese in the wider labour market' (Pang, 1999, pp. 54–5). And as Lyman (2000) has noted elsewhere, Chinese in the USA are being kept out of mainstream blue-collar jobs by a 'lingering sinophobic animus'. Furthermore, as one UK government report warned:

> One concern over their [the Chinese] future occupational integration in Britain is that they may be trapped in the traditional catering trade (Home Affairs Committee, 1985) in spite of their expressed aspirations for top professional jobs (Chan 1986).
>
> (Cheng, 1996, p. 179)

Finally, our analyses provide some interesting implications for educational thinking around aspirations and social class. For instance, the British-Chinese pupils and parents' constructions of their aspirations seem to challenge more traditional and policy models of aspirations as individualised decisions that tend to be based upon personal interest and aptitude. Instead, aspirations appeared to be the product of complex interpersonal and collective relations and the negotiation of competing demands and desires. Furthermore, our analyses suggest that some theories of social class reproduction and education do not always 'fit' or extend neatly to explain British-Chinese social mobility. This is something that we shall return to in the next chapter.

7 Understanding and addressing educational inequalities

Racisms, sexisms and classisms

Introduction

As noted earlier (Chapter 1) recent educational policy approaches concerning the achievement of minority ethnic pupils have tended to advocate that schools should focus their energies on 'raising aspirations' or providing 'positive role models' rather than, for instance, addressing racism(s) and structural inequalities. Where racism is discussed, it is notable that higher achieving groups of pupils, like many British-Chinese young people, remain absent from these discussions. This is presumably because it is commonly assumed that achievement levels act as a barometer, reflecting the social problems and inequalities experienced by particuar BME communities. In other words, the relatively high recorded achievement of many British-Chinese pupils is taken to signal that they do not constitute (or experience) any significant problems – and hence are not requiring of any specific attention or resources.

In contrast, a significant literature has emerged in relation to other minority ethnic pupils' experiences of racism and schooling (e.g. Wright, 1987a, 1987b; Osler, 1989; Rassool, 1999; Siraj-Blatchford, 1993; Youdell, 2003). Within this, particular attention has been given to Black girls (e.g. Ali, 2003; Mirza, 1992), Black boys (e.g. Blair and Bourne, 1998; Majors, 2001; Osborne, 2001; Sewell, 1997; Wright, 1987b) and South Asian boys (e.g. Archer, 2003; Alexander, 2000) and girls (e.g. Basit, 1997a 1997b; Bhatti, 2000; Dwyer, 1998; Haw, 1997; Shain, 2003). Yet very little recognition or consideration has been devoted to understanding and mapping British-Chinese pupils' experiences of racism within education. This is perhaps because, as discussed in Chapter 3, Chinese pupils have been viewed as – what has been termed in the USA – a 'model minority' (see Gibson, 1988; Hing, 1993), whose 'success' is taken to indicate that they do not encounter any substantial inequalities.

A number of researchers have, however, drawn attention to evidence demonstrating that Chinese families in Britain are subject to considerable discrimination and inequalities in relation to health, housing and employment (e.g. Cheng, 1996; Parker, 2000; Tam, 1998; Chau and Yu, 2001; Cheng and Heath, 1993; Song, 1999). Sociological and ethnographic studies have also graphically highlighted the extent of racism experienced by British-Chinese young people working within their family catering businesses (e.g. Parker, 1995, 2000; Song, 1999). And Benton's (1998) book provides a comprehensive history and discussion of the Chinese presence in Britain, noting how the history of British racism has shaped not only popular representations but also the material lives of Chinese in Britain. This chapter attempts to help redress the gap in knowledge and awareness about the racism(s) encountered and experienced by British-Chinese pupils within the education system.

In this chapter we suggest that, despite their apparently high achievement, British-Chinese young people are located within complex power geometries and experience intertwining inequalities of 'race', class and gender. As our analyses will argue, these axes of social difference are integrally intermeshed with one another, hence pupils' experiences of, and responses to, racism(s) are gendered and classed. We map out how racism is an everyday, 'banal' experience for many British-Chinese young people, although the racism(s) experienced may take quite complex and contradictory forms. These range from 'traditional' forms of racism (e.g. explicit forms of verbal abuse; biologically based discourses of difference) through to more subtle and shifting forms (e.g. more covert forms of racism; culturally grounded discourses). In particular, we posit that British-Chinese pupils are positioned within a pernicious racist discourse of orientalism, the local manifestation of which comprises 'negative positives' and a gendered, cultural exoticisation of British-Chinese boys and girls. Finally, we consider British-Chinese pupils' resistances to their positioning within racist discourses and we discuss pupils' and parents' proposed responses to racism, teasing out the implications that these raise for educators.

Everyday racisms: 'they always call me chink'

The majority of teachers that we interviewed did not think that Chinese pupils experienced much racism – although as we shall discuss shortly, the accounts of British-Chinese pupils and parents painted a quite different picture. Some teachers, like Ms Ogden for example, suggested that British-Chinese pupils are not teased and bullied as much as other groups of pupils. This perception seemed to be rooted in the notion that because British-Chinese pupils are in a minority, they do not attract much attention from other pupils:

MRS SINGLETON: I think the numbers in our school aren't big enough for them to be seen as a significant group by other children. But I mean they're definitely, I mean here you probably saw for yourself, we're more Black than anything else at this school, and it's a mixture of Caribbean and particularly very strongly West African countries represented now, so.

INTERVIEWER: Sure.

MRS SINGLETON: So, you know, those are the dominant cultures. I think, you know, if you've only got one Chinese kid in your class, I think probably the others just think 'oh they've got an interesting language, I don't understand any of it, but –'.

INTERVIEWER: You don't think there's much racism or anything like that?

MRS. SINGLETON: No, no, no I don't think so.

A number of teachers also felt that British-Chinese pupils were immune from social class inequalities. For instance, Ms Lynch imagined that most Chinese families come from affluent backgrounds:

I think the Chinese tend to be a well off group, don't they? Economically they can give their children the advantages and a secure home life rather than having to struggle.

Another teacher, Ms Benjamin, also recounted her surprise at finding out that Hui, a high achieving British-Chinese girl in her class, lived on a notoriously deprived and crime-ridden council estate:

> So I said I would pick her up and one of the things that stunned me was where she lived – because [its] one road in the borough where all very difficult, predominantly White working-class families live, kind of drug infused, it's a horrible place. And I've dealt with several families who come from that road, they come to this school ... So when I had to pick her up from there I was surprised because, you know, obviously it kind of smashed my view of the place, because here's Hui living in the middle of it all.

However, whilst almost all teachers shared the assumption that British-Chinese pupils did not experience much racism, some teachers recognised the spread of class backgrounds within their British-Chinese pupil populations:

> I think they're pretty much similar, maybe, maybe a little bit but I mean the boys we have generally they're from the type of backgrounds where their parents work in catering, restaurant work, mini-cabbing, all that sort of stuff and shop keeping. We do have parents that are professional teachers and officers but they are few and far between, I mean it's just natural from where we're based, I mean we're on the doorstep of the city but that's not our intake. Our intake is this side, it's in [inner London Boroughs], so, I think that's reflected in the boys.
>
> (Ms Perkins)

Contrary to their teachers' assumptions, the British-Chinese pupils described racism as a relatively common occurrence. It was certainly not extraordinary, it formed a backdrop to their everyday school lives and, in this sense, might be described as 'everyday' (Essed, 1991) – although this did not reduce the negativity of the experience. For instance, Chui and Alice complained of the other pupils in their schools:

> Well, they tend to be racist, they can be racist but other than that usually it's fine. ... Well I mean sometimes they could be very rude but that's quite – that's, yeah, rude.
>
> (Chui)

> There are girls who make fun if you're Chinese, and that's really bad. It really gets you down sometimes.
>
> (Alice)

The young people commonly described experiencing racist abuse that was organised around their embodiment of difference. For instance, abuse was often targeted at their physiognomy/appearance and/or their ability to speak Chinese and/or having an 'accent'. Eye shape and size and skin colour were mentioned as a particular focus of racist taunts:

> Yeah, skin colour again and sometimes like funny accent and stuff.   (Donald)

Yeah, oh, and [they say] that all Chinese people tend to have slitty eyes. (Amy)

...people will treat you differently, they do really. Especially like treat you according to your appearance, because we obviously look different by these really small eyes ... people are always looking at me ... especially if I was with my sister and we are talking in Chinese and people are just staring at you. Yeah it is embarrassing. (Sarah)

They just look at maybe their like colour and maybe how they speak and their eyes and their faces, what shape that it is and yeah. (Susan)

They think, they say that we have got very small eyes. Yeah, sometimes they say that. Actually they are not that small ... But because like we have got different colours then sometimes they will sort of make a fuss because we look quite different. (Wai)

Various pupils also complained about the tendency for non-Chinese pupils to lump together all 'Oriental' people on the basis of an assumed physiological similarity. Pupils described feeling uncomfortable and annoyed by this homogenisation of an enormous diversity of regional, ethnic, cultural and national differences that they felt internally differentiate 'Chinese' people and delineate Chinese from other East Asian racialised communities:

They always keep asking are you Chinese or Japanese, that's one of the most annoying things you can get. It's like you know, one, it doesn't matter. And secondly, you know, why are you asking a silly question. (Phil)

Yes really, it is kind of different 'cos all the English people think ah China is all the same difference. (Sarah)

All of these forms of racism that are organised around physiognomy can be categorised as falling within 'old', 'traditional' discourses of racism (that draw on myths of shared biology and common physiological ancestry) and which construct racialised boundaries through the embodiment of difference/Otherness. These persistent 'old' forms of racism were also intermeshed with more 'modern', contradictory and subtle forms of racisms (e.g. see Billig, 1988; Billig *et al.*, 1988; Cohen, 1988; Wetherell and Potter, 1992), organised around 'culture'. A key element within these discourses of cultural racism was the issue of language – and this featured strongly within the pupils' accounts of their experiences of racism. For instance, young people described how they were regularly assumed to be unable to talk English by other pupils ('I get angry sometimes but then I just prove them wrong because I can speak English', Barbara), by some teachers, and more generally by members of the public whom they encountered outside school ('some people expect you, like you can't talk English or anything, like they treat you differently', Elizabeth).

Those pupils who came from overseas, and for whom English was not their first language, also experienced ridicule and abuse on account of their accent and fluency ('sometimes they – like if you don't understand – they will sometimes just laugh at you, yes', Wai). In this way, language was used as a marker of difference within a discourse of cultural racism to question Chinese young people's 'Britishness' and their right to 'belong'. The issue of language was often raised by staff as a potential area of concern with respect to British-Chinese pupils' social and educational development and their academic achievement. A few teachers expressed some concern that living in 'ethnic enclaves' does not help British-Chinese pupils to learn English and various teachers worried that British-Chinese pupils were weaker in the area of literacy (as compared to numeracy) due to their bi/tri-lingualism. Of course this view has been criticised by numerous commentators (see e.g. Cummins, 2001 for an overview of debates, see also work by the Community Languages Resource Group, London). Indeed, as research by Li Wei (e.g. 1995) demonstrates, over the last decade Chinese pupils' achievement in English has not only caught up but overtaken that of other ethnic groups.

Orientalism (and 'local' or 'micro' formations)

In addition to the 'old' racist discourses discussed above, British-Chinese young people also recounted experiencing quite complex and subtle forms of racism. In this section, we would like to argue that their experiences can be read as falling within a discourse of Orientalism – the specific and particular manifestation of which we shall refer to as a 'local' Orientalism.

Our terminology here demands some contextualising and explanation. We are making an obvious and explicit reference to Edward Said's 1978 classic text, *Orientalism*, and yet we are also attempting (what we would hope he would recognise and approve of as) a 'contrapuntal'[1] reading of his work – taking up, adapting and applying his general premises within a specific, 'local' context.

The essence of this conceptual 'stock' refers to Said's conceptualisation of Orientalism as a pervasive, general, transhistorical pattern of Western thinking, which divides the world into 'us' (the West/ Occident) and 'them' (the Orient). For Said, Orientalism concerns the politics of knowledge, that is how the West seeks to subjugate the Orient through representations and knowledge of the other, which are intimately tied to the exercise of cultural, social, political and military power. In other words, Orientalism refers to an intellectual, as well as social/political, form of colonialism.

The power of Orientalism, according to Said, lies in its recycling and repetition of negative, homogenising representations of the Orient across a range of fields, times and contexts ('its internal repetitious consistency about its constitutive will-to-power over the Orient', 1978, p. 222), which is used to justify colonialism, oppression and subjugation of the Orient. This is not to say that he proposes that specific representations of the Orient remain fixed, static and unchanging across time and context. Rather, Orientalism persists as a general pattern of unequal power relations, in which the Orient may be constructed in multiple ways, yet is always, consistently positioned as inferior. This persistent power of Orientalism as a set of social relations rests upon the 'flexible positional superiority' (1978, p. 7) of the West. In other words, the specific constructions and ways in which the Orient is represented as inferior (and the West as superior) are generated and shaped within specific sociocultural relations and particular times and spaces. However, one common theme that Said does identify – and which we pick up specifically within our analyses below – is that of the masculine nature of Orientalism and its constructions of the Orient as 'both feminised and eroticised: seductive, available, penetrable' (p. 281; Williams, 2004).

However, our application of the notion of Orientalism also departs from Said in several ways. For instance, Said was particularly interested in the exercise of Orientalism through cultural and intellectual practices (e.g. as conveyed for instance through the ideas espoused, or silenced, within literature, philosophy and scholarship) and he tended to work at a more 'macro', socio-political level. We, however, wish to extend this premise to inform an analysis of how Orientalism (as a pattern of relations and characteristic set of ideas) filters through, pervades and is reproduced within popular life and policy thinking. Furthermore, we shall attempt to consider how Orientalist discourses are not merely espoused by dominant group members, but how they are experienced, taken up and resisted by those subsumed within them – as articulated within the talk of pupils, parents and teachers.

Finally, we should also note that whilst Said adopts a 'macro' approach to Orientalism, and uses a broad categorisation of the world into the Orient and the Occident, we are taking a more 'micro' approach and are examining a very particular manifestation of Orientalism, namely specific cultural, historical discursive racist constructions of (British) Chinese people. In other words, we are concerned with a highly localised form of Orientalism (socially and geographically) as experienced at the individual, subjective level. As such, we might better be characterised as hailing Said's ideas, rather than working directly within his framework, hence our provisional terming of 'Orientalism' through the descriptor 'local' (or 'micro').

As we discuss in detail below, this local/micro Orientalist discourse comprises two key components: (i) 'negative-positives'; and (ii) a gendered, cultural exoticisation of British-Chinese masculinities and femininities. These two elements work to homogenise, reify and 'exoticise' British-Chinese pupils in narrow, yet paradoxical, ways. The paradox in this construction arises from the nature of their exoticisation. On the one hand, the cultural exoticisation of British-Chinese boys and girls comprises *explicitly sexual/erotic*, heterosexualised constructions of British-Chinese masculinity and femininity. As we shall discuss further below, pupils often reported feeling pressured by their classmates to 'perform' these culturally exoticised identities. On the other, as we shall discuss below, through the application of 'negative positives', British-Chinese pupils were also educationally exoticised, but in a distinctly *unsexual/ non-erotic* way (by their teachers and peers). In other words, they may be exoticised in the sense that they are held up as a rare and unusual educational species (as clever, high-achieving, hard-working pupils) who are to be marvelled at, akin to a rare animal in a zoo. The nature and content of this educational 'exoticisation' is, however, remarkably un-erotic in that it is un-flamboyant and de-sexualised – constructing pupils as 'geeks', passive, shy and repressed educational automatons.

Negative positives (clever – geek)

The subtlety and 'slipperiness' of the racism(s) experienced by many of the British-Chinese young people derives from its expression through, what we term, 'negative positives'. In other words, British-Chinese pupils often experienced being stereotyped in narrow, homogenising ways, but the nature and content of these stereotypes was seemingly (on the surface at least) 'positive'. This form of racism stands in stark contrast to the more 'usual' phenomenon of teachers tending to hold lower expectations of minority ethnic pupils – and the negative impact that such expectations can have on achievement (Connolly, 1998; Blair, 2001a, 2001b; Blair and Bourne, 1998; Ofsted, 1999; Osborne, 2001; Tikly *et al.*, 2004).

The most common version of this 'negative positive' stereotype positioned British-Chinese pupils as 'clever'. Indeed, almost three-quarters of pupil respondents described being positioned within a popular assumption that (British) Chinese pupils are 'naturally' clever, high achievers and/or hard working. This association has been noted internationally, for instance Hing (1993) refers to young Asian[2] Americans being stereotyped as 'whizz kids'. Many young people described being positioned within this discourse of 'natural Chinese cleverness' by their peers:

> My friends and stuff and other people they think 'oh you're clever because you're Chinese … They go 'I've revised just as much as you but you get a higher mark just because you're Chinese'. Erm, a lot of people kind of joke with that, yeah.
>
> (Carmen)

> Sometimes they think like Chinese people are more clever than them. I don't know why, but … like in school sometimes you hear about it and stuff like that.
>
> (Helen)

> They always think that and it's quite annoying.
>
> (Alice)

These expectations (for British-Chinese pupils to be clever and high achievers) were also rife among teachers (see also Archer and Francis, 2005a). For instance, the young people complained of their teachers 'they expect us to be smart' (Waiman) and 'they expect us to be brighter' (Alice) – cf. Wrench and Hassan, 1996.

> I think most teachers expect the Chinese pupils to do better. I think they, yeah, I think because of like the stereotype where they think Chinese pupils do better than maybe like the sort of lower class White people, and Black people tend to do worse. And so yeah, their expectations are quite high, I think, for us.
>
> (HoiLing)

As we saw in Chapter 4, parents too were aware of this discourse of 'natural Chinese cleverness' operating within teachers' expectations of their children. A teacher's 'reassuring' comment to Pui Keung at a parents' evening that there is no need to worry on account of 'your race – you're Chinese – and generally speaking Chinese people seem to do well in education', demonstrates how this stereotype was even voiced quite freely and openly in some instances. Presumably the assumed 'positivity' of the stereotype (the notion that 'Chinese people seem to do well in education') makes it socially acceptable.

As we shall now discuss, however, this discourse of natural Chinese cleverness was experienced in negative terms by the British-Chinese pupils and parents themselves. In particular, the stereotype was felt to homogenise and distort young people's academic experiences, misrepresent their efforts and achievements and created a pressure of expectation that was experienced as oppressive. Moreover, the notion of cleverness was also pathologised and formed the flip side to a more overtly negative discourse of 'Chinese geeks'.

Many of the young people interviewed recounted feeling distinctly uneasy with the discourse of natural Chinese cleverness and frequently complained about the extremeness of the perception. As LaiFong put it, 'there's never a balance', adding 'but my friends know that I'm not like that, I'm like in the middle somewhere'. Some of the pupils who were high achievers (as many of the sample were – see Chapter 2), felt that the stereotype not only detracted from their own efforts and application, but also the struggles with learning that they also encountered. For example, ChingChing recounted how her peers 'think that Chinese people can do everything. And they think that nothing's hard for them'. She argued, however, that her good marks were attributable to her hard work, and not a naturally 'good brain'.

Frances similarly resisted also being positioned in this way and, interestingly, suggested that some pupils' hostility towards British-Chinese pupils' achievement might be rooted within jealousy and anxiety and a desire to justify their own (comparative) lack of achievement. When asked how she thought the other pupils at her school perceived British-Chinese pupils, Frances replied that they seemed 'terrified' of their high achievement:

> Terrified. It's not our fault if we're getting the marks because we study for it but sometimes they can be pretty lazy.   (Frances)

From a psycho-social perspective (e.g. Lucey *et al.*, 2003), Frances' extract might be read as exemplifying how racist discourses can be generated by a psychic splitting and projection onto other groups in order to protect the self from potentially negative judgements or self-blame for under-achievement. Hence the attribution and projection of natural Chinese cleverness allows other pupils to evacuate any responsibility/blame for under-achievement from the self (e.g. denying that laziness or a lack of hard work might be a potential counter-explanation for achievement differentials). These feelings of anxiety may be further ratcheted up within the current educational policy context that is obsessed with achievement and relentless testing – where (narrow) quantified forms of 'achievement' (in the form of scores, ratings, grades) are constantly publicly on display and opened up to scrutiny (see Reay and Wiliam, 1999).

A number of British-Chinese pupils also felt that the stereotype was straitjacketing of their own experiences and asserted that they themselves did not feel clever, or that they were not equally able across all subjects, and hence emphasised how they did not fit the stereotype. For example, Sarah maintained '[they] like think ah you must be really clever but I am not really. ... They think Chinese people are really different from others ... They think I am clever but I am not'. These sentiments echo Yip's (1997) critique of the 'model minority' discourse in the USA, in which she argues that such stereotypes homogenise and deny the diversity that exists within such communities.

The pressure to conform to the stereotype – particularly due to teacher expectations – created considerable tension and anxiety for British-Chinese pupils, and several worried that they did not or could not perform to these high expectations. For example, Nora described feeling uncomfortable as 'sometimes if you do really badly in tests and they do kind of look at you strange'. This pressure was summed up by Donna:

> [I'm seen as] clever, but I'm not clever. It's like 'no, you're wrong' … 'Cos like a lot of people think Chinese people are clever. … Sometimes [I] feel that I have to try and be clever, to like be up to their standard. But sometimes, it is difficult. But I just try [to do] what I do best really…. My Chinese friends don't expect me to be clever, they just, you know. If you can't do it then you just do your best really.
> (Donna)

The almost unbearable weight of expecatation was felt by pupils to encompass their behaviour, application and achievement:

> [Teachers expect] good behaviour and stuff like that and probably thinking that we achieve very great numbers, and expect us to get better grades than others and get good behaviour and hard-working.
> (David)

Hence whilst seemingly positive (after all, teachers are constantly encouraged to hold high expectations for all pupils), the specifically homogenous, racialised nature of these stereotypical teacher expectations of British-Chinese pupils were experienced by the young people as a considerable burden and pressure. As Charles put it, 'it's a big pressure sometimes like teachers like expect you to get like high grades'. Similarly, Shirley lamented:

> Once you kind of do it [achieve highly] they kind of expect it from you consistently and then if you don't do it, they kind of make, they'll comment about like why you didn't achieve it and all this rubbish but yeah.

Many pupils were also painfully aware that the stereotype of 'Chinese cleverness' fed into, or overlapped with, a racist discourse of 'Chinese geeks':

> I think that sometimes there is like racism … It's just that sometimes I feel that Chinese people are labelled as geeks. And there's racism because like the White people don't really necessarily like them, and cleverer than them, so they start labelling them as geeks. And they can bullied, they can be bullies … I think that some Chinese, some non-Chinese think Chinese people are geeks, like always doing their work. I mean my friends don't think that of me or anything … But sometimes they do think of us as geeks and swots, and it's like always doing well and everything. [Interviewer: Right] Because that's, that's jut stereotyping.
> (HoiLing)

In this way, pupils experienced how the discourse of 'natural Chinese cleverness' could slip seamlessly into a more pejorative essentialism that embodied this ability within the derided figure of the 'Chinese geek'. This pathologisation of 'Chinese cleverness' (as 'geeks') was also evident in some of the teachers' talk, with several suggesting that British-Chinese pupils tend to be seen as 'bookworms' (e.g. 'maybe boys would think of them as being you know, like bookworms or something like that', Mr Anderson).

Whilst well-meaning, as Gillborn (1990) and Connolly (1998) point out in relation to South Asian pupils, even seemingly 'positive' racialised stereotypes (e.g. of pupils as well behaved, high achievers) can be problematic for those subsumed within them. This is because these broad-brush assumptions mask a diversity of experiences and, as Nira Yuval-Davis writes, such constructions 'homogenise and naturalise social categories and groups and deny shifting boundaries as well as internal power differences and conflicts of interest' (1994, p. 179). Furthermore, as noted above, 'positive' stereotypes are also often just one end of a sliding scale, revealing a more pejorative and/or pathologised expression at the other end.

Negative positives (hard-working/quiet – passive/repressed)

As noted in the preceding section, British-Chinese pupils were often keen to attribute their educational success to 'hard work'. We have seen in Chapter 5 that they were likely to describe themselves as 'good pupils'. Teachers also praised British-Chinese pupils for being hard-working, aspirational and well-behaved pupils:

> Well without generalising really, thinking about the ones that I've ever taught, they always appear to be very hard-working, have, you know, very good aspirations, want to succeed, want to do very well, and seem to achieve it.
>
> (Mrs Barlow)

However, both pupils and parents alike also complained about the ways in which they are commonly stereotyped as excessively quiet, diligent and hard-working and exhibted a strong resistance to the stereotype that all Chinese pupils are 'naturally' quiet, shy and excessively diligent.

> I think they might think we are quiet.   (Nancy)

> People think the Chinese work hard ... It's a little bit to do with the image but it depends who the person is really, things like that.   (TsingYee)

> Well I think if they don't know you very well then they would think oh, you know, they are really just hard-working and doing nothing [else] actually, but it's not true.   (Maggie)

The source of this resistance can be traced to the various negative assumptions that are layered within the seemingly 'positive' stereotype. Pupils were concerned, for instance, that popular representations of British-Chinese as quiet and shy position them as weak, effeminate, powerless and 'victims'. A number of young people explicitly discussed how this popular stereotype exposed them to increased racism and bullying, precisely because they were assumed to be 'soft targets':

I know some people that think [that] Chinese [are] easily picked on like ... 'cos we're Chinese, so they think, you get – you know – you get them people that think they're bad and they're big and they're strong and they've everything, like everyone must be scared of them, them people [Interviewer: who gets picked on?] Like the typical White people and Chinese people, people that ain't Black basically ... Yeah, so they pick, [we're] more easily picked on because we won't do nothing about it and we will be scared of them ... I don't like it.   (Lucy)

Some teachers' constructions of 'Chinese quietness' also contained echoes of notions of subservience and passivity:

I have to say that they like to please. I don't know if that a cultural thing you know. Whether it is regarded as being polite to people.   (Mrs Brennan)

British-Chinese pupils' 'hard-work' and 'dedication' was further pathologised, with several teachers expressing concerns about British-Chinese pupils' hard-working approach to their studies, suggesting that perhaps they are too focused on schoolwork, to the detriment of their overall development. For instance, queries were raised about whether this dedication to academic studies is too one-sided:

They're very focused and they're prepared to work very hard and, you know, do a lot of work all the time. And again, I can't speak for all of them, but I would say, it would be interesting to look at how many of them take part in a lot of extra-curricular activities, and whether they look beyond just the academic side of the curriculum.   (Mrs Barlow)

British-Chinese pupils themselves were also painfully aware of being positioned in this way by their teachers – as problematically passive, quiet and repressed (see Archer and Francis, 2005; Chapter 3):

I think they [teachers] probably [think] – because I've been told lots of times that they see us really hard-working and we should relax more and play more and go out.   (Rebecca)

Questions were raised by some teachers as to whether this hard work and focused dedication can be psychologically and physically unhealthy for young people. For instance, Mrs McCluskey suggested that, anecdotally in her experience, there is 'a lot of pressure to succeed', which could impact negatively on the mental health of some British-Chinese pupils ('we do find there are some mental health problems with Chinese students ... there are a lot of girls that find, you know, under such pressure that – life is tough for kids these days').

Notions of quietness, diligence and passivity were also positioned negatively through their association with being the 'wrong' sort of learner. As detailed in Chapter 3, teachers commonly described British-Chinese boys and girls as quiet, passive and repressed pupils, positioning them, we argued, like educational automatons. Parents, like Carmen, also described how teachers encouraged them to change their children's behaviours, to try and make them 'less passive' in class (see Chapter 4).

Drawing on the trichotomy described in Chapter 3, we would argue that this popular discourse (of passive/quiet/repressed British-Chinese pupils) feeds directly into the othering and pathologisation of British pupils' learner identities. This is because, as feminist literature has identified, the 'ideal' pupil is constructed in dominant educational discourse as male, assertive and confident, against which other pupils are judged negatively (Walkerdine, 1988, 1990; Francis, 2000a).

Cultural exoticism

The second component within the discourse of 'New Orientalism' concerns the cultural exoticisation of British-Chinese boys and girls. This element was strongly gendered and highly heterosexualised – comprising dominant constructions and fantasies of racialised Others in terms of their (hetero)sexual desirability which British-Chinese pupils are called upon (or demanded) to publicly perform. As we shall now discuss, for girls, these performances focused on their embodiment of 'culture' and demands to perform culturally 'pure' and 'exotic' identities. In contrast, demands were placed on British-Chinese boys to perform a Chinese racialised hegemonic masculinity, through displays of martial arts and triadism.

British-Chinese girls recounted their embarrassment and dismay at being constantly required by other pupils to perform particular forms of Chinese culture. For example, girls complained that they were regularly harassed to 'speak Chinese' or to 'write Chinese' against their wishes, for the amusement of their peers:

> … people always want you to speak Chinese to them and … and then when you don't want to they are like 'oh you are sad' or what. I don't know, there are pupils that have tried to force me but I never did do it. [Interviewer: are they interested or they just want to know?] I don't know, I just think they want a laugh, I don't know. (MayPing)

> Because they are always thinking, ah, the amount of girls in this school always asking me about Chinese, writing in Chinese – because I can write Chinese and speak Chinese. They are always like thinking 'ah, can you write my name in Chinese?' like that, like always like that. So it is kind of … it is quite annoying actually … Yeah trying to make me do stuff. Ah, it is really embarrassing in lesson and you just keep writing in Chinese and you know. (Sarah)

> I think one disadvantage is people asking how to say things in Chinese or something. (Kitty)

These demands were tied to notions of an 'authentic' (exotic) identity, such that those girls who were unable or unwilling to perform found that their Chinese identities were called into question:

> They expect you to know Chinese … Oh, what does this say? And if you don't know then they're like, are you really Chinese? But I can speak Chinese and read it, so I'm alright. But they're all, there are some girls who can't and they don't feel

the same towards them as they do towards to me because they don't see them as real Chinese people.   (Alice)

As Anthias and Yuval-Davis (1992) argue, dominant discourses tend to construct ethnic boundaries through gender, such that women become positioned as 'cultural carriers', bearing the responsibility for the expression, embodiment and transmission of 'culture'. Hence girls were berated and verbally/symbolically attacked when they attempted to resist the demands made by other pupils that they perform 'Chinese culture'.

In contrast, British-Chinese boys described how other pupils would relentlessly demand that they perform exoticised versions of a 'hard' Chinese masculinity. These centred predominantly around the performance of martial arts, with the assumption being made that all British-Chinese boys would be 'naturally' skilled in these forms of fighting. Like the British-Chinese boys interviewed by Parker (1998b), boys in our study complained of being relentlessly dubbed 'Bruce Lee' by their peers:

> When I came to this school they all ask me to do karate so … They want to start fight and stuff you know like [they say] 'come on Bruce Lee, come on Bruce Lee'. …Yeah, I know if they do like, like do [it] once, one times or two times I [can] get over it, but they do it loads of times. Every time they see me it's just 'hey chink' and it's like really annoying to me, I hate that.   (Donald)

> Well like you know, they like say this, like – you know Jackie Chan, yeah? Like he's on the films and sometimes like when people just go in and like see that, they go 'oh Charles, like Jackie Chan is well good are you as good as him like?' You know, stuff like that you know.   (Charles)

> … sometimes it gets really annoying when people come up to me and say … do you wanna fight me and things like that.   (Man)

As exemplified in these extracts, not only were British-Chinese boys homogenised as all being skilled in martial arts, but all martial arts (which may come from diverse countries and traditions – e.g. karate, kung fu) were lumped together as signifiers of 'Oriental masculinity'. As noted in the above extracts, this exoticisation of a 'martial arts Chinese masculinity' was epitomised by the embodied fantasy film figures of Bruce Lee and Jackie Chan. The prevalence of this construction was also indicated by one teacher's reference to a 'Jackie Chan masculinity' to describe British-Chinese boys' identities.

Donald and Charles' experiences also point to the relationship between desire and fear (see Fanon, 1970) that underlies racist constructions such as these. That is, the (exoticised, fantasy) discourse of martial arts Chinese masculinity is both desired by other boys (as epitomising 'hardness', a desirable exotic form of masculinity), yet it is also feared (as the racialised Other; and because it challenges other dominant racist constructions of 'passive' and effeminate British-Chinese masculinity). Hence it is loathed/ridiculed and constantly challenged as a means for reducing its power and containing it. Indeed, the potency of this myth was evidenced through the boys' experiences of being constantly demanded to fight. They were thus positioned as a resource for other boys in order to engage in tests of manhood and the performance of hegemonic masculinities in the playground.

Resistances and responses to racism

The young people and parents proposed a range of different potential responses to racism – although, as we shall discuss, it was notable that most of the suggestions placed the onus of responsibility for action upon British-Chinese individuals (rather than schools, policy makers or White society). This, we suggest, reflects the power of dominant discourses to constrain the range of explanations for/responses to racism that are made 'thinkable' within contemporary society. It thus indicates that more needs to be done to encourage schools and policy makers to start looking at how this burden of responsibility might be shifted.

In this final part of the chapter we will look at the various ways in which pupils resisted racisms and the strategies they advocated or employed to 'deal' with it. Some discourses were voiced by boys and girls alike (namely the strategy of 'working extra hard' to overcome the ethnic penalties caused by racism, and the notion of 'ignoring it'. Both boys and girls also resisted (gendered) stereotypical notions of British-Chinese femininity and masculinity by 'being otherwise'. However, there was also a specifically gendered dimension to pupils' proposed responses, with girls advocating strategies such as 'move elsewhere' and 'assimilate/ learn to fit in', whereas boys were more likely to 'make friends with abusers' and 'fight back/perform hegemonic masculinities'. The material and psychic consequences and implications of these are discussed in turn.

'Work extra hard'

Boys and girls (although particularly girls) advocated a strategy of 'working extra hard' in order to try and overcome the problems and obstacles to success caused by structural racial inequalities. These pupils recognised that they would face ethnic penalties within the labour market ('especially in this country, most jobs are like for the English people', Alice), and felt that these might be challenged and overcome through sustained effort and application on their own part:

> Sometimes I think I have to work harder and I do feel a bit like out of place sometimes 'cos … like English people in England [pause] [Interviewer: yeah, so when you say you have to work harder, is that –] So that I like I get past the prejudices and things.   (MaiLai)

> Because I think like some of the English, I can't say all the English, some English do look down at Chinese people so that is [why we] work hard.   (Sarah)

Mr Baxter also discussed his perception that minority ethnic boys in his independent (fee-paying) school felt that they had to work harder:

> They do tend to be quite hard working and studious and so on, which contrasts sometimes with, well, quite a lot of the boys who are not from ethnic minority

groups. I don't know whether there's a kind of correlation between if you come from an ethnic minority group and you're in a school where you are in a minority you *perhaps feel you've got to work a little bit harder*, or you may owe it to your parents, or something like that. Whereas maybe the majority of the school just think well, 'OK they pay the fees, so I'll just sit back and let it all wash over me and get four As at A2 and off I go' sort of thing (emphasis added).

In many ways, this strategy of 'working extra hard' is paying off as British-Chinese pupils are achieving highly and progressing into professional careers. However, we would also caution that this does not absolve society from addressing the unequal conditions that necessitate British-Chinese young people having to work 'extra' hard. Indeed, we might read the requirement of having to work extra hard as a form of injustice, highlighting the lack of a level playing field in education and employment.

'Ignore it'

A number of pupils and parents suggested that, at an interpersonal level, the best way to deal with racism on an everyday basis was to 'ignore it'. For example, Chui maintained 'just ignore it' and MeiYee claimed 'I don't really like to take notice of them [pupils being racist]'.

On the one hand, this discourse enables British-Chinese young people to rhetorically dismiss racism. Yet, on the other hand, advocating that racism is 'ignored' can leave inequalities protected and unchallenged. Moreover, it relies upon the individual or collectivity experiencing racism(s) to 'deal with it' themselves – as opposed, for example, to requiring the culprits to acknowledge and change their discourse and behaviours. The 'ignore it' response may also hint at the potential fruitlessness of complaining about racism(s). As noted by Ali Rattansi:

> A frequent complaint of Black students is that their reports of racial abuse and violence are habitually ignored or their racialised elements denied by White teachers.
>
> (Rattansi, 1992, p. 21)

Furthermore, we would suggest that the requirement for young people to 'ignore' racism can generate a level of psychic stress, as it requires considerable suppression and control of the emotions and demands a high degree of work on the self. As Tsing Yee's quote, below, illustrates, there are numerous costs associated with learning to 'deal with it' and 'move on':

> I don't really think much about me being Chinese. I just get on with life really, I don't think about me with my race and things like that. I just fit in with friends and things like that. … As I was younger, people like used to make comments and stuff like that used to affect me, but I've learnt to like deal with that and so it doesn't really matter no more. All I really want is to learn and achieve my goal on my own. … it was just that there were certain people I was seeing you know

[were racist], but I think I've learned to deal with that so, so move on.

(TsingYee)

Positivistic social psychological theories have proposed that assimilation and acculturation of minority ethnic groups into the dominant societal culture provides the most psychologically and socially beneficial form of adaptation and integration (e.g. Phinney, 1990; Hogg *et al.*, 1988). However, such approaches have been strongly criticised for privileging dominant groups and values and pathologising minority ethnic communities (see e.g. Mullard, 1985; Archer, 2003). Such assumptions protect the status quo and place the onus of responsibility upon minority groups, who must change themselves in order to learn to 'pass' in mainstream society (learn to 'fit in') and cope with racism/discrimination (learn to 'deal with it'). Certainly, the problematic power of these dominant assumptions is evident within TsingYee's talk.

'Being otherwise'

Across the sample, boys and girls resisted the narrow and homogenising ways that they are positioned by racist discourse by asserting themselves as 'being otherwise'. For instance, as noted earlier, they often explicitly rejected their positioning as 'naturally clever' and/or reframed their hard work in more positive terms.

Girls also resisted their positionings as 'passive' and 'repressed' through the performance of a diversity of agentic femininities. For instance, within the interviews we experienced many of the girls as lively, talkative and opinionated. A few girls emphasised and recounted instances of conflict between themselves and their teachers (disrupting the discourse of the passive/quiet repressed British-Chinese female pupil). A number also actively resisted the idea that their perceived 'quietness' in class is problematic or indicative of passivity. For instance, being quiet in class was described as both a necessary, 'normal' strategy for getting on and achieving, but also a potential response to racism.

Girls also took up and challenged dominant explanations for why they may not spend as much time socialising in public places as their White peers. Like the British Muslim girls reported in Archer (2003b), the girls rejected the notion that this implied repression or oppression, reframing it instead as a means for avoiding dangers (including racism) and 'staying safe'. Notwithstanding the implied demonisation of White, working-class locales implicit within the following extract (see Reay and Lucey, 2000, 2001), it does illustrate how Ms Benjamin's assumptions about one of her pupils, Hui, were shifted after visiting the neighbourhood where Hui lived:

> ... it also made me think, oh gosh, no wonder you're worried about coming out, where you're going to be, the parents are worried about that as well, because I would be. You know, some of the ... public are incredibly racist and homophobic.

As we shall be discussing shortly below, a number of boys actively resisted stereotypes of passive and 'geek' identities through the performance of culturally entangled, popular 'laddish' masculinities. Others also tried to disrupt the narrow binary within which they were positioned – as either 'boffin/geek' or 'triad' (see Chapter 5), by trying to inhabit both spaces. Although, as David's extract below suggests, this was often confounded in practice, being more a case of being located within both sides of the dualism, rather than occupying a more liberatory alternative 'third space':

> The good ones always think they're smart, but one word 'boffin'. But if they're bad yeah, one word again 'tag' … They call me both so, some they call me boffin, some they call me tag.
>
> (David)

Girls' discourses: 'move elsewhere'

Unlike the boys, girls tended to advocate quite practical, applied strategies for how they might overcome racism in the labour market when it came to their future careers. For instance, MaiLai and Alice suggested that they might move elsewhere – i.e. to a 'less racist' country – in order to achieve their goals and aspirations. Moving back to China or Hong Kong was imagined to be a particularly appropriate, realistic and desirable option, offering in particular the chance to become part of the mainstream majority (to be seen as 'normal', as MaiLai puts it):

> I think it depends where you, which country you are in (Interviewer: Right) Because I think that me being in England that it is like a sort of disadvantage people see you like quite differently. But if I was somewhere like in my own country like Hong Kong or something it's like normal. (MaiLai)

The USA was also described as a potential possibility, due its being popularly perceived as a more 'multi-ethnic' and meritocratic nation (see also the same view among young British Muslims, Archer, 2003).

> My mum said if you're going to be something like that you've got to move on, either go back to Hong Kong or go to America where it's more multi-cultural. (Alice)

We feel that it is also worth noting that neither MaiLai nor Alice were from professional 'middle-class' backgrounds, in which geographical mobility might be a taken-for-granted practice associated with the mobile, flexible, culturally omnivorous self (see Skeggs, 2004). Rather, we would suggest that their use of this discourse of global mobility as a means for progressing their future careers, reveals the traces of diasporic habitus. That is, it illuminates global imagined communities (international spaces where British-Chinese young people might be seen as/feel 'normal') and the role of racism in the UK as a localised, contextualising discourse that prompts creative responses. In other words, the discourse is both a product of histories of migration and experiences of racism, as well as a response to these. The notion of 'going back' was also closely linked to a discourse of 'giving back' – to parents' (for their migrational sacrifices) and to the imagined Chinese/Hong Kong diaspora. It is also interesting to note that whilst the 'myth of return' is no longer a powerful or pervasive discourse among South Asian communities in Britain, it seems to have more purchase among British-Chinese young people (notably girls). Whether this gender dimension is just a product of the relatively small sample, or whether it reflects women's greater propensity to be positioned as the bearers or carriers of 'culture', is an interesting point for further debate.

Boys' discourses: make friends with abusers and fight back/ perform hegemonic masculinities

A number of boys resisted and responded to being positioned within racist discourses through the construction and performance of hegemonic masculinities. This tended to involve a tactic of trying to 'make friends with abusers' and, particularly, to ingratiate themselves with the 'popular' boys through successful performances of 'cool' masculinity, in order to prevent further harassment. As Chui explained, an individual's success in avoiding or preventing racist abuse was dependent upon their ability to make friends with someone from the most popular peer group. But this approach was not without its difficulties: indeed, as we shall discuss in a case study shortly, Donald found that his 'friends' refused to stop calling him 'chink' despite his apparently successful performances of 'hard', 'cool' masculinity and despite his protestations and requests for them to stop. Futhermore, we will argue that this strategy contained a range of negative psychic costs and consequences for the boys involved.

The strategy of 'fighting back' and 'performing hegemonic masculinities' was advocated by a number of boys, who resisted popular negative stereotypical assumptions about Chinese masculinity through the embodiment of 'harder' masculinities and by gaining status as 'bad' pupils:

> I don't know. They see other Chinese kids as like geeks and 'cos they tend to do good in school, but me and my friends, they tend to see us as bad pupils.
>
> (Hong)

These masculinities were performed and enacted on the body through particular forms of style, appearance, dress, use of language, music and allusions to gang membership. For instance, dyed hair could signify that 'you think that they've got an attitude and meanness' (Hui).

> … Chinese people … with bleached hair, cool, … it really depends like … if you're like hard.
>
> (LaiFong)

The boys took up culturally entangled, complexly racialised forms of style and appearance, which borrowed from popular 'Black' masculinity (what Majors and Billson (1992) term 'cool pose') and from Hong Kong popular/gangster style, interweaving these with the exoticised tropes of Chinese masculinity outlined earlier (e.g. Triadism, martial arts). In this way, boys like Donald and Hong might be read as resisting racist (gendered, racialised) stereotypes of British-Chinese masculinity (e.g. as 'passive', 'victims' and 'boffins/geeks') through the performance of a stylised 'hard', British-Chinese masculinity.

However, these performances generated a paradox between competing discourses of masculinity and 'race' because (as noted earlier) boys admitted that they disliked being positioned within a discursive equation of Chinese masculinity with martial arts prowess. And yet this discourse offered them a potential 'hard' masculine identity, through which they might resist racist discourses. Furthermore, these performances could create psychic conflict and stress, not least because they required a degree of splitting and dissociation from 'Chinese identity'.

The most extreme example of ethnic identity splitting and dissociation can be found within Donald's account. Donald provides an illustrative case of the difficult negotiation of self-hood and the resultant psychic cost/burden involved in taking up the strategies of making friends with abusers and fighting back through the performance of hegemonic forms of masculinity. As we recounted in Chapter 5, Donald was one of only a handful of British-Chinese boys in a suburban school with a predominantly White pupil population. The school contained a relatively large concentration of Korean pupils, whom Donald derided for their poor English and (what he saw as) their poor efforts to perform cool or 'gang' masculinities. Donald also dissociated himself from other British-Chinese pupils at the school, whom he described in scathing and derogatory terms, saying 'I never have like Chinese friends':

> Yeah, they [Chinese pupils] all have thick glasses and study at school … they're all geeks … everyone knows that, they've got big glasses … they're real like Chinese geeks.

Donald thus dissociated from other (British) Chinese pupils and identified instead with a group of 'hard', laddish White boys. He heavily invested in performances of 'laddish', hard and 'cool' constructions of masculinity, for instance he described with bravado his persistent truanting, fights and conflict with teachers. However, his performances of 'laddish' masculinity and his membership of the group were contradictory and precarious. For instance, he stayed explicitly committed to maintaining his achievement levels. He also named these laddish White boys as his friends and yet they were overtly racist and violent towards him. For instance, he complained bitterly that they called him 'chink' and took no heed of his protestations that he hated this. They also teased him relentlessly about kung fu and martial arts, calling him 'Bruce Lee', and could be violent towards him.

Donald was painfully caught within the ambiguities and ambivalences of racism(s) – which left him with few options or resources with which to overcome his difficulties or escape his situation. For example, he uncomfortably recounted his attempts to negotiate between trying to stay friends with his abusers and to be seen as 'cool' whilst also retaliating (e.g. physically fighting back) when they are racist to him. He also described how he felt compelled to stay silent about his experiences and not seek help from the school in order not to jeopardise his performances of popular masculinity (to avoid being a 'grass'). As a result, Donald appears to occupy a very difficult and painful space: isolated and at the mercy of racist 'friends', without the support of the school/teachers. Yet, he is not just a passive victim within this scenario – as his active performance of particular forms of 'hard' masculinity are implicated in perpetuating his involvement in the cycle of abuse and his reluctance to seek help through other means:

It doesn't make me feel bad, it just make me attack ... like if they call me chink....
I just get annoyed and punch them ... I wouldn't tell the teacher ... Some
cowards do that, I wouldn't do that ... No, just no point, they're my friend, I
don't want them to ... get in trouble and I'll get in trouble, because they might
beat me up.   (Donald)

His extracts suggest the psychic violence caused by the internalisation of racisms
and feelings of powerlessness. Yet they also flag up the complex and contradictory
role of hegemonic forms of masculinity – which appear to offer a response to racist
constructions of Chinese masculinity, but which are based upon a derogation of
Other Chinese boys and which also play into cycles of violence and keep racism
'underground'. In this sense, hegemonic masculinity operates as a seductive object or
identity position, one which Donald both desires and loathes, to which he continues
to strive but can never fully attain.

Thus, we suggest that in spite of British-Chinese boys' protests at being located
within the boffin/triad dualism, some boys used 'hybridised' laddish constructions of
masculinity (that draw on particular exoticised cultural tropes) as a form of cultural
currency with which to access masculine capital. These discourses were thus implicated
in both the production of racisms *and* some boys' attempts to resist racisms.

Furthermore, we suggest that these responses are inherently exclusionary
because the ability to engage in them depends upon possessing particular embodied
resources (e.g. physical strength) and relies upon being recognised by dominant
others as being 'cool' – something that is obviously unachievable for many boys.
As a response, the performance of 'hard'/popular masculinities might also be
read as ultimately self-defeating because those boys who did perform aspects of
'hard'/'bad' British-Chinese masculinities were drawn into conflict with teachers
and schools and served to perpetuate dominant dualistic constructions of British-
Chinese masculinity.

Finally, we would like to emphasise that whilst many British-Chinese boys
actively positioned themselves within a discourse of 'clever'/'good' British-Chinese
masculinity and explicitly resisted the 'laddish' boys' versions of masculinity, to an
extent all the boys remained trapped within this dualism. For example, Phil criticised
boys like Donald, saying 'they look really silly and stupid, yeah ... some of them
are trouble makers'. Yet the power of the binary (and its currency within teachers'
constructions, as noted earlier and in Chapter 3) still leaves him positioned within
the 'clever/geek' discourse, which does not allow him to generate masculinity capital
with an exchange value. Thus, we would argue, British-Chinese boys continue to
experience a representational injustice and (like British-Chinese girls) continue to be
denied spaces within which to perform (and be acknowledged as having) a diversity
of ways of being.

Conclusion: the challenge for schools

In this chapter we have argued for a need to shift the burden of responsibility
for responding to, or engaging with, racism(s) away from minority ethnic pupils

themselves and on to institutions and structures. We have highlighted that there is a considerable amount of physical and symbolic violence against British-Chinese young people which is going unaddressed. Instead, pupils are being required to engage in considerable and costly individualised responses, bearing the burden and responsibility for learning to 'deal with it' themselves.

Underpinning these failings is the issue that we feel the education system as a whole needs to engage more meaningfully with the complexity of racialised identities and inequalities – and the ways in which these are bound up with axes of gender (and class). Without more complex understandings of these intersections, educationalists may unwittingly reinforce oppressive relations. As an illustration, we would like to close this chapter with a discussion of the following extract, in which Ms Ellis describes her confusion and frustration with the apparent 'failure' of a particular muticultural inititative aimed at British-Chinese pupils:

> We had a terrible problem for years and years when I would ask them [British-Chinese girls] to present assemblies for the Chinese New Year – because we try to celebrate all cultures. And I would always get the Chinese girls for the Chinese New Year, but they were just so quiet and so shy. And you know, it was that sad because it was [reinforcing] the Chinese sort of stereotype.

Reading this extract now, in light of the preceding analyses, we might encourage teachers like Ms Ellis to reflect upon whether asking girls to publicly 'perform culture' might be problematic (e.g. given that girls experience the demand to 'perform culture' as oppressive, which we have argued falls within a discourse of cultural exoticisation). We might also suggest that the reading of this resistance as 'quiet and shy' and reinforcing 'the Chinese sort of stereotype' might also usefully be interrogated and reflected upon more critically. Furthermore, the assumption that only Chinese students would be involved in performing and celebrating Chinese New Year could be re-examined for cultural biases and assumptions – as, indeed, might the whole multiculturalist approach to 'celebrating difference' which relies upon simplistic, reified and homogenising assumptions around minority ethnic 'cultures' (see Rattansi, 1992).

The Macpherson Report (1999) has been important in foregrounding institutional racism and the Race Relations Amendment Act (2000) now outlaws direct and indirect racial discrimination and places general duties on public organisations to work towards the elimination of unlawful discrimination and to promote equality of opportunity and good relations between ethnic groups. Yet our data suggests that racism remains a potent and detrimental force within British schools. Of course, British-Chinese pupils are not distinctive from other minority ethnic pupils in this respect. However, British-Chinese pupils are frequently absent from discussions around racism and their experiences are rarely documented.

It is important to note, however, that there were also spaces of hope in the study data. For example, Ms Ellis was, of course, keenly concerned to try and do something to promote positive race relations within the school. Several pupils, like Grace, also defended their teachers' egalitarianism, saying 'no, the teachers probably treat everyone, like pupils in the school like the same way as like the British people. Even if they come from a different culture or whatever'. However, we would maintain that our findings highlight the urgent need for schools and policy makers to embrace their responsibility for challenging racisms on numerous levels. We have drawn attention to how even seemingly 'positive' stereotypes about British-Chinese pupils can have negative consequences for these pupils, with increased feelings of pressure among students and negatively stereotyping and homogenising the British-Chinese as an ethnic group. British-Chinese pupils' and parents' own accounts suggest that they may not be making much of a 'fuss' for schools to deal with racism(s), as they seem to be internalising and reproducing dominant discourses that emphasise dealing with racism at a personal/individual level. This, we would argue, actually places an even greater importance upon the need for schools and policy to address the issue. The feelings of isolation recounted by many pupils also highlight an increased need for mainstream attention to be brought to bear on actively finding ways to bring to light and challenge the multiplicity of inequalities being experienced by British-Chinese young people. Indeed, the views of British-Chinese pupils and their parents demand that practitioners question their everyday assumptions and practices with respect to 'high achieving groups', as well as those who traditionally achieve less well.

8 Implications

Broadly speaking, the aims of this book have been three-fold: (i) to analyse the case of a high-achieving minority ethnic group within the British education system, examining the factors facilitating and sustaining this achievement; (ii) to theorise their subjectivities and positionings within the British education system; and (iii) to bring British-Chinese experiences to bear within wider debates on 'race' and achievement. In this final chapter we set out to consider some implications of our findings for research, policy and practice.

Key messages

Given that an overview of the key content and structure of our different chapters was set out in some detail within the Introduction, we do not intend to rehearse such synopses here (see instead section 'structure of the book' in the preface). Rather, we wish instead to draw attention to important contributions that our analyses might make to the field of 'race', ethnicity and education (and to the study of social identities in education more broadly).

British-Chinese educational achievement

First, we have provided an account of the various factors facilitating British-Chinese educational achievement. We have unpicked how British-Chinese families generate, and are able to draw on, a combination of capitals (social, cultural and economic) to motivate and perpetuate high achievement. These capitals interweave to produce highly effective resources – albeit with costs, both psychic and economic. These costs are illustrated by parents' hard labour to resource and assist their children's learning, and in the high expectations and consequent hard work that pupils undertake to comply with the family project of upward mobility and 'escape' via educational achievement. Readers may question how far these practices and capitals differ to those utilised by other (less highly achieving) minority ethnic groups in relation to their children's education. For example, we have reported evidence that Black and other minority ethnic mothers are highly engaged in their children's education, and often utilise economic and other forms of capital to facilitate their children's achievement (e.g. Crozier, 2000, 2005) – although these approaches may still be read by schools as exemplifying 'the wrong cultural currency' (Reay, 1998b). We acknowledge these similarities, but would also highlight socio-cultural practices such as the socially competitive practice of 'face' as potentially distinctive delineators of British-Chinese subjectivities in relation to educational credentials. Furthermore, (British) Chinese constructions of education might be distinguished from the constructions of some other ethnic collectivities by the way in which these practices are underpinned and informed by the powerful identity-based discourse of 'Chinese valuing of education'. This discourse was used by parents and pupils within the construction and maintenance of diasporic identity boundaries, to demarcate their difference from other ethnic groups in Britain and, within this, to reinforce cultural pride and affirmation. The discourse also instilled a construction of educational achievement as expected and demanded as a member of the (British) Chinese community – i.e. educational achievement is incorporated into the diasporic habitus as 'something *we* (the British-Chinese) do'. The production of this discourse (as a key aspect of cultural distinction) and the various capitals which British-Chinese families mobilised to materialise this discourse in relation to their children, worked together as strong facilitators of achievement.

A further distinctive factor relates to the stereotypes applied to British-Chinese pupils by their teachers (and peers). We have analysed how these seemingly 'positive' stereotypes of Chinese children (e.g. as high-achieving, quiet, diligent, obedient pupils) operate as 'negative positives', narrowly and offensively stereotyping pupils in a way which they often experience as pressurised, insulting and uncomfortable. We have also drawn attention to how Western ('raced', classed and gendered) models of 'the ideal pupil' and 'the proper approach to learning' produce British-Chinese pupils as 'not achieving in the right way' – even though their tendency to high achievement is acknowledged. But we further suggest that the racial stereotypes applied to British-Chinese learners may also function as 'positive negatives', in the sense that high expectations on the part of teachers can perpetuate self-fulfilling prophecies. Teachers' beliefs in British-Chinese pupils as being 'high achievers', 'valuers of education' and 'hard workers' are likely to manifest in classroom interactions that affirm British-Chinese engagement and achievement, and further support British-Chinese pupils' own investment in the discourse of 'Chinese valuing of education' (which we have identified as making a profound contribution to their achievement). While all racial stereotypes are offensive in their narrowness and their reproduction of the racist/imperialist/Orientalist discourses on which they are built, some are clearly more facilitative or detrimental to educational achievement than others. Those applied to the British-Chinese, while pathologising British-Chinese identities and methods of achievement, are at least facilitative of that achievement. Whereas, as research indicates, for other groups of BME pupils (especially Black children), the content and nature of the stereotypes and discourses applied to them may mean that the reverse is the case. Indeed, statistics within a report recently published by the DfES, *Ethnicity and Education Report* (2005), reveal how Black children's achievement is incrementally slowed and curtailed as they progress through the education system – whereas the achievement of British-Chinese pupils accelerates.

Hence we wish to emphasise the power of these stereotypes and the discourses that underpin them. It is sobering to think that such constructions are likely to be applied from children's very first experiences of the education system. Connolly's (1997) work has shown that stereotypes around 'race' and classroom behaviour are expressed by primary school teachers, and we would suggest that research also urgently needs to explore the perceptions of early years childcare practitioners regarding 'race' and ability/educational achievement.

Experiences of racism(s)

Given the prevalence of the assumptions by teachers that British-Chinese children are not subject to racism in school, and the silence on high-achieving minority ethnic groups in policy literature, our British-Chinese respondents' articulation of the extent and variety of racism that they experience is likely to come as a shock to many educationalists. We hope to have shown how even ostensibly 'positive' stereotypes can have negative effects, impacting detrimentally on pupils' experiences of schooling, their interactions with peers, and their perceptions of their teachers. Furthermore, we have underlined how the 'negative positive' stereotypes applied to the British-Chinese build on Orientalist, exoticising and pathologising discourses on 'Eastern' ethnicities. However, we have also argued that 'old' racisms – based on essentialised constructions of bodily differences, and expressed as explicit racist abuse – remain a common and 'everyday' experience for British-Chinese pupils in London schools.

Theoretical insights

Clearly, we have found the perceptive work of Edward Said (1978) invaluable in analysing the discursive positioning of the British-Chinese within an English educational environment. In this sense, our application of his work is novel as we have applied his macro explanation of the Western readings and 'Otherings' of the East to a specific diasporic context, developing an account of the ways in which Orientalist technologies position British-Chinese subjectivities as pathological in relation to studenthood and learning. Our discourse analytical approach has enabled the teasing out of the various characteristics applied to the Chinese, delineating dichotomous Western ('normal'/natural) and Eastern ('Other'/pathological) imagined subjectivities and approaches to learning. Our qualitative focus has thus provided an insight to the micro experiences that both construct and result from the macro perspectives that Said analyses. Interviews with pupils, parents and teachers have been used to illustrate the ways in which discursive constructions inform teachers' readings of pupils' behaviours, and how such readings are experienced by British-Chinese pupils and parents. Hence we have proposed how British-Chinese pupils and parents are read within dominant discourses as having the 'wrong' approach to learning – even as they are succeeding in terms of educational achievement.

One aspect of this analysis that we consider to be particularly innovative is the conceptual model of the 'trichotomy', outlined in Chapter 3 to explain the positioning of different racialised bodies within Western discourses on learning. We posit that the straightforward notion of a discursively constructed dichotomy (the naturalised dominant subject versus the Other) is insufficiently nuanced to explain the different positionings of various minority ethnic groups within discourses on 'race' and educational achievement (or indeed on 'race' more broadly). While we have branded this model a 'trichotomy', it actually retains the dichotomous split between Self (Western) and Other. However, we have identified a further binary divide between the 'othered' – in this case 'achieving BME pupils' (e.g. the Orientalised 'culture rich' Chinese and Indians, who appear as feminised within this discourse) and 'under-achieving BME pupils' (e.g. Black Caribbean pupils who are often represented in hyper-sexualised and/or masculinised terms). Hence there is, if you like, a 'thick' binary dividing line between the Western Self and 'Others', but then a further dividing boundary between constructions of achieving and under-achieving Others. Our analysis is also pioneering in terms of the incorporation of attention to discursive positionings according to social class, gender and 'race' (as well as the characteristics associated with these positions) within the same model. We feel that the model has provided us with an effective tool to facilitate a nuanced analysis of the ways in which subjects – who are delineated by their embodiment[1] of 'race', gender and social class – may be differently discursively produced in relation to learning and educational achievement. Thus we have theoretically 'opened up' the dichotomy – and invite the identification of further binaries which may be evident and identified within both Subject and Other positions.

Employing the model has also enabled us to argue that the dominant educational 'ideal learner' discourse is not solely conceputalised in terms of the 'mind' (i.e. as an attitude, internal psychological orientation or disposition, as various psychological/ teaching and learning orientated theories might propose). Rather, we have argued that the 'ideal learner' is an inherently embodied discourse, which always excludes minority ethnic pupils and denies them from inhabiting positions or identities of 'success' with any sense of permanency or authenticity.

Implications for policy makers

The fact that high achievement among minority ethnic groups is absent from current education policy literature reveals much about national policy makers' thinking on such groups. Indeed, this absence would appear to speak volumes to their thinking on minority ethnic groups in general. For instance, the common reduction of 'BME pupils' into discussions around under-performance and 'disadvantage' reveals the deficit positioning of all minority ethnic children within such discourses. The absence of any substantial acknowledgement or discussion of high-achieving BME pupils seems to us to be indicative of the following set of pernicious underlying assumptions, namely that:

1   BME children in general are low achieving (and hence high-achieving BME pupils are unusual/anomalies);
2   BME achievement should not be celebrated or valorised because it is produced by 'oppressive home cultures' and/or by innappropriate learning styles (i.e. BME achievement is produced in the 'wrong' way);

3 BME pupils who are achieving must be 'doing fine' and do not require any additional attention or concern;

4 high achievement among BME pupils indicates that the education system is 'working fine' and there are no unduly worrying social justice issues; and

5 the existence of BME 'achievement' means that the blame for under-achievement must, therefore, lie with (other) BME families/ communities and pupils.

We hope that this book will have provided evidence to explode each of these travesties.

Importantly, our data has demonstrated that high-achieving groups are subject to racism in schools as much as other BME children. Albeit that, in the case of the British-Chinese, their experiences of racism tend not to be recognised or known about by teachers. We would argue that such unawareness and lack of reflection on the issues that may face (high-achieving) BME children in the British education system is facilitated by the current policy obsession with 'standards and achievement'. Policy makers' prioritisation of these discourses over issues of social justice and inclusion is amply illustrated by the current UK political administration's increasing acceptance of schools' use of exclusion as an aspect of promoting 'high standards' (indeed, the government has created a competitive and punitive policy context that increasingly pushes and encourages schools to use exclusions in this way). This situation continues despite sustained critiques of the deeply racialised nature of exclusion rates[2] and the institutionalised racism which creates these discrepencies (see e.g. Tikly *et al.*, 2004). Furthermore, it is this overwhelming focus on 'standards and achievement' that renders invisible (and irrelevant) the equality issues faced by (high-achieving) British-Chinese pupils and their families. Clearly, this approach is unacceptable from a social justice perspective and we hope that an application of our research might help to contribute to putting issues of 'race' and racism 'back on the map' for education policy and for teacher education.

We would suggest, then, that policy makers:

• Apply nuance to issues of ethnicity and achievement in policy documents, recognising high achievement as well as under-achievement, and avoiding propagating a deficit view of BME pupils as 'problem' children.

• Take radical steps to address stereotyping in the teaching profession. The Race Equality Advisory Forum (2006) recommends urgent compulsory race equality training across the public sector. Yet the amount of time dedicated to issues of social justice and equity is being increasingly squeezed in teacher-education programmes and teacher educators complain that it is impossible to devote adequate time to reflection on such issues. Yet, as we have discussed throughout this book, a raft of research continues to demonstrate the pernicious effects of teachers' low expectations and negative stereotypes on the engagement and subsequent achievement of Black children. Our own study has also shown how the pervasive 'negative positive' stereotypes applied to British-Chinese pupils have a dramatic (negative) impact on British pupils' educational experiences, and on perceptions of them by other pupils. The stereotypes are also a key aspect in the pathologisation of Chinese approaches to learning.

- Take radical steps to address racism(s) in schools. A great deal of research has shown how experiences of racism on the part of pupils and teachers has a profound impact on the engagement and experiences of BME pupils. Our work has also helped to demonstrate that experiences of racism affect pupils from diverse BME backgrounds – regardless of their achievement. This issue has to be addressed at a policy level in terms of ensuring that socially just practices are demanded and maintained in schools. We also return to the importance of ensuring that more attention is given to issues of 'race' and racism within teacher education curricula – as 'frontline' workers, teachers need to be aware of the issues and equipped to recognise and address racism when it is reported or observed within schools.
- Develop awareness of the way in which the 'standards and achievement' discourse is further privileging White, middle-class, masculine values (and hence the achievement of White/middle-class/male children) and recognise how it is marginalising inclusion and equity issues within education.[3] Addressing these concerns will be crucial for ensuring the engagement and achievement of all BME children in the British education system.

Practitioners

Our evidence suggests that the main onus for practitioners ought to be on encouraging reflection and developing a critical awareness about their interactions with BME pupils and parents; their 'commonsense' assumptions; and the various potential manifestations of racism within schools. In terms of addressing stereotyping:

- As noted above, far more time and space needs to be devoted to social justice issues within teacher education courses.
- INSET sessions are also required to provide teachers with information and the opportunity to reflect on the popular constructions and stereotypes that are applied to different groups of pupils (and the negative impact of such discourses on pupils' educational experiences and achievement). It is essential that such training is not simplistic or patronising – it needs to respect and engage with teachers' professional knowledges and experiences, whilst also facilitating more complex conceptualisations of racialised identities and enabling teachers to translate these concerns into their own everyday professional practices (see Ladson-Billings, 1995 for a discussion of the challenges in this respect).
- Such training needs to be extended to managers and governors, and to teaching assistants, as well as to class teachers. The Race Equality Advisory Forum (2006) recommends that an anti-racist approach be adopted in all such training, exploring 'personal, cultural and institutional racism' (p. 2), and assisting participants in identifying strategies to address and challenge such racisms. Furthermore, it would seem important and pertinent for schools to reflect on diversity issues with regard to the recruitment, retention and promotion of BME teachers and

other staff. Schools might, for instance, usefully identify and tackle 'concrete ceilings' and interrogate whether there is an appropriate representation of BME staff (at all levels) in relation to the school's pupil population.

- Space might usefully be given (e.g. in appropriate classroom lessons and/or in whole-school contexts) to discuss issues of racism with pupils, highlighting the pernicious effects of stereotyping, and providing pupils with the opportunity to discuss and reflect on their experiences and on the impact of racism(s). It is vital that such discussion be carefully facilitated and boundaries maintained, given the danger for such discussion, if poorly managed, to perpetuate stereotypes and even facilitate racism (Epstein, 1992). For guidance and suggestions on the content and handling of such sessions with pupils, Epstein's (1992) contribution remains an excellent reference point.

- This work (developing a more critical awareness of 'race' and racism within practitioners' professional lives and the lives of pupils) will necessarily need to engage with issues of whiteness and the role of whiteness in the re/production of educational privilege. However, as various commentators and researchers note, this endeavour may meet with considerable resistance – for instance, the resistances of White student teachers to anti-racist interventions and pedagogy is flagged up by researchers working in various international contexts (e.g. Gaine, 2000, 2001; Ladson-Billings, 1996; McIntosh, 1990; Solomona *et al.*, 2005). Such work thus needs to be undertaken with the utmost care – it is not something that can be 'done' in a single session, rather it should be 'mainstreamed' and embedded, e.g. threaded throughout an entire course; formalised within institutional structures and policy communities; made into part and parcel of 'who we are and what we do'. This is what Warrington and Younger (2005) term a sociocultural 'whole school approach'.

- There also seems to be considerable scope for schools to reassess their range of practices and engagement with BME families, in an attempt to bring the two parallel tracks (Ran, 2001) into closer alignment and understanding. Some parents may be more comfortable and/or confident than others in interacting with the school, and these patterns may be 'raced' and classed. Furthermore, such encounters may be read differently by educationalists, depending on interactions of 'race', class and gender between parents and teachers. There may be gulfs of understanding between BME parents and schools and important work might be undertaken to help bridge these gaps. Hence we suggest that education professionals might critically reflect on the extent of BME parental involvement with schools and join with families in dialogue to identify the key issues and seek ways to redress them. For instance, when trying to identify where and how the gaps reflect resourcing, structural or other issues, it might be useful to question why some parents feel excluded by the dominant culture of teacher-parent interactions, or the PTA committee. Does the governing body represent the diversity of pupils/families within the school, and why or why not?

As we observed at the outset, this book does not itself offer toolkits for initial teacher education or 'best practice',[4] but there is a raft of excellent material already existing for teachers and teacher educators to draw on in this regard. Examples include the Multiverse website (http://www.multiverse.ac.uk/), which provides a resource for teachers and teacher trainers on 'race' and equalities, and is packed with information on policy and legislation, research findings, and training materials etc. The Anti-racist Toolkit (http://www.antiracisttoolkit.org.uk) is another useful resource, with ideas for training and documentary materials, as well as extensive links to other relevant websites. Many books specialising in teacher education also offer effective and user-friendly training ideas to encourage understanding, reflection and good practice in relation to race equality and addressing racism in education (e.g. Brown, 2001; Gaine, 1995; Gaine and George, 1998).

All Local Education Authorities and schools are expected to comply with the Race Relations (Amendment) Act 2000, which demands the promotion of 'race' equality. Governing bodies are obliged to ensure that policies on race and sex discrimination are in place. But far more needs to be done to ensure that racism can be adequately acknowledged and addressed within schools. Indeed, as Skelton and Francis (2003) observe, the 'splintering and repackaging' of issues which were once addressed as 'equal opportunities' has added to the burden on teachers. Policy makers, headteachers, governors, and other educational managers need to ensure that teachers are provided with appropriate time and resources to understand, subscribe to and implement equal opportunities policies. For instance, it ought to be ensured that school policy documents provide effective, user-friendly systems that facilitate the recognition of racism(s) and ensure that action can be swiftly and easily taken to address concerns.

As noted previously, the DfES (2004) highlights 'parental and community involvement' as a key aspect of race equality policy for schools, yet often schools are not effective in engaging and facilitating the involvement of BME parents. Educational policy makers and professionals need to be aware of the issues impeding positive interactions between BME families and schools and should endeavour to ensure that such issues are considered and addressed in their policies.

The task that we are proposing in this book is substantial and multifaceted. It necessitates enacting associational, relational and distributional forms of social justice – i.e. ensuring that BME pupils and their families: (i) have an equal 'voice' and say within schools (e.g. regarding input into educational policies, and how children are taught); (ii) are not subject to racial stereotypes and assumptions; (iii) possess the requisite resources to enable them to participate on an equal footing with other pupils and families. This project also demands a widening of current dominant conceptualisations and approaches to 'achievement' and a more nuanced appreciation of issues of achievement/under-achievement with respect to BME pupils. As such, we strongly argue for an explicit social justice concern with 'race' (and racism) to be brought to bear within educational policy agendas. Finally, we hope that this book does justice (in all its multiple meanings) to the lives and experiences of British-Chinese pupils and families everywhere.

Notes

Preface

1 Albeit note that we use this terminology guardedly, to resist its simplistic multiculturalist connotations.
2 Migrant Chinese workers have been the victims of tragic events in the past few years, such as those who died in a lorry at Dover and the Chinese cockle pickers who died on the sands of Morecambe Bay.
3 *The Times*, Saturday 28 February 2004, p. 8

1 'Race' and achievement

1 Although, of course, many schools remain 'informally' skewed in terms of the mix (or homogeneity) of their racialised pupil populations.
2 And this pattern continues at AS/A level (DfES, 2005). Research has indicated that minority ethnic groups are more likely than White students to enter higher education (Bhattacharyya *et al.*, 2003; Connor *et al.*, 2004), but even here the picture is far from straightforward: Archer *et al.* (2003), Bhattacharyya *et al.* (2003) and Connor *et al.* (2004) show how minority ethnic students tend to be concentrated in the less-prestigious 'new' (post-1992) university sector, and how their qualifications may also be less 'prestigious'.
3 As Gillborn (2001) observes, in using programmes such as 'Excellence in Cities' as examples as to how minority ethnic achievement will be facilitated, the Government conflates 'minority ethnic' with 'urban'.
4 Although within this focus on ethnicity rather than gender there is particular attention to the performance of Black boys (e.g. Polite and Davis, 1999; Majors, 2001; Osborne, 2001; Ferguson, 2000; Conchas and Noguera, 2004).
5 In fact, as Arnot *et al.* (1999) discuss, girls had been out-performing boys at a majority of subjects prior to the introduction of the 'National Curriculum' in 1988, but because they tended to pursue less prestigious subject areas this point went unnoticed. The introduction of the mandatory curriculum forced girls to pursue science subjects to GCSE level for the first time, leading to a rapid improvement in their performance in science subjects that was not matched by a simultaneous improvement at language subjects among boys.
6 In this case, dual heritage women in further education.
7 Recent examples of such practices in the UK include the various 'tough' measures and punishments to deal with 'yobbish behaviour', including 'ASBOs' (Anti-Social Behaviour Orders). These can be applied to almost any behaviour that does not fit the dominant social model – a model which arguably reflects the norms of the White middle-classes (Francis, 2006). For example, it has recently been suggested that ASBOs be applied to car drivers who play their music too loudly. Further examples include the jailing or electronic tagging of parents whose children persistently truant; and Tony Blair's intention 'to cut child benefit of persistent truants' (Grice, 2005).

8   There is no evidence to show that single-sex education benefits boys. Findings on this matter remain extremely mixed and often contradictory (Younger *et al.*, 2005; Francis and Skelton, 2005), with research showing that where there are clear signs of improved achievement from single-sex classes, this in fact tends to concern the performance of *girls*.

9   However we read the figures on gender and achievement, it remains hard to conceive boys generally as marginalised: a huge body of research shows how hegemonically masculine boys continue to dominate classroom life, and indeed to succeed occupationally beyond school.

2 Theoretical perspectives on race, gender, class and achievement

1   Whilst adopting different terminologies (masculinities/masculinity) we hold a common conceptual position. The differences in terminology reflect the contrasting ways in which we each seek to emphasise and convey either this *plurality* of performances (Louise – masculinities) or the point that it is the *performances* which are plural, not 'types' of masculinity (Becky – masculinity).

2   *The Times*, Saturday 28 February 2004, p. 8

3   As discussed in Archer and Francis (2006), the category 'chef' accounted for around 15 per cent of the sample, but this designation can comprise a broad range of socio-economic levels within it. Also, a small number of pupils' responses (around 6 per cent) could not be categorised due to either unclear or refused responses.

4   These two pupils were both from small business owner families.

3 Teachers' views on pupils identities and achievement

1   The publication of the novel *The Satanic Verses* by UK/Indian author Salman Rushdie prompted an international outcry, as some prominent Muslim clerics and commentators described it as blasphemous and insulting to Islam. The Ayatollah Khomeni issued a *fatwah*, or death warrant, against the author and there was intense and widespread media coverage of subsequent instances of public unrest and demonstrations by Muslims in Britain.

2   As Phoenix (1987) and other Black feminist writers critically discuss, Black families have long been associated with 'unstable' and pathologised family structures, with the prevalence of Black lone parent families being commonly over-estimated. Black families are popularly stereotyped as posing a potential threat or danger to (particularly male) children's identities by the assumed absence of Black fathers.

3   As Skeggs (2005, p. 967) notes, there has been a recent increased focus on unhealthy eating and drinking habits, where programmes such as *You Are What You Eat* (Channel 4) 'predominantly expose working-class families, especially mothers, as incapable of knowing how to look after themselves and others, as irresponsible'.

4   Her interview pre-dated the popular TV series *Jamie's School Dinners* (Channel 4) that has been credited with instigating an overhaul of the school dinner system in the UK.

5   For critical discussion of notions of a 'Chinese work ethic', see for instance Wong, 1994; Parker, 1998a; Chau and Yu, 2001.

6   See article by Ranson *et al.* (2004) on social class and parental interactions with schools.

7   http://www.standards.dfes.gov.uk/sie/eic/EiCOverview/

4 Minority ethnic parents' views of the British education system

1   See also 'Pushy middle class mothers', Woman's Hour, Thursday 13 March 2003, see http://www.bbc.co.uk/radio4/womanshour/2003_10_thu_02.shtml.

2   It is interesting to consider this delineation of 'Other' (non-White and Middle-Class) parents between what Stoer and Cortesao (1999) analyse as seen by policy makers as

'hostile' or 'responsible' working-class parenthood, in terms of Bauman's (2005) work on the neo-liberal policy delineation of the deserving and undeserving poor, and the pernicious penalties accrued as a result of being designated 'undeserving'.

3 Supplementary school, as it is commonly termed, or 'Complementary school' as Creese *et al.*, constructively term it.

4 Many of the pupil respondents also said that they attended Chinese school, and many more said that they had attended when they were younger.

5 Some of the parents in our study had themselves spent time in the British education system: indeed a few had experienced some years of primary education in Britain.

6 The remaining eight parents gave ambivalent responses, including that the British education system is 'alright' or 'not bad'; that selective schools are good quality but comprehensives poor; and comments that the education system provides 'a lot of freedom' or 'less pressure than in Hong Kong' but without attaching an evaluation to such comments.

7 Shun Hei is referring to the high suicide/trauma rate among Hong Kong pupils following their exam results.

5 Young people's educational identities

1 (In examining the table there are some complexities to bear in mind: there are more female than male respondents [48:32], and where a couple did not identify any subjects, many pupils chose more than one. Moreover, while many English schools have generic 'Double Science' as part of their GCSE curriculum, some schools teach the science subjects separately, with the result that some pupils have identified various science disciplines ['chemistry' etc.] while the majority refer simply to 'science'. Although it would be possible to lump these separate choices in with 'science', there are gender implications in the choices [e.g. girls tend traditionally to enjoy and pursue biology, and boys chemistry and physics] which are pertinent and which would be hidden by condensing these choices together.)

2 See Francis 2000b for details.

3 Maths was often noted by pupil and parent respondents as something which Chinese people are good at, or are stereotypically seen to be good at. Some pupils discussed how parents take maths, and achievement at maths, particularly seriously. Also, teachers as well as pupils frequently observed that Chinese first-generation immigrant pupils who have been schooled in China tend to be particularly advanced at maths, and ahead of British peers.

4 See Francis and Archer (2005c) for a more detailed discussion of British-Chinese pupils' least popular subjects at school.

5 E.g. see www.setwomenresource.org.uk.

6 Some of our data directly contradicts this view, as many of the pupils critically analysed and questioned the views of their parents during the interviews, and indeed some of the parents mentioned such behaviour in their children during their interviews.

7 Of course we might also reflect here on our role here as researchers – and the possibility that the young people were concerned to challenge or resist the potential stereotypes of British-Chinese pupils that we might, as White women, be holding (see also Archer, 2002a, 2003 for discussions on this issue). It should also be noted that we did not conduct observation of the pupils to assess the extent to which we might concur with the relationship between pupils' self-constructions and their observed school and classroom behaviours.

8 See Hall (1992) for a critical discussion on the collapse of Englishness and Whiteness within popular discourse.

9 See Archer, *et al.*, forthcoming for a discussion on urban young people's constructions of identity through styles such as 'hoodies' and 'bling'.

10 As Alexander (2000) writes, "'The Gang' exists more as an idea than a reality – a mode of interpretation rather than an object, more fiction than fact. It becomes impossible to disprove and imbued with the residual power of commonsense "Truth'" (p. xiii). We frame our constructions of the boys' involvement with Triadism within these conceptual terms, being wary that such terms can operate as a powerful explanatory framework that can be used to pathologise those young people subsumed within it, which can 'silence or render suspect alternative accounts, erasing cultural, historical and individual specificities in favour of a racialized all-purpose framework, in which young men [are] viewed as all the same, all as bad as each other, and all equally to blame ...' (Alexander, 2000, pp. xii–xiii).

6 Linking identities, aspirations and achievement

1 This use of the media was overwhelmingly cited by working-class girls; however, May (who came from a more middle-class family) also suggested that it was her consumption of lifestyle magazines that had given her the idea to become a writer or to work in fashion: 'I don't know because when I came here I just liked reading and I just started buying magazines and I just thought I want to be a writer and the buyer for the shops. I read about it, I read about someone who does that job in the magazine and so I thought I like that job' (May).
2 This encompassed: following in the footsteps of a parent, sibling or other relative, or friend of the family. Alternatively, simply being advised of a particular route, not wanting to do what parents have done; or building aspirations upon roles already performed in the family (e.g childcare, teaching music).
3 Note that we are using a Bourdieuian conceptualisation of social capital here, rather than the approaches of Coleman (1988), Puttnam (1993) and Zhou and Bankston (1994).
4 Indeed, these notions of mobility through education appear to operate as an international discourse that suggests Britain now replaces the USA as the educational place of choice for overseas Chinese (*The Times*, 2003).

7 Understanding and addressing educational inequalities

1 Said's notion of contrapuntal reading refers to one who is 'combinatory, historically contextualised, politically informed, culturally sensitive, non-reductive' (Williams, 2004, p. 279).
2 In America, 'Asian' denotes East Asian migrants (e.g. Chinese), whereas the term in Britain is used to refer to South Asian from e.g. Bangladesh, India and Pakistan.

8 Implications

1 We use the term 'embodiment' deliberately rather than using Butler's (1990) notion of performance here, to underscore the *determined* aspects of this discursive positioning according to 'race' (and other aspects of social identity). Although we agree that social identifications such as gender, class and 'race' are performed and maintained by constant repetition of performance; the notion of embodiment reinforces the material (as well as discursive) aspects of these positionings and the constraints on agency for subjects to refute their discursive positionings within the Western Gaze.
2 See Blair, 2001b for a comprehensive discussion on 'race' and exclusion.
3 Indeed, it might even be said that Standards and Achievement discourses are silencing those on equality, since the latter are often positioned as impeding and distracting from 'the core business of learning'.
4 Note that we adopt a highly critical perspective on the notion of 'best practice' – particularly as it is envisaged within new managerialist policy discourses (see e.g. Davies, 2003; Archer, 2003).

References

AAUW (American Association of University Women) (1992) *How Schools Short-change Girls* (Washington, DC, AAUW).

Ahmad, F. (2001) Modern Traditions? British Muslim Women and Academic Achievement, *Gender and Education* 13(2): 137–52.

Ahmed, S. (1999) 'She'll wake up one of these days and find she's turned into a nigger': passing through hybridity, *Theory, Culture and Society* 16(2): 87–106.

Ainley, P. (1998) Towards a learning or a certified society? Contradictions in the New Labour modernisation of lifelong learning, *Journal of Education Policy*, 13: 559–73.

Alexander, C. (1996) *The Art of Being Black: The Creation of Black British Youth Identities* (Oxford, Oxford University Press).

Alexander, C. (2000) *The Asian Gang* (Oxford/New York, Berg).

Ali, S. (2003) To be a girl: culture and class in schools, *Gender and Education* 15(3): 269–83.

Anderson, B. (1991) *Imagined Communities: Reflections on the Origins and Spread of Nationalism* (London, Verso).

Ang, I. (2001) *On Not Speaking Chinese: Living between Asia and the West* (New York, Routledge).

Ang-Lygate, M. (1996) Waking from a dream of Chinese shadows, *Feminism and Psychology* 6(1): 56–60.

Anthias, F. (1992) Beyond feminism and muliticulturalism: locating difference and the politics of location, *Women's Studies International Forum* 24(4): 619–41.

Anthias, F. (2001) New Hybridities, old concepts: the limits of 'culture', *Ethnic and Racial Studies* 24(4): 619–41.

Anthias, F. and Yuval-Davis, N. (1992) *Racialized Boundaries: Race, Nation, Gender, Colour and Class and the Anti-racist Struggle* (London, Routledge).

Anti-Racist Toolkit (2006) http://antriracisttoolkit.org.uk/html/020101.htm

Archer, L. (2001) 'Muslim brothers, black lads, traditional Asians': British Muslim young men's constructions of race, religion and masculinity, *Feminism and Psychology* 11: 79–105.

Archer, L. (2002a) It's easier that you're a girl and that you're Asian: interactions of race and gender between researchers and participants, *Feminist Review* 72: 108–32.

Archer, L. (2002b) Change, culture and tradition: British Muslim pupils talk about Muslim girls' post-16 'choices', *Race, Ethnicity and Education* 5(4): 359–76.

Archer, L. (2003) *Race, Masculinity and Schooling: Muslim Boys and Education* (Buckingham, Open University Press).

Archer, L. (2005) Re/theorising 'difference' in feminist research, *Women's Studies International Forum* 27: 459–73.

Archer, L. and Francis, B. (2005a) 'They never go off the rails like other ethnic groups': teachers' constructions of British Chinese pupils' gender identities and approaches to learning', *British Journal of Sociology of Education* 26(2): 165–82.

Archer, L. and Francis, B. (2005b) British Chinese pupils' and parents' constructions of racism, *Race, Ethnicity and Education* 8(4): 387–407.

Archer, L. and Francis, B. (2006) Challenging classes? Exploring the role of social class within the identities and achievement of British Chinese pupils, *Sociology* 40(1).

Archer, L. and Leathwood, C. (2003). Identities, inequalities and higher education, in L. Archer, M. Hutchings and A. Ross (eds) *Higher Education and Social Class: Issues of Exclusion and Inclusion* (London, RoutledgeFalmer).

Archer, L. and Yamashita, H. (2003) Theorising inner-city masculinities: 'race', class, gender and education, *Gender and Education* 15(2): 115–32.

Archer, L., Halsall, A., Hollingworth, S. and Mendick, H. (2005) *Dropping Out and Drifting Away: An Investigation of Factors Affecting Inner-City Pupils' Identities, Aspirations and Post-16 Routes,* Final Report for The Esmee Fairbairn Foundation (London, IPSE).

Archer, L., Halsall, A. and Hollingworth, S. (2007) Class, gender, (hetero)sexuality and schooling: working class girls' engagement with schooling and post-16 aspirations, *British Journal of Sociology of Education*.

Archer, L., Halsall, A. and Hollingworth, S. (forthcoming) Inner-city femininities and education: 'race', class, gender and schooling in young women's lives, *Gender and Education*.

Archer, L., Hollingworth, S. and Halsall, A. (forthcoming) University's not for me – I'm a Nike Person. Inner-city young people's negotiations of 'new' class identities and educational engagement, *Sociology*.

Archer, L., Hutchings, M. and Ross, A. (2003) *Higher Education and Social Class: Issues of Exclusion and Inclusion* (London, RoutledgeFalmer).

Archer, L., Leathwood, C. and Hutchings, M. (2001) Engaging with commonality and difference: theoretical tensions in the analysis of working class women's educational discourses, *International Studies in Sociology of Education* 11(1): 41–62.

Archer, L., Pratt, S. and Phillips, D. (2001) Working class men's constructions of masculinity and negotiations of (non)participation in higher education, *Gender and Education* 13(4): 431–49.

Arnot, M., David, M. and Weiner, G. (1999) *Closing the Gender Gap?* (Cambridge: Polity Press).

Arshad, R., Almeida Diniz, F., Kelly, E., O'Hara, P., Sharp, S. and Syed, R. (2004) *Minority Ethnic Pupils' Experiences of School in Scotland* (Edinburgh, Scottish Executive).

Avis, J. (1996) Learner identity, vocationalism and global relations: students in FE, *British Journal of Education and Work* 9(3): 35–46.

Back, L. (1996) *New Ethnicities and Urban Culture: Racisms and Multiculture in Young Lives* (London, UCL Press).

Ball, S. (1999) Labour, learning and the economy: a 'policy sociology' perspective, *Cambridge Journal of Education* 29: 195–206.

Ball, S. (2003) *Class Strategies and the Education Market* (London, RoutledgeFalmer).

Ball, S.J. and Vincent, C. (1998) 'I heard it on the grapevine': 'hot' knowledge and school choice, *British Journal of Sociology of Education* 19: 377–400.

Ball, S.J., Maguire, M. and Macrae, S. (2000) *Choices, Transitions and Pathways: New Youth, New Economies in the Global City* (London, Falmer Press).

Ball, S.J., Reay, D. and David, M. (2002) 'Ethnic choosing': minority ethnic students, social class and higher education choice, *Race, Ethnicity and Education* 5(4): 333–57.

Barber, M. (1994) *Young People and their Attitudes to School* (Keele, Keele University).

Barrett, L. (1998) *Blackness and Value: Seeing Double* (Cambridge, Cambridge University Press).

Barthes, R. (1981) *Camera Lucida: Reflections on Photography* (New York, Hill and Wang).

Basit, T. (1997a) 'I want more freedom but not too much': British Muslim young women's constructions of race, religion and femininity, *Gender and Education* 9(4): 425–9.

Basit, T. (1997b) *Eastern Values, Western Milieu: Identities and Aspirations of Adolescent British Muslim Girls* (Aldershot, Ashgate).

Bastiani, J (1997) *Home School Work in Multicultural Settings* (London, David Fulton).

Bauman, Z. (2001) *Community: Seeking Safety in an Insecure World* (Cambridge, Polity Press).

Bauman, Z. (2005) *Work, Consumerism and the New Poor: Second Edition* (Buckingham, Open University Press).

Beck, U. (1992) *The Risk Society* (London, Sage).

Benson, S. (1996) Asians have culture, West Indians have problems: discourses on race inside and outside anthropology, in T. Ranger, Y. Samad and O. Stuart (eds) *Culture, Identity and Politics: Ethnic Minorities in Britain* (Aldershot, Avebury).

Benton, G. (1998) *The Chinese in Europe* (Basingstoke, Palgrave).

Bhabha, H. (2001) Locations of culture: the post-colonial and the postmodern, in S. Malpas (ed.) *Postmodern Debates* (Basingstoke, Palgrave).

Bhabha, H. (1990) *Nation and Narration* (London, Routledge).

Bhabha, H. (1996) Rethinking authority: interview with Homi Bhabha, *Angelaki* 2(2): 59–65.

Bhachu, P. (1985) *Twice Migrants: East African Sikh Settlers in Britain* (London, Tavistock).

Bhattacharyya, G., Ison, L. and Blair, M. (2003) *Minority Ethnic Attainment and Participation in Education and Training: The Evidence* (London, DfES).

Bhatti, G. (2000) *Asian Children at Home and at School* (London, Routledge).

Bhavnani, K.-K. (1988) Empowerment and social research: some comments, *Text* 8: 41–50.

Billig, M. (1988) The notion of 'prejudice': some rhetorical and ideological aspects, *Text* 8: 91–111.

Billig, M., Condor, S., Edwards, D. (1988) *Ideological Dilemmas: A Social Psychology of Everyday Thinking* (London, Sage).

Blair, M. (2001a) The education of Black children: why do some schools do better than others?, in R. Majors (ed.) *Educating Our Black Children* (London, RoutledgeFalmer).

Blair, M. (2001b) *Why Pick on Me? School Exclusion and Black Youth* (Stoke-on-Trent, Trentham Books).

Blair, M. and Bourne, J. (1998) *Making the Difference: Teaching and Learning Strategies in Successful Multi-Ethnic Schools* (London, DfEE).

Bleach, K. (1998a) Why the likely lads lag behind, in K. Bleach (ed.) *Raising Boys' Achievement in Schools* (Stoke-on-Trent, Trentham Books).

Bloomer, M. and Hodkinson, P. (2000) The complexity and unpredictability of young people's learning careers, *Education + Training* 42(2): 68–74.

Boaler, J. (1997) Reclaiming school mathematics: the girls fight back, *Gender and Education* 9(3): 285–305.

Bordo, S. (1990) Feminism, Postmodernism and Gender scepticism, in L.J. Nicholson (ed.) *Feminism/ Postmodernism* (London, Routledge).

Bourdieu, P. (1986) *Distinction: A Social Critique of the Judgement of Taste* (London, Routledge and Kegan Paul)

Bourdieu, P. (1990) *The Logic of Practice* (Cambridge, Polity Press).

Bourdieu, P. (1992) *Language and Symbolic Power* (Cambridge, Polity Press).

Bourdieu, P. (1993) Concluding remarks: for a sociogenetic understanding of intellectual works, in C. Calhoun, E. Lipuma and M. Postone (eds) *Bourdieu: Critical Perspectives* (Cambridge, Polity Press).

Bourdieu, P. and Passeron, J.-C. (1977) *Reproduction in Education, Society and Culture* (London, Sage).

Bourdieu, P. and Wacquant, L. (1992) *An Invitation to Reflexive Sociology* (Chicago, University of Chicago Press).

Bradley, H. (1996) *Fractured Identities* (Cambridge, Polity Press).

Brah, A. (1994) Difference, diversity and differentiation, in D. James and A. Rattansi (eds) '*Race', Culture and Difference* (London, Sage).

Brah, A. (1996) *Cartographies of Diaspora* (London, Routledge).

Brah, A. and Minhas, R. (1986) Structural racism or cultural difference? Schooling for Asian girls, in G. Weiner (ed.) *Just a Bunch of Girls* (Milton Keynes, Open University Press).

Brewer, R. (1993) Theorizing race, class and gender: the new scholarship of Black feminist intellectuals and Black women's labour, in S.M. James and A.P.A. Busici (eds) *Theorizing Black Feminisms: The Visionary Pragmatism of Black Women* (London, Routledge).

Brittan, A. (1989) *Masculinity and Power* (New York, Cassell).

Brown, B. (2001) *Combatting Discrimination* (Stoke-on-Trent, Trentham Books).

Burman, E. (1992) Feminism and discourse in developmental psychology: power, subjectivity and interpretation, *Feminism and Psychology* 2: 45–59.

Burman, E. and Parker, I. (1993) *Discourse Analytical Research* (London, Routledge).

Burr, V. (1995) *An Introduction to Social Constructionism* (London, Routledge).

Butler, J. (1990) *Gender Trouble* (New York, Routledge).

Butler, J. (1993) *Bodies That Matter: On the Discursive Limits of Sex* (London, Routledge).

Butler, J. (1997) Performative acts and gender constitution, in K. Conboy, N. Medina and S. Stanbury (eds) *Writing on the Body: Female Embodiment and Feminist Theory* (New York, Columbia University Press).

Byers, S. (1998) Co-ordinated action to tackle boys' underachievement. Speech at the 11th International Congress for School Effectiveness and Improvement, University of Manchester Institute of Science and Technology, 5 January.

Carr, S. (2005) Missionaries do the cheerleading for Blair, *The Independent*, 1/2/05, p. 18.

Carrigan, T., Connell, R. and Lee, J. (1985) Towards a new sociology of masculinity, *Theory and Society*, 14: 551–604.

Cealey-Harrison, W. and Hood-Williams, J. (1998) More varieties than Heinz: social categories and sociality in Humphries, Hammersley and beyond, *Sociological Research Online* 3(1) www.socresonline.org.uk/3/1/contents.

Chan, Y.M. (2000) Self-esteem: a cross-cultural comparison of British-Chinese, White British and Hong Kong Chinese Children, *Educational Psychology* 20(1): 59–74.

Chaplin, R. (2000) Beyond Exam Results? Differences in the social and psychological perceptions of young males and females at school, *Educational Studies* 26: 177–90.

Chapman, T.K. (2005) Peddling backwards: reflections of Plessy and Brown in the Rockford public schools de jure desegregation efforts, *Race. Ethnicity and Education* 8(1): 29–44.

Chau, R. and Yu, S. (2001) Social exclusion of Chinese people in Britain, *Critical Social Policy* 21(1): 103–25.

Cheng, Y. (1996). The Chinese: upwardly mobile, in C. Peach (ed.) *The Ethnic Minority Populations of Great Britain* (London, HMSO).

Cheng, Y. and Heath, A. (1993) Ethnic origins and class destinations, *Oxford Review of Education* 19(2): 151–65.

Clarricoates, K. (1987) Child culture at school: a clash between gendered worlds, in A. Pollard (ed.) *Children and Their Primary Schools* (Lewes, Palmer).

Coard, B. (1974) *How the West-Indian Child is Made Educationally Subnormal in the British School System: The Scandal of the Black Child in Schools in Britain* (Grenada, New Beacon for the Caribbean Education and Community Workers' Association).

Cohen, P. (1988). The perversions of inheritance: studies in the making of multi-racist Britain, in P. Cohen, and H.S. Bains *Multi-Racist Britain* (London, Macmillan).

Cohen, T. (2005) Is school biased against boys? *Daily Mail* http://www.dailymail.co.uk/pages/ standard/article.html.

Coleman, J.S. (1988) Social capital in the creation of human capital, *American Journal of Sociology* 94(suppl. 95): 95–120.

Collins, C., McLeod, J. and Kenway, J. (2000) *Factors Influencing the Educational Performance of Mmales and Females in Schools and their Initial Destinations after Leaving School* (Canberra, DETYA).

Conchas, G. and Noguera, P. (2004) Understanding the exceptions: how small schools support the achievement of academically successful Black boys, in N. Way and J. Chu (eds) *Adolescent Boys* (New York, NYU Press).

Connell, R. (1987) *Gender and Power* (Cambridge, Polity Press).

Connell, R. (1989) Cool guys, swots and wimps: the interplay of masculinity and education, *Oxford Review of Education* 15: 291–303.

Connell, R. (1995) *Masculinities* (Cambridge, Polity Press).

Connell, R.W. (2007) Understanding men: gender sociology and the new international research on masculinities, in C. Skelton, B. Francis and L. Smulyan (eds) *Handbook of Gender and Education* (London, Sage).

Connolly, P. (1995) Boys will be boys?: Racism, sexuality, and the construction of masculine identities amongst infant boys, in M. Blair and J. Holland (eds) *Equality and Difference: Debates and Issues in Feminist Research and Pedagogy* (Clevedon, Multilingual Matters).

Connolly, P. (1998) *Racism, Gender Identities and Young Children* (London, Routledge).

Connolly, P. (2004) *Boys and Schooling in the Early Years* (London, RoutledgeFalmer).

Connor, H., Tyers, C., Modood, T. and Hillage, J. (2004) *Why The Difference? A Closer Look at Higher Education Minority Ethnic Students and Graduates*, Research Report 552 (London, DfES).

Cowan, A. (2004) Pushy parents are the best promoters, *The Scotsman*, Wednesday 23 June 2004.

Crozier, G. (2000) *Parents and Schools: Partners or Protagonists?* (Stoke-on-Trent, Trentham Books).

Crozier, G. (2003) Researching Black parents: making sense of the research and the researcher, *Qualitative Research* 3(1): 79–94.

Crozier, G. (2005) Beyond the call of duty: the impact of racism on black parents' involvement in their children's education, in G. Crozier and D. Reay (eds) *Activating Participation* (Stoke-on-Trent, Trentham Books).

Crozier, G. and Reay, D. (2005) Introduction, in G. Crozier and D. Reay (eds) *Activating Participation* (Stoke-on-Trent, Trentham Books).

Cummins, J. (1986) Empowering minority students: a framework for intervention, *Harvard Educational Review* 56, 18–36.

Cummins, J. (2000) *Language, Power, and Pedagogy: Bilingual Children in the Crossfire* (Clevedon, Multilingual Matters).

Cummins, J. (2001) *Negotiating Identities: Education for Empowerment in a Diverse Society*, 2nd edition (Los Angeles, CA, California Association for Bilingual Education).

Daily Mail (2003) 'Boys learn better next to girls', *FeMail*, http://www.dailymail.co.uk/pages/standard/article.html.

Davies, B. (1989) *Frogs and Snails and Feminist Tales* (Sydney, Allen and Unwin).

Davies, B. (1993) *Shards of Glass* (Sydney, Allen and Unwin).

Davies, B. (2003) Death to critique and dissent? The policies and practices of new managerialism and of 'evidence-based practice', *Gender and Education* 15: 91–103.

Davies, B. and Saltmarsh, S. (2006) Gender and literacy, in C. Skelton, B. Francis and L. Smulyan (eds) *Handbook of Gender and Education* (London, Sage).

Department for Education (1994) *Our Children's Education: the Updated Parent's Charter* (London, HMSO).

Department for Education and Employment (1998) *Teachers: Meeting the Challenge of Change* (London, DfEE).

Department for Education and Skills (2003) *Using the National Healthy School Standard to Raise Boys' Achievement* (Wetherby, Health Development Agency).

Department for Education and Skills (2004) *Schools Race Equality Policies: From Issues to Outcomes* (London, HMSO).

Department for Education and Skills (2005a) http://www.standards.dfes.gov.uk/ethnic minoritis/raising_achievement.

Department for Education and Skills (2005b) *Higher Standards, Better Schools for All* (London, The Stationery Office).

Department for Education and Skills (2005c) http://www.standards.dfes.gov.uk/ethnic minoritis/raising_achievement/whats_new/EMAG_Gd_Prtc_pubs04/.

Department of Education and Science (1991) *The Parents' Charter: You and Your Child's Education* (London, HMSO).

Department of Education and Science (DES) (1981) *West Indian Children in Our Schools* (London, HMSO) (The Rampton Report).

DES (Department of Education and Science) (1985) *Education for All* (The Swann Report) (London, HMSO).

Devine, F. and Savage, M. (2000) *Renewing Class Analysis* (Oxford, Blackwell).

Dewan, I. (2005) An investigation into concepts of personhood and equity, with specific reference to mixed-race women in post-compulsory education, unpublished PhD thesis, (London, University of Greenwich).

Du Gay, P. (1996) *Consumption and Identity at Work* (London, Sage).

Dwyer, C. (1998) Contested identities: challenging dominant representations of young British Muslim, in T. Skelton and G. Valentine (eds) *Cool Places: Geographies of Youth Cultures* (London, RoutledgeFalmer).

Dwyer, C. (2000) Negotiating diasporic identities: young British South Asian Muslim women, *Women's Studies International Forum* 23(4): 475–86.

Edgell, S. (1993) *Class* (London, Routledge).

Edley, N. and Wetherell, M. (1995) *Men in Perspective: Practice, Power and Identity* (London, Prentice Hall/Harvester Wheatsheaf).

Edwards, R., Alldred, P. and David, M. (2000) Children's understandings of parental involvement in education, in *Children 5–16 Research Briefing* (Swindon, ESRC).

Eggleston, J., Dunn, D., Anjali, M. and Wright, C. (1986) *Education for Some* (Stoke-on-Trent, Trentham Books).

Epstein, D. (1992) *Changing Classroom Cultures: Anti-racism, Politics and Schools* (Stoke-on-Trent, Trentham Books).

Epstein, D. (1998) Real boys don't work: 'underachievement', masculinities and the harassment of 'sissies', in D. Epstein, J. Elwood, V. Hey and J. Maw (eds) *Failing Boys?* (Buckingham, Open University Press).

Epstein, D., Elwood, J., Hey, V. and Maw, J. (1998) Schoolboy frictions: feminism and 'failing boys', in D. Epstein, J. Elwood, V. Hey and J. Maw (eds) *Failing Boys?* (Buckingham, Open University Press).

Epstein, D., O'Flynn, S. and Telford, D. (2003) *Silenced Sexualities in Schools and Universities* (Stoke-on-Trent, Trentham Books).

Essed, P. (1990) *Everyday Racism: Reports from Women of Two Cultures* (Alameda, CA, Hunter House).

Essed, P. (1991) *Understanding Everyday Racism* (Newbury Park, Sage).

Ethnic Communities Oral History Project (1994) *Such a Long Story: Chinese Voices in Britain* (London, Hammersmith and Fulham Council).

Eysenck, H.J. (1971) *Race, Intelligence and Education* (London, Maurice Temple Smith Publications).

Fanon, F. (1986) *Black Skin, White Masks* (London, Pluto Press).

Ferguson, A. (2000) *Bad Boys: Public Schools in the Making of Black Masculinity* (Michigan, University of Michigan Press).

Fine, M., Weis, L., Powell, L. and Mun Wong, L. (1997) *Off White: Readings on Race, Power and Society* (London, Routledge).

Fletcher, R. (1995) Changing the lives of boys, in R. Browne and R. Fletcher (eds) *Boys in Schools: Addressing the Real Issues* (Sydney, Finch Press).

Foucault, M. (1978) *The Will to Knowledge: The History of Sexuality* vol. 1 (trans. R. Hurley) (Harmondsworth, Penguin).

Foucault, M. (1980) *Power/Knowledge: Selected Interviews and Other Writings 1972–1977* (New York, Pantheon).

Francis, B. (1998) *Power Plays* (Stoke-on-Trent, Trentham).

Francis, B. (1999) Lads, lasses and (New) Labour: 14–16 year old student responses to the 'laddish behaviour and boys' underachievement' debate, *British Journal of Sociology of Education* 20: 355–73.

Francis, B. (2000a) *Boys, Girls and Achievement* (London, RoutledgeFalmer).

Francis, B. (2000b) The gendered subject: students' subject preferences and discussions of gender and subject ability, *Oxford Review of Education* 26(1): 35–47.

Francis, B. (2001) Commonality *and* difference? Attempts to escape from theoretical dualisms in emancipatory research in education, *International Studies in Sociology of Education* 11(2): 157–71.

Francis, B. (2002) Is the future really female? The impact and implications of gender for 14–16 year olds' career choices, *Journal of Education and Work* 15(1): 75–88.

Francis, B. (2006) Heroes or zeroes? the discursive positioning of 'underachieving boys' in English neo-liberal education policy, *Journal of Education Policy* 21(2): 187–200.

Francis, B. (2007) The nature of gender, in C. Skelton, B. Francis and L. Smulyan (eds) *Handbook of Gender and Education* (London, Sage).

Francis, B. and Archer, L. (2005a), British-Chinese pupils' and parents' constructions of the value of education, *British Educational Research Journal* 31(1): 89–107.

Francis, B. and Archer, L. (2005b) Negotiating the dichotomy of boffin and triad: British-Chinese pupils' constructions of 'laddism', *The Sociological Review* 53(3): 495–520.

Francis, B. and Archer, L. (2005c) British-Chinese pupils' constructions of gender and learning, *Oxford Review of Education* 31(4): 497–515.

Francis, B. and Skelton, C. (2005) *Reassessing Gender and Achievement* (London, Routledge).

Francis, B. and Skelton, C. (eds) (2001) *Investigating Gender: Contemporary Perspectives in Education* (Buckingham, Open University Press).

Francis, B., Hutchings, M., Archer, L. and Melling, L. (2003) Subject choice and occupational aspirations among pupils at girls' schools, *Pedagogy, Culture and Society* 11(3): 425–41.

Fraser, N. (1993) Clintonism, welfare and the antisocial wage: the emergence of a neo-liberal political imagery, *Rethinking Marxism* 6(1): 9–23.

Fraser, N. (1994) Reinventing the welfare state, *Boston Review* 19(1): 1–7.

Fraser, N. (2000) Rethinking recognition, *New Left Review* 3: 107–20.

Fricker, M. (1994) Knowledge as construct: theorizing the role of gender in knowledge, in K. Lennon and M. Whitford (eds) *Knowing the Difference: Feminist Perspectives in Epistemology* (London, Routledge).

Frosh, S., Phoenix, A. and Pattman, R. (2002) *Young Masculinities* (Basingstoke, Palgrave).

Gaine, C. (1995) *Still No Problem Here* (Stoke-on-Trent, Trentham Books).

Gaine, C. (2000) Anti-racist education in 'white' areas: the limits and possibilities of change, *Race, Ethnicity and Education* 3(1): 65–81.

Gaine, C. (2001) 'If it's not hurting it's not working': teaching teachers about 'race'. *Research Papers in Education* 16(1): 93–113.

Gaine, C. and George, R. (1998) *Gender, Race and Class in Schooling: An introduction for Teachers* (London, RoutledgeFalmer).

Gewirtz, S. (2001) Cloning the Blairs: New Labour's programme for the re-socialization of working class parents, *Journal of Education Policy* 16(4): 365–78.

Gibson, M.A. (1988) *Accommodation Without Assimilation: Sikh Immigrants in an American High School* (Ithaca, NY, Cornell University Press).

Gill, R. (1995) Relativism, reflexivity and politics: interrogating discourse analysis from a feminist perspective, in S. Wilkinson and C. Kitzinger (eds) *Feminism and Discourse* (London, Sage).

Gillborn, D. (1990) *Race, Ethnicity and Education: Teaching and Learning in Multiethnic Schools* (London, Unwin Hyman).

Gillborn, D. (2001) Racism, policy and the (mis)education of Black children, in R. Majors (ed.) *Educating Our Black Children* (London, RoutledgeFalmer).

Gillborn, D. (2005) Education policy as an act of white supremacy: whiteness, critical race theory and education reform, *Journal of Education Policy* 20(4): 485–505.

Gillborn, D. and Gipps, C. (1996) *Recent Research on the Achievement of Ethnic Minority Students* (London, Ofsted/Institute of Education).

Gillborn, D. and Mirza, H. (2000) *Educational Inequality: Mapping Race, Class and Gender* (London, HMI).

Gillborn, D. and Youdell, D. (2000) *Rationing Education: Policy, Practice, Reform and Equity* (London, Routledge).

Giroux, H. (2002) Neoliberalism, corporate culture and the promise of higher education: the university as a democratic public sphere, *Harvard Educational Review*, winter 2002: 425–64.

Gleeson, K., Archer, L., Riley, S. and Frith, H. (2005) Visual methodologies: special issue, Editorial, *Qualitative Research in Psychology* 2(3): 187–98.

Goldthorpe, J. (1996) Class analysis and the reorientation of class theory: the case of persisting differentials in education attainment, *British Journal of Sociology* 47(3): 481–505.

Gorard, S. (2000) One of us cannot be wrong: the paradox of achievement gaps, *British Journal of Sociology of Education* 21(3):391–400.

Gorard, S., Rees, G. and Salisbury, J. (1999) Reappraising the apparent underachievement of boys at school, *Gender and Education* 11(4): 441–59.

Gramsci, A. (1971) *Selections from the Prison Notebooks* (London, Lawrence and Wishart).

Grice, A. (2005) Brown warns Milburn over 'gimmicks', *The Independent*, 1/2/05, p. 19.

Griffin, C. (1998) Representations of youth and the 'boys' underachievement debate: just the same old stories? Paper presented at 'Gendering the Millennium' Conference, University of Dundee, 11–13/11/98.

Gurian, M. (1996) *The Wonder of Boys: What Parents, Mentors and Educators Can Do to Raise Boys into Exceptional Men* (New York: Tarcher/Putnam).

Gurian, M. (2002) *Boys and Girls Learn Differently!* (San Francisco, Jossey Bass).

Halberstam, J. (2005) *In a Queer Time and Place* (New York, New York University Press).

Hall, S. (1990) Culture, identity and diaspora, in J. Rutherford (ed) *Identity, Community, Culture, Difference* (London, Lawrence & Wishart).

Hall, S. (1992) New Ethnicities, in J. Donald and A. Rattansi (eds) *'Race', culture and difference* (London, Sage).

Hall, S. (1992) New ethnicities, in J. Donald and A. Rattansi (eds) *'Race', Culture and Difference* (London, Sage).

Hall, S. (1993) 'What is this "black" in black popular culture?', *Social Justice* 20(1–2): 101–14.

Hall, S. (1996) Introduction: who needs 'identity'?, in S. Hall and P. du Gay (eds) *Questions of Cultural Identity* (London, Sage).

Hamilton, C., Rejtman, R. and Roberts, M. (1999) *Racism and Race Relations in Predominantly White Schools* (Colchester, Children's Legal Centre).

Haraway, D. (1990) A manifesto for cyborgs: science, technology and socialist feminism in the 1980s, in L.J. Nicholson (ed.) *Feminism/Postmodernism* (London and New York, Routledge).

Harding, S. (1986) *The Science Question in Feminism* (Milton Keynes, Open University Press).

Harding, S. (1991) *Whose Science? Whose Knowledge?* (Buckingham, Open University Press).

Haw, K. (1996) Exploring the educational experiences of Muslim girls: tales told to tourists – should the white researcher stay at home? *British Educational Research Journal* 22(3): 319–30.

Haw, K. (1998) *Educating Muslim Girls* (Buckingham, Open University Press).

Hayes, D. and Lingard, B. (2003) Introduction: rearticulating gender agendas in schooling: an Australian perspective, *International Journal of Inclusive Education* 7(1): 1–6.

Hernstein, R. and Murray, C. (1982) *The Bell Curve: Intelligence and Class Structure in American Life* (New York, Simon & Schuster).

Hewitt, R., (1996) *Routes of Racism* (London, Institute of Education).

Hey, V. (2002) Horizontal solidarities and molten capitalism: the subject, intersubjectivity, self and the other in late modernity, *Discourse* 23(2): 227–41.

Hing, B. (1993) *Making and Remaking Asian America through Immigration Policy, 1850–1990* (Stanford, CA, Stanford University Press).

Hoff Sommers, C. (2000) *The War Against Boys (How Misguided Feminism is Harming Our Young Men)* (New York, Simon and Schuster).

Hogg, M., Abrams, D. and Patel, Y. (1988) Ethnic identity, self-esteem and occupational aspirations of Indian and Anglo-Saxon British adolescents, *Genetic, Social and General Psychology Monographs* 113: 487–508.

Holland, J., Ramazanoglu, C, Sharpe, S. and Thomson, R. (1998) *The Male in the Head* (London, Tufnell Press).

Hollway, W. and Jefferson, T. (2000) *Doing Qualitative Research Differently* (London, Sage).

hooks, b. (1982) *Ain't I a Woman?* (London, Pluto).

hooks, b. (1992) *Black Looks* (London, Turnaround Press).

Hopkins, P. (2004) Young Muslim men in Scotland: inclusions and exclusions, *Children's Geographies* 2(2): 257–72.

House of Representatives Standing Committee on Education and Training (2002) *Boys: Getting it Right: Report on the Inquiry into the Education of Boys* (Canberra, Commonwealth Printer).

Jackson, C. (2006, forthcoming) 'Wild' girls? An exploration of 'ladette' cultures in secondary schools, *Gender and Education*.

Jackson, S. and Scott, S. (2004) Sexual antinomies in late modernity, *Sexualities* 7(2): 233–48.

Jensen, A. R. (1973) *Educability and Group Differences* (London, Harper Collins).

Kibria, N. (2002) *Becoming Asian American: Second-Generation Chinese and Korean American Identities* (Baltimore, MD and London, Johns Hopkins University Press).

Kimmel , M.S. (1994) Masculinity as homophobia: fear, shame and silence in the construction of gender identity, in H. Kaufman and M. Brod (eds) *Theorizing Masculinities* (London, Sage).

Ladson-Billings, G. (1994) *The Dreamkeepers: Successful Teachers of African American Children* (San Francisco, Jossey-Bass).

Ladson-Billings, G. (1995) What can we learn from multicultural education research?, *Educational Leadership* 51(8): 22–6.

Ladson-Billings, G. (1996) Silences as weapons: challenges of a black professor teaching white students, *Theory into Practice* 35(2): 79–85.

Lave, J. and Wenger, E. (1992) *Situated Learning: Legitimate Peripheral Participation* (Cambridge, Cambridge University Press).

Lawler, S. (1999) Getting out and getting away: women's narratives of class mobility, *Feminist Review* 63: 3–24.

Lawler, S. (2005) Rules of engagement: habitus, power and resistance, *Sociological Review* 52(Supplement 2): 110–28.

Lees, S. (1992) *Sugar and Spice* (London, Penguin).

Levitas, R. (2005) *The Inclusive Society,* 2nd edition (Basingstoke, Palgrave).

Lewis, P. (2000) An enquiry into male wastage from primary ITE courses at a university college and success indicators for retention, paper presented to Recruitment and Retention of Teachers Seminar Conference at University of North London, 19 January.

Li Wei (1995) Variations in patterns of language choice and code-switching by three groups of Chinese/English speakers in Newcastle upon Tyne, *Multilingua* 14(3): 299–325.

Lightbody, P. and Durndell, A. (1996) Gendered career choice: Is sex-stereotyping the cause or the consequence? *Educational Studies*, 22: 133–46.

Lingard, B., Martino, W., Mills, M. and Bahr, M. (2002) *Addressing the Educational Needs of Boys*, report to Department of Education, Science and Training (Canberra, DEST).

Lucey, H. (2001) Social class, gender and schooling, in B. Francis and C. Skelton (eds) *Investigating Gender* (Buckingham, Open University Press).

Lucey, H. (2004) Differentiated citizenship: psychic defence, social division and the construction of local secondary school markets, in *The Open University Faculty of Social Science Course Materials, DD305 Personal Lives and Social Policy* (Milton Keynes, The Open University Press).

Lucey, H. and Reay, D. (2002) A market in waste: psychic and structural dimensions of school-choice policy in the UK and children's narratives on 'demonised' schools, *Discourse* 23: 23–40.

Lucey, H., Melody, J. and Walkerdine, V. (2003) Uneasy hybrids: psychosocial aspects of becoming educationally successful for working class young women, *Gender and Education* 15(3): 285–300.

Luttrell, W. (2005) 'No offence': White women teachers' conflicts about authority, presented at the Gender, Power and Difference Conference, University of Cardiff, 29–31/3/05.

Lyman, S.M. (2000) The 'Chinese question' and American labor historians, *New Politics* 7(4).

Lynch, K. and O'Neill, C. (1994) The colonisation of social class in education, *British Journal of Sociology of Education* 15: 307–24.

Mac an Ghaill, M. (1988) *Young, Gifted and Black: Student–Teacher Relations in the Schooling of Black* Youth (Buckingham, Open University Press).

Mac an Ghaill, M. (1994) *The Making of Men* (Buckingham, Open University Press).

Macpherson, W. (1999) The Stephen Lawrence Enquiry: Report of an Enquiry by Sir William Macpherson (London, The Stationery Office).

Mahony, P. (1998) Girls will be girls and boys will be first, in D. Epstein, J. Elwood, V. Hey and J. Maw (eds) *Failing Boys?* (Buckingham, Open University Press).

Mahony, P. and Hextall, I. (2000) *Reconstructing Teaching* (London, RoutledgeFalmer).

Mahony, P. and Zmroczek, C. (1997) *Class Matters* (London, Taylor & Francis).

Majors, R. (2001) Introduction, in R. Majors (ed.) *Educating Our Black Children* (London, RoutledgeFalmer).

Majors, R. and Billson, J.M. (1992) *Cool Pose: The Dilemmas of Black Manhood in America* (New York, Lexington Books).

Mama, A. (1995) *Beyond the Masks: Race, Gender and Subjectivity* (London, Routledge).

Martino, W. (1999) 'Cool boys', 'party animals', 'squids' and 'poofters': interrogating the dynamics and politics of adolescent masculinities in schools, *British Journal of Sociology of Education* 20: 240–63.

Martino, W. and Pallotta-Chiarolli, M. (2003) *So What's a Boy?* (Buckingham, Open University Press).

Maynard, M. and Purvis, J. (1994) *Researching Women's Lives from a Feminist Perspective* (London, Taylor & Francis).

McIntosh, P. (1990) White privilege: unpacking the invisible knapsack, *Independent School* (Winter 1990): 31–6.

Mendes, P. (2003) *Australia's Welfare Wars: The players, the Politics and the Ideologies* (Sydney, University of New South Wales).

Mendick, H. (2006) *Masculinities in Mathematics* (Maidenhead, Open University Press).

Mercer, K. (ed.) (1988) *Black Film/ British Cinema* (London, Institute of Contemporary Arts).

Miles, R. (1989) *Racism* (London, Routledge).

Mills, M. (2001) *Challenging Violence in Schools* (Buckingham, Open University Press).

Mills, M. (2003) Shaping the boys' agenda: the backlash blockbusters, *International Journal of Inclusive Education* 7: 57–73.

Mirza, H. and Reay, D. (2005) Doing parental involvement differently: Black women's participation as educators and mothers in black supplementary schooling, in C. Crozier and D. Reay (eds) *Activating Participation* (Stoke-on-Trent, Trentham Books).

Mirza, H.S. (1992) *Young, Female and Black* (London, Routledge).

Modood, T. (1992) *Not Easy Being British* (Stoke-on-Trent, Trentham Books).

Modood, T. (1994) The end of a hegemony: the concept of 'black' and British Asians, in J. Rex and B. Drury (eds) *Ethnic Mobilisation in a Multicultural Europe* (Aldershot, Avebury Press).

Modood, T., Berthoud, R., Lakey, J., Nazroo, J., Smith, P., Virdee, S. and Beishon, S. (1997) *Ethnic Minorities in Britain* (London, Policy Studies Institute).

Mullard, C. (1985) Multiracial education in Britain, in M. Arnot (ed.) *Race and Gender: Equal Opportunities Policies in Education* (Milton Keynes, Open University Press).

Multiverse (2006) http://www.multiverse.ac.uk/.

Nayak, A. (2001) Ice-white and ordinary: new perspectives on ethnicity, gender and youth cultural identities, in B. Francis and C. Skelton (eds) *Investigating Gender* (Buckingham, Open University Press).

NS-SEC (2001) *The National Statistics Socio-economic Classification*, available at: http://www.statistics.gov.uk/methods_quality/ns_sec/ (Accessed 19 June 2006).

O'Brien, M. (2003) Girls and transition to secondary-level schooling in Ireland: 'Moving on' and 'moving out', *Gender and Education* 15: 249–67.

OECD PISA 2000 (2003) *Literacy Skills for the World of Tomorrow* (Paris, OECD).

Ofsted (1999) *Raising the Attainment of Minority Ethnic Pupils: Schools and LEA's Response* (London, Ofsted).

Ofsted (2003a) *Yes He Can – Schools Where Boys Write Well* (London, Ofsted Publications).

Ofsted (2003b) *Boys' Achievement in Secondary Schools* (London, Ofsted Publications).

Okeye, P. (2005) Parental support in raising achievement, *The Bulletin* (London, The Resource Unit for Supplementary and Mother-tongue Schools).

Oliver, M. (1992) Changing the social relations of research production, *Disability, Handicap and Society* 7(2): 101–14.

Omi, M. and Winant, H. (1986) *Racial Formation in the United States* (London, Routledge).

Osborne, J. (2001) Academic disidentification: unravelling underachievement among Black boys, in R. Majors (ed.) *Educating Our Black Children* (London, RoutledgeFalmer).

Osgood, J. , Francis, B. and Archer, L. (2006) Gendered identities and work placement: why don't boys care?, *Journal of Education Policy* 21(3): 305–22.

Osler, A. (1989) *Speaking Out: Black Girls in Britain* (London, Virago).

Owen, D. (1994) *Chinese People and 'Other' Ethnic Minorities in Great Britain: Social and Economic Circumstances* (Warwick, Centre for Research in Ethnic Relations, University of Warwick).

Paechter, C. (1998) *Educating the Other: Gender, Power and Schooling* (London, Falmer Press).

Paechter, C. (2000) *Changing School Subjects: Power, Gender and Curriculum* (Buckingham, Open University Press).

Pakulski, J. and Waters, M. (1996) The reshaping and dissolution of social class in advanced society, *Theory and Society* 25(5): 667–91.

Pang, M. (1999) The employment situation of young Chinese adults in the British labour market, *Personnel Review* 28: 41–57.

Parker, D. (1995) *Through Different Eyes: The Cultural Identities of Young Chinese People in Britain* (Aldershot, Ashgate).

Parker, D. (1998a), Emerging British Chinese identities: issues and problems, in E. Sinn (ed.) *The Last Half Century of Chinese Overseas* (Hong Kong, Hong Kong University Press).

Parker, D. (1998b) Rethinking British Chinese identities, in T. Skelton and G. Valentine (eds) *Cool Places: Geographies of Youth Cultures* (London, RoutledgeFalmer).

Parker, D. (2000) The Chinese takeaway and the diasporic habitus: space, time and power geometrics, in B. Hesse (ed.) *Un/settled Multiculturalisms* (London, Zed Books).

Parker-Jenkins, M., Hawe, K., Barrie, A. and Khan, S. (1997) Trying twice as hard to succeed: perceptions of Muslim women in Britain. Paper presented at the British Educational Research Conference University of York, September 1997.

Parsons, C., Godfrey, R., Annan, G. and Wennerstrom, V. (2003) *Minority Ethnic Exclusions and the Race Realtions (Amendment) Act 2000: Interim Summary* (London, DfES).

Phillips, T. (2005) Opinion, *Education Guardian* 31/5/05, p. 5.

Phinney, J. (1990) Ethnic identity and adolescents and adults: review of research, *Psychological Bulletin* 108(3): 494–514.

Phoenix, A. (1987) Theories of gender and black families, in G. Weiner and M. Arnot (eds) *Gender Under Scrutiny* (London, Hutchinson).

Phoenix, A. (1994) Practising feminist research: the intersection of gender and race in the research process, in M. Maynard and J. Purvis (eds) *Researching Women's Lives from a Feminist Perspective* (London, Taylor & Francis).

Pickering, J. (1997), *Raising Boys' Achievement* (London, Network Educational Press).

Polite, V. and Davis, J. (1999) *African American Males in School and Society* (New York, Teachers College Press).

Pollack, W. (1998) *Real Boys* (New York, Owl Books).

Puttnam, R. (1993) *Making Democracy Work* (Princeton, NJ, Princeton University Press).

Qualifications and Curriculum Authority (1998) *Can do Better: Raising Boys' Achievement in English* (London, QCA).

Race Equality Advisory Forum (2006) http://www.scotland.gov.uk/library3/society/equality/reaf-04.asp.

Rampton. B. (1995) *Crossing: Language and Ethnicity Among Adolescents* (London, Longman).

Ran, A. (2001) Travelling on parallel tracks: Chinese parents and English teachers, *Educational Research* 43(3): 311–28.

Ranson, S., Martin, J. and Vincent, C. (2004) Storming parents, schools and communicative inaction, *British Journal of Sociology of Education* 25(3): 259–74.

Raphael Reed, L. (1998) 'Zero tolerance': gender performance and school failure, in D. Epstein., J. Elwood, V. Hey, and J. Maw (eds) *Failing Boys? Issues in Gender and Achievement* (Buckingham, Open University Press).

Rassool, N. (1999) Flexible identities – exploring race and gender issues among a group of immigrant pupils in an inner-city comprehensive school, *British Journal of Sociology of Education* 20(1): 23–36.

Rattansi, A. (1992) Changing the subject: racism, culture and education, in J. Donald and A. Rattansi (eds) *'Race', Culture and Difference* (Buckingham, Open University Press).

Reay, D. (1996) Dealing with difficult difference: reflexivity and social class in feminist research, *Feminism and Psychology* 6(3): 443–56.

Reay, D. (1997) The double-bind of the 'working class' feminist academic: the success of failure or the failure of success?, in P. Mahony and C. Zmroczek (eds) *Class Matters* (London, Taylor & Francis).

Reay, D. (1998a) Always knowing and never being sure: familial and institutional habituses and higher education choice, *Journal of Education Policy* 13: 519–29.

Reay, D. (1998b) *Class Work* (London, Falmer Press).

Reay, D. (2001a) Nice girls, spice girls, tomboys and girlies, *Gender and Education* 13(2): 153–66.

Reay, D. (2001b) Finding or losing yourself? working class relationships to education, *Journal of Education Policy* 16(4): 333–46.

Reay, D. (2002) Shaun's story: troubling discourses of white working-class masculinities, *Gender & Education*, 14: 221–33.

Reay, D. (2003) Troubling, troubled and troublesome? Working with boys in the primary classroom, in C. Skelton and B. Francis (eds) *Boys and Girls in the Primary Classroom* (Buckingham, Open University Press).

Reay, D. (2004) 'It's all becoming a habitus': beyond the habitual use of habitus in educational research, *British Journal of Sociology of Education* 25(4): 431–44.

Reay, D. and Ball, S.(1998) Making their minds up: family dynamics of school choice, *British Educational Research Journal* 24: 431–48.

Reay, D. and Lucey, H. (2000) 'I don't like it here but I don't want to be anywhere else': children living on inner London council estates, *Antipode* 32(4): 410–28.

Reay, D. and Lucey, H. (2001) Stigmatised choices: social class and local secondary school markets. Paper presented at Addressing Issues of Social Class and Education: Theory into Practice, University of North London, 26 June.

Reay, D., and Lucey, H. (2003) The limits of 'choice': children and inner city schooling, *Sociology* 37(1): 121–42.

Reay, D. and Mirza, H. (1997) Uncovering genealogies of the margins: Black supplementary schooling, *British Journal of Sociology of Education* 18(4): 855–74.

Reay, D. and Mirza, H. (2005) Doing parental involvement differently: black women's participation as educators and mothers in black supplementary schooling, in G. Crozier and D. Reay (eds) *Activating Participation* (Stoke-on-Trent, Trentham Books).

Reay, D. and Wiliam, D. (1999) 'I'll be a nothing': structure, agency and the construction of identity through assessment, *British Educational Research Journal* 25(3): 343–54.

Reay, D., Davies, J., David, M. and Ball, S. (2001) Choices of degree or degrees of choice? Class, 'race' and the higher education choice process, *Sociology* 35(4): 855–74.

Reay, D. (2005) Thinking class, making class, *British Journal of Sociology of Education* 26(1): 139–43.

Renold, E. (2001) 'Square girls', femininity and the negotiation of academic success in the primary school, *British Educational Research Journal* 27(5): 577–88.

Renold, E. (2005) *Girls, Boys and Junior Sexualities* (London, RoutledgeFalmer).

Rich, A. (1986) Compulsory heterosexuality and lesbian existence, *Signs: Journal of Women in Culture and Society* 5(4): 631–60.

Rose, N. (1999) *Powers of Freedom* (Cambridge, Cambridge University Press).

Rose, S. (2001) Escaping evolutionary psychology, in H. Rose and S. Rose (eds) *Alas Poor Darwin: Arguments Against Evolutionary Psychology* (London, Vintage).

Rosenthal, R. and Jacobson, L. (1968) *Pygmalion in the Classroom: Teacher Expectation and Pupils' Intellectual Development* (London, Holt).

RS31 (London, Department for Education and Employment).

Runnymede Trust, The (1986) *The Chinese Community in Britain: the Home Affairs Committee Report in Context* (London, The Runnymede Trust).

Russell, J. (2006) If we treat schools like market stalls, we will end up with vegetables, *The Guardian*, 14/1/06, p. 14.

Said, E. (1978) *Orientalism* (New York, Pantheon).

Said, E. (1984) *The World, the Text and the Critic* (London, Faber and Faber).

Savage, M. (2000) *Class Analysis and Social Transformation* (Buckingham, Open University Press).

Sayer, A. (2005) Class, moral worth and recognition, *Sociology* 39(5): 947–63.

Sennett, R. and Cobb, J. (1977) *The Hidden Injuries of Class* (Cambridge, Polity Press).

Sewell, T. (1997) *Black Masculinities and Schooling: How Black Boys Survive Modern Schooling* (Stoke-on-Trent, Trentham Books).

Sewell, T. (1998) Loose canons: exploding the myth of the 'black macho' lad, in D. Epstein, J. Elwood, V. Hey and J. Maw (eds) *Failing Boys?* (Buckingham, Open University Press).

Shain, F. (2003) *The Schooling and Identity of Asian Girls* (Stoke-on-Trent, Trentham Books).

Sham, S. and Woodrow, D. (1998) Chinese children and their families in England, *Research Papers in Education* 13(2): 203–26.

Siraj-Blatchford, I. (ed.) (1993) *'Race', Gender and the Education of Teachers* (Buckingham, Open University Press).

Skeggs, B. (1997) *Formations of Class and Gender* (London, Sage).

Skeggs, B. (2004) *Class, Self, Culture* (London, Routledge).

Skeggs, B. (2005) The making of class and gender through visualizing moral subject formation, *Sociology* 39(5): 965–82.

Skelton, C. (2001) *Schooling the Boys* (Buckingham, Open University Press).

Skelton, C. (2003) Male primary teachers and perceptions of masculinity, *Educational Review* 55: 195–209.

Skelton, C. and Francis, B. (2003) Introduction, in C. Skelton and B. Francis (eds) *Boys and Girls in the Primary Classroom* (Buckingham, Open University Press).

Solomona, P., Portelli, J., Daniel, B.J. and Campbell, A. (2005) The discourse of denial: how white teacher candidates construct race, racism and 'white privilege', *Race, Ethnicity and Education* 8(2): 147–69.

Song, M. (1997), 'You're becoming more and more English': investigating Chinese siblings' cultural identities, *New Community* 23(3): 343–62.

Song, M. (1999) *Helping Out: Children's Labor in Ethnic Businesses* (Philadelphia, Temple University Press).

Spender, D. (1982) *Invisible Women: The Schooling Scandal* (London, Writers and Readers).

Spivak, G. (1993) Can the subaltern speak?, in P. Williams and L. Chrisman (eds) *Colonial Discourse and Post-Colonial Theory* (Hemel Hempstead, Harvester Wheatsheaf).

Stanworth, M. (1981) *Gender and Schooling* (London, Hutchinson).

Stoer, S. and Cortesao, L. (1999) The reconstruction of home/school relations: Portuguese conceptions of the 'responsible parent', *International Studies in Sociology of Education* 9(1): 23–38.

Tam, S.K. (1998) Representations of 'the Chinese' and 'ethnicity' in British racial discourse, in E. Sinn (ed.) *The Last Half Century of Chinese Overseas* (Hong Kong, Hong Kong University Press).

Taylor, M. (1987) *Chinese Pupils in Britain* (Berkshire, NFER-Nelson).

Thomas, K. (1990) *Gender and Subject in Higher Education* (Buckingham, Open University Press).

Thompson, M. (2000) *Raising Cain: Protecting the Emotional Life of Boys* (New York, Ballantine Publishing Group).

Tikly, L., Caballero, C. and Haynes, J. (2004) *Understanding the Educational Needs of Mixed Heritage Pupils* (London, DfES).

Tikly, L., Osler, A., and Hill, J. (2005) The Ethnic Minority Achievement Grant: a critical analysis, *Journal of Education Policy* 20(3): 283–312.

Tomlinson, S. (1977) Race and education in Britain 1960–77: an overview of the literature, *Sage Race Relations Abstracts* 2(4): 3–30.

Troyna, B. and Hatcher, R. (1992) *Racism in Children's Lives* (London, Routledge).

Vincent, C. and Ball, S. (2005) *Childcare, Choice and Class Practices* (London, Routledge).

Vincent, C. and Martin, J. (2005) Parents as citizens: making the case, in G. Crozier and D. Reay (eds) *Activating Participation* (Stoke-on-Trent, Trentham Books).

Walker, B. and MacLure, M. (2005) Home-school partnerships in practice, in G. Crozier, and D. Reay (eds) *Activating Participation* (Stoke-on-Trent, Trentham Books).

Walkerdine, V. (1988) *The Mastery of Reason* (Cambridge, Routledge and Kegan Paul).

Walkerdine, V. (1989) *Counting Girls Out* (London, Virago).

Walkerdine, V. (1990) *Schoolgirl Fictions* (London, Verso).

Walkerdine, V. (2003) Reclassifying upward mobility: femininity and the neoliberal subject, *Gender and Education* 15: 237–47.

Walkerdine, V. and Lucey, H. (1989) *Democracy in the Kitchen* (London, Virago).

Walkerdine, V., Lucey, H. and Melody, J. (2001) *Growing Up Girl. Psychosocial Explorations of Gender and Class* (Basingstoke, Palgrave).

Warrington, M. and Younger, M. (2000) The other side of the gender gap, *Gender and Education* 12: 493–507.

Watson, J. (1977) The Chinese: Hong Kong villagers in the British catering trade, in J. Watson (ed.) *Between Two Cultures* (Oxford, Basil Blackwell), pp. 181–213.

Weeks, D. and Wright, C. (1998) *Improving Practice: A Whole School Approach to Raising The Achievement of African Caribbean Youth* (London, Runnymede Trust).

Weeks, J. (1981) *Sex, Politics and Society: The Regulation of Sexuality since 1800* (Harlow, Longman).

Weeks, J. (1986) *Sexuality* (London, Routledge).

Wei, L. (1994) *Three Generations, Two Languages, One Family: Language Choice and Language Shift in a Chinese Community in Britain* (Clevedon, Multilingual Matters).

Weiler, K. (1993) Feminism and the struggle for a democratic education: a view from the United States, in M. Arnot and K. Weiler (eds) *Feminism and Social Justice in Education* (London, Falmer Press).

Werbner, P. and Modood. T. (eds) *Debating Cultural Hybridity: Multicultural Identities and the Politics of Anti-racism* (London, Zed Books).

Westwood, S. (1990) Racism, black masculinity and the politics of space, in J. Morgan and J. Hearn (eds) *Men, Masculinities and Social Theory* (London, Unwin Hyman).

Wetherell, M. and Potter, J. (1992) *Mapping the Language of Racism* (London, Harvester Wheatsheaf).

Whitehead, J. (1996) Sex stereotypes, gender identity and subject choice at 'A'-level, *Educational Research* 38: 147–60.

Whitehead, J. (1998) Masculinity, motivation and academic success: a paradox. Paper presented at the Gendering the Millennium Conference, University of Dundee, Sept.

Whitehead, S. (2002) *Men and Masculinities* (Cambridge, Polity Press).

Wikeley, F. and Stables, A. (1999) Changes in school students' approaches to subject option choices: a study of pupils in the West of England in 1984 and 1996, *Educational Research* 41: 287–99.

Williams, P. (2004) Edward Said (1935–2003), in J. Simmons (ed.) *Contemporary Critical Theorists: From Lacan to Said* (Edinburgh, Edinburgh University Press).

Willis, P. (1977) *Learning to Labour: How Working Class Kids Get Working Class Jobs* (Farnborough, Saxon house).

Wong, L. (1994) Di(s)-secting and Dis(s)-closing 'Whiteness', *Feminism and Psychology* 4(1): 133–53.

Woodrow, D. and Sham, S. (2001) Chinese pupils and their learning preferences, *Race, Ethnicity and Education* 4(3): 377–94.

Wrench, J. and Hassan, E. (1996) *Ambition and Marginalisation: A Qualitative Study of Underachieving Young Men of Afro-Caribbean Origin*, Research Study RS31 (London, Department for Education and Employment).

Wright, C. (1987a) Black students – white teachers, in B. Troyna (ed.) *Racial Inequality in Education* (London, Allen and Unwin).

Wright, C. (1987b) The relations between teachers and Afro-Caribbean pupils, in G. Weiner and M. Arnot (eds) *Gender Under Scrutiny* (Milton Keynes, Open University Press)

Wright, C. (1997) The relations between teachers and Afro-Caribbean pupils, in M. Arnot and G. Weiner (eds) *Gender Under Scrutiny: New Enquiries in Education* (London, Hutchinson).

Yates, L. (1997) Gender equity and the boys debate: what sort of challenge is it?, *British Journal of Sociology of Education* 18(3): 337-47.

Youdell, D. (2003) Identity traps, or how black students fail, *British Journal of Sociology of Education* 24(1): 3–20.

Youdell, D. (2004) Engineering school markets, constituting schools and subjectivating students: the bureaucatic, institutional and classroom dimensions of educational triage, *Journal of Education Policy* 19(4): 407–31.

Younger, M. and Warrington, M. (1996) Differential achievement of girls and boys at GCSE, *British Journal of Sociology of Education* 17: 299–314.

Younger, M., Warrington, M. and McLellan, R. (2005) *Raising Boys' Achievements in Secondary Schools: Issues, Dilemmas and Opportunities* (Maidenhead, Open University Press/McGraw Hill).

Yuval-Davis, N. (1994) Women, ethnicity and empowerment, *Feminism and Psychology* 4(1): 179–97.

Yuval-Davis, N. (1997) Ethnicity, gender relations and multiculturalism, in P. Werbner and T. Modood (eds) *Debating Cultural Hybridity: Multicultural Identities and the Politics of Anti-racism* (London, Zed Books).

Zhou, M. and Bankston, C. L. (1994) Social capital and the adaptation of the second generation: the case of Vietnamese youth in New Orleans, *International Migration Review* 28(4): 821–45.

Index